LocoScripting People
Managing lists with a PC or Amstrad PCW

Jane Clayton and Richard Clayton

Sigma Press § Wilmslow

Copyright © 1992 Jane Clayton and Richard Clayton
The moral right of the authors has been asserted.

All rights reserved. No part of this publication may be reproduced, stored in a retrieval system, or transmitted in any form or by any means, electronic, mechanical, photocopying, recording or otherwise, without prior written permission.

First published in 1992 by:
Sigma Press, 1 South Oak Lane, Wilmslow, Cheshire SK9 6AR, England.

British Library Cataloguing in Publication Data:
A CIP catalogue record for this book is available from the British Library.

ISBN: 1-85058-305-6

Cover design by:
Design House, Marple Bridge.

Distributed by:
John Wiley & Sons Ltd., Baffins Lane, Chichester, West Sussex, England.

Printed by:
The Cromwell Press, Melksham, Wiltshire

Whilst the authors have made every effort to ensure that the "programs" and procedures in this book work as described they are not in a position to judge whether they would be suitable for any particular purpose or whether they will continue to work under all possible conditions or circumstances. The programs are presented "as is" without warranty of any kind either express or implied.

The names, addresses, telephone numbers and other details given in examples are entirely fictitious and no association with any real people is intended or should be made.

This book was typeset and laid out electronically by the authors. The cooperation of Locomotive Software in making this possible is gratefully acknowledged.

Amstrad is a registered trademark of Amstrad plc.
PCW8256,PCW8512,PCW9512,PcW9256 and PcW9512+ are trademarks of Amstrad plc.
LocoScript, Loco and Locomotive are registered trademarks of Locomotive Software Ltd.
LocoScript 2, LocoSpell, LocoMail, LocoFile, LocoLink, LocoScript PC and $^{Loco}Script$ Professional are trademarks of Locomotive Software Ltd.

Preface

If you are using, or only thinking of using, the LocoScript program on a PC or an Amstrad PCW to manage lists of people, then this book was written for you. The people might be subscribers to your magazine, business contacts, or maybe just your Christmas card list. The practical problems of handling any list of people have much in common. However, this book is particularly concerned with how to administer the records for the members of a club or society. It shows you step by step how you can use your computer to keep track of your members' names, addresses, interests; and whether they have paid their subscription or not!

The early chapters point out the advantages of keeping your records on a computer. We explain what information you should seek from your members; how to set up a datafile to record this; and how to enter the details onto the machine. In chapter 5 we explain about indexing the data for easy access, then in chapter 6 we emphasise the importance of keeping a backup of your material so that you will not have to type it all in again.

Chapters 7 to 10 explain how to use your information in different ways to produce alphabetically ordered lists of the membership. We show you how to get these reports in different orders, and how you can include everyone or make a selective list of just the people you need. Chapter 11 contains programs to count your membership, category by category. Chapters 12 to 14 are concerned with the slightly specialised topic of printing sticky labels, then chapters 15 to 17 cover how to write the same letters time and again without re-typing, and the all-important topic of sending out the renewal notices.

Chapters 18 & 19 deal with setting up and using specialised "alternative item" indexes. We explain how to find all the people who have common interests, or who have offered help to the club in various categories. We also show you how to use just one record to cope with members who all live at the same address.

The LocoScript system allows you to change your mind about how you record various items. We explain how to do this for single items of information and also how to make more drastic changes of layout. These topics are covered in chapters 20 to 23.

You may not be starting a club or society completely from scratch, and so we explain in chapter 24 how to use the previous records, whether they have been kept manually or on some other sort of computer system.

All the programs in the book have been tested, but we know that at some point you will meet error messages when things fail to work first time. So there is a chapter devoted to error messages; what they mean, and suggestions of what to do next.

The Data Protection Act lays down the rules of who must register their use of computers to maintain personal information. We explain how you can keep the right side of the law, and how to get more information if you need it.

We have a chapter on obtaining supplies of paper, envelopes, labels and software. Finally, there is a glossary, an index of our "programs" so that you can find them quickly, and then a normal index.

Amongst all the computer material we've also tried to add as much practical advice and tips as we can about the realities of dealing with lists of people. We even tell you how to avoid sticking stamps onto your renewal notices!

The book is intended as a working reference book, and it is aimed at ordinary mortals who are merely using their computer as a tool. You do not need to be a 'typist', one finger typing is quite OK, and certainly you should never be afraid of 'computers'.

> Jane didn't learn to use a PCW until late in life – and even now she will freely admit that her grandsons know more about computers than she does, but she would hate to be without her PCW. "I learnt a lot by trial and error, but that is why we have written this book; so you can profit by my mistakes!"
>
> Richard has been fascinated by computers since he was a teenager, and he built much of the LocoScript software. But his expertise has not been used to blind you with science. "Everyone can learn to use the little programs we have devised for this book. Even Jane!"

We are both sure that this book will save you time and effort. And give you back your evenings!

Richard & Jane Clayton
September 1992.

Contents

1. **What can computers do for you?** — 1
   How computers can save you work;
   How you can produce otherwise impractical lists;
   What computers won't do for you;
   What hardware and software to use.
2. **Setting up from scratch** — 5
   What you need to record and why;
   The pros and cons of membership numbers;
   Classes of membership;
   How to get this information and keep it up to date.
3. **Designing the LocoFile card** — 11
   Setting up a datafile to hold your information.
4. **Entering the data** — 19
   How to type in the data and amend it;
   How to find entries which have "disappeared".
5. **Indexing** — 25
   How to set up an index;
   Date indexes;
   What indexes you need;
   Looking up an entry.
6. **Backing up your data** — 31
   Why you backup and how often;
   How to copy discs and files;
   How to use a backup.
7. **Simple lists** — 37
   Simple lists of members' names and other details;
   How to get different orders and different details.
8. **Selective lists I** — 49
   Skipping the unwanted records;
   Using prompts to make general purpose programs;
   Mailmerge comparisons.
9. **Selective lists II** — 59
   Using indexes for speed.

10.	**Splitting lists into sections**	**67**
	Splitting output into batches;	
	Splitting lists by class or other criteria.	
11.	**Counting records**	**77**
	Counting members in each membership class;	
	How to correct errors in your datafile.	
12.	**Introducing envelopes and labels**	**81**
	Window envelopes;	
	Getting the most out of the Post Office.	
13.	**Labels on a PCW**	**85**
	Label paper types;	
	1-across labels, continuous and sheets;	
	n-across labels, continuous and sheets;	
	Generating labels in batches;	
	Generating labels selectively.	
14.	**Labels on the PC**	**107**
	Label paper types;	
	The labels program;	
	Generating labels in batches;	
	Generating labels selectively;	
	Dealing with blank lines in labels.	
15	**Writing letters to everyone**	**121**
	Putting datafile information into a letter;	
	Making parts of the letter optional;	
	Testing the letters;	
	Writing master documents;	
	Sending letters to only some people.	
16	**Renewals**	**131**
	The renewal notice;	
	Entering the people who paid ;	
	Reminding those that did not;	
	Covenants for charities.	
17.	**Writing special letters**	**139**
	How to avoid copy typing by using Extract;	
	Using Fill to write letters.	
18.	**Alternative item indexes I : Special interests**	**145**
	How to set up lists of interests;	
	Indexing with alternative main items;	
	Listing and counting special interests;	
	How to use "Find" to locate records.	

Contents

19.	**Alternative item indexes II : Family memberships** Putting several people on the same datafile card; Making lists of children and parents.	**155**
20.	**How to change your mind** How to change the size and position of items; Putting in new items or removing unwanted ones; Squashing the datafile; Making lists with temporary items.	**161**
21.	**New data for old** How to change item contents by global exchange; Solving problems when inserting data; How to change item contents automatically.	**167**
22.	**New items for old** How to create new items; How to merge items; How to split addresses into single lines; How to put the town in the town item.	**175**
23.	**Splitting up datafiles** Removing lapsed members to a separate datafile.	**185**
24.	**Taking over an existing list** Taking over a manual list; Taking over a computer list – inserting the data; How to handle CSV format; How to transfer a computer list to your machine.	**189**
25.	**Troubleshooting** What messages you get and what they mean; How to find the errors in your programs; Converting datafile names.	**199**
26.	**Legal implications** The Data Protection Act – do you need to register?	**213**
27.	**Supplies and suppliers** Paper labels and envelopes; Backup, transfers and software.	**217**
	Glossary	**225**
	Index of programs	**227**
	Index	**229**

LocoScripting People

1
What can computers do for you?

Introduction

If you need "lists" of people for any reason – membership lists, lists of help offered, even your own Christmas card lists, you can of course sit down with pen and paper, or pen and a record book, and write them out. If you need a neater version for other people and you have a typewriter then you can type them. But this is time consuming, and if you are not a brilliant typist you will make mistakes. More importantly, people will get married and change their name, people will move house, or people will need to be added and there won't be room on "their" page in the book. This is where the PC or PCW comes into its own. These machines are not just for games, and equally not just for "big" clubs or lists. They are so cheap nowadays that you can justify owning one for quite tiny uses.

So why use a computer rather than a pen or typewriter? First and foremost it will save you work. Yes, you will have to put the entries on the computer in the first place, but once on, they are there forever and you can use them again and again.

Next, having put on the entries, you can check them and correct mistakes. You will never again have to re-type a whole page, or spend a fortune on Tipp-ex. You correct the mistake and it stays corrected.

Even more important than either of the above benefits, is the fact that once entered, you can use the data to produce lists, totals and reports which are impractical under any manual system. We know of a small charity where a helper has spent many hours writing out lists of people in given areas, so that they can be told of coffee mornings. Jane produced a list for the same purpose, but broken down by towns and villages, in about ten minutes from when she first decided to do it.

You don't have to be a programmer to use a computer, nor have a college degree. The little routines we call programs in this book are simple to understand and adapt to your own needs. Although we explain how they work, you need not ever worry about understanding them, because you can just copy what we have written. It does not even really matter that a few look a little bit long and complicated. You only have to type them in once!

What computers won't do for you

Computers are stupid. If you have mis-typed a name or address, a computer won't tell you. When you ask it to look up the address, it won't necessarily find the mis-typed version. It will do **exactly** as you asked – so you have to do the thinking before you ask. However, it will then do what you asked as many times as needed, and do it accurately and quite fast!

The computer cannot tell you things it does not know! If you want a list of coffee morning helpers, then you will need to add this information to the relevant members' records.

The computer can't keep things up to date if you don't tell it what has changed. You have to type in the address changes, otherwise the computer will keep on churning out labels to the old address.

The system is programmed to show error messages when something does not work – but these have to cover so many eventualities, and the messages are so brief, that you must learn to understand what has gone wrong. We have a chapter on **troubleshooting** (the computer jargon for dealing with error messages and unexpected events) – so you can always refer to this, but you will save time by learning the more common messages. You will have made the mistake – not the computer.

Software and hardware

We have written this book assuming that you are using either some sort of Amstrad PCW or an IBM-compatible ("industry standard") PC. In the jargon, this is your **hardware**. We have also assumed that you are using the LocoScript word processing program as your **software**. If you are using some other software, then you may well get some benefit from the more general information we give, but the program examples won't be any good to you.

On a PCW you need to be using LocoScript 2, LocoMail and LocoFile. If your PCW is a 9512 or 9512+, then it came with the first two of these, but you will need to buy

LocoFile in addition. If you have a 8256, 8512 or 9256, then it is necessary to purchase all three. If you are still struggling on with the ancient LocoScript '1' supplied with these machines then you will find LocoScript 2 simple to learn, a great deal faster and easier to use, and of course it will continue to read your old documents. See chapter 27 for supplier details.

There have been three versions of LocoScript for the PC. In 1990 LocoScript PC v1.0 was sold both separately and "bundled" as a special promotion with the Amstrad 1640. In 1991 LocoScript PC v1.5 was produced, with a number of extra features. In 1992 *LocoScript* Professional superseded all these earlier versions. You can upgrade any of the earlier versions to Professional for a small charge (see chapter 27). Although most of the programs in this book will work with any version of LocoScript PC, the new Professional version has such a lot of improvements, especially if you are going to produce labels, that we have assumed that you have upgraded.

As well as possessing the right software, we have to assume that you have some knowledge of how it works! If word processing is completely new to you, please spend a little time working through the examples/tutorial that come with the products. You do not need to have a deep knowledge of why they work, but it will help enormously if you have seen what happens when you use them. You also need the practice in how to get into (or out of) files, how to change what you have typed in, and the reassurance that you need not panic if you press the wrong key!

Where we've given keystrokes for the various operations we've put them in for the PCW (and then if they are different for the PC in brackets). In a few cases you will find that the PC keystrokes are only appropriate for the Professional version, but in general all the versions of the PC program work the same way. We usually give the keys to press once, but thereafter we tend to assume that you will know what we mean when we say "go into datafile set-up". If in doubt, then the manuals which came with your software will help you out.

You may also find that going back to the tutorial examples after starting to use our programs as set out in this book, will deepen your understanding and some things will suddenly make sense where before it merely seemed like magic.

2
Setting up from scratch

If you are starting up a society, club, or whatever from scratch, you should first sit down and think about what your "society" is going to do and what you need to know about your members. From experience we would suggest that this is an individual effort, even if when you have come up with some ideas, these need to be considered by others.

Names and addresses

The most obvious requirement is for the name and address of members.

Make sure that you note the preferred form of title. Mr, Mrs, Miss, Ms, Rev, Dr. are the commonest choices. Also make sure that you are given initials. It is no joke to find that you have five entries for Mr and Mrs Smith, and even worse if they are all in the same town or area. The Treasurer will tell you that Mr R Smith has paid and that John Smith has resigned. You are then stuck unless the Treasurer has kept a record of the name and address. You will look incompetent if you continue sending newsletters to the one who has resigned and keep on sending renewal reminders to the one who has paid.

Make sure that the name is clearly spelt out for you – there are variants on the obvious names like Green, Reid and Moore but also on less obvious ones like Armatage and Armitage. Nothing annoys people more than having their name mis-spelt. Don't be afraid to ask people to spell their name for you if you are taking it down at a meeting or over the telephone. You can also check that you have it right by reading out to them what you have written down.

For the address, make sure that you have a full address, including the postcode. If you are using a form for people to write down their name and address, always make a space asking for the postcode. Without this, people tend to leave it out, but if the space is there to be filled, most people will complete it. This will be a useful item on which to sort your membership at a later stage – and if the society grows, you can get rebates on your postage if you are able to sort it by postcodes.

On the subject of forms – do make sure you ask for the details you need. If you leave something out – even something as obvious as Name – then people will complete the form and fail to put a name. (Jane will vouch for this – she did it once!)

What else will you need to know ?

Decisions need to be taken before you start to think about computer systems and they are not easy. The better the information you start with, the less re-thinking of your system at a later date.

We have compiled a checklist to give you some ideas, but this cannot cover all eventualities. You need to consider your society and decide what information you need – and perhaps even how you will acquire it.

Checklist:

- Title, Initials, Surname;
- Name of company or another society, if this is relevant;
- Address (3 lines is usually enough);
- Town;
- Postcode;
- Telephone number;
- Subscription/Membership number (if being used);
- Start date and/or expiry date;
- Type of membership;
    e.g. individual, family (others at the same address), social, corporate, society, gratis, life.
- Method of payment;
    If necessary distinguish between standing orders and covenants.
- Date and amount paid;
- A code to identify how the member came to join;
- Interests;
- Skills offered (including offers of help);
- Free form space.
    It is always useful to have a general space for recording things which do not really fit into any other category.

Setting up from scratch

Subscription/membership numbers

On a manual system, it is usual to give members a number on joining. A numbered card is perhaps used to admit members to meetings. It certainly is a quick reference and identification of a member. If you have an existing society, you may wish to continue using the system you already have.

When you put your entries onto the computer, you will see that the computer numbers the records. There is no reason why this record number cannot also be the membership number. However, we do not really recommend it.

The main problem is that the record number is totally under the control of the computer. For example, if you delete a record you cannot re-use the number. Auditors like this sort of thing because for other uses of datafiles it discourages fraud. But it can be most inconvenient if you wish to reallocate the same number to an ex-member who has now rejoined. You will also find that if you restructure your datafile using the techniques of chapter 21 then you get a whole new set of numbers. The final inconvenience is that the PCW cannot put the record number into a computer generated list (the PC can).

If you do decide to use membership numbers then we recommend that you put them into a separate item and generate their values yourself. But will you actually use a membership number? They do have advantages; for instance if you need to access Mr Smith quickly and you know his membership number, then you can use the membership index and go straight to the correct Smith without having to page through all the others in your records. Similarly, entering payments at renewal time can be speeded up if you have put the membership number on your renewal notices.

If you decide to use membership numbers, there is no need to feel that you should re-use numbers when members have resigned, or that numbers need to be consecutive. You can go on allocating new numbers for ever. Even if you end up with a lot more digits than you started with, it is very easy to change the size of the membership number box.

You don't need to use numbers in order to know your total membership. Chapter 11 shows you how to get the computer to count the members for you, category by category if you wish; and of course if you use the [F5] `Inspect document` command on your datafile it will instantly tell you the total number of records, and hence the overall count of members.

Classes of membership

How you define your members depends to a large extent on the purposes of your society. You may wish to differentiate between individuals and family members, or it may be between individuals and companies, or active and social members.

You may decide to have a special rate for students and perhaps for O.A.P.'s, or the new "in word" the unwaged. You may wish to give certain people free membership or free copies of your publication. You may give Life membership to someone for services rendered, a special donation, or for a lump sum of a given amount. These are all things which should be discussed and exact criteria laid down. Not doing so can lead to problems and bad feeling at a later stage.

It is important to record on the computer the subscriber's membership type because you will need to know which members need to be sent renewal notices and those which must not. There may be differing rates for different groups, and you need to be able to put the correct rate on the renewal notice. (See chapter 16.)

If you are a registered charity, you could ask your members to pay by standing order and sign a deed of covenant, which will increase the income you get from their subscription. Again, see chapter 16 for details of this.

Corporate members and other societies

If you have a lot of corporate members, you need the company name as a separate item (and indexed) so that you can look it up. You will probably need the company or society name more than the individual to whom notices are addressed, particularly if your contact is with a post or officer rather than a definite individual. You can then send renewal notices to the company rather than to an individual.

You may have reciprocal arrangements with other societies. You need a consistent scheme so that you can easily cope when the next village's W.I. acquires a new Hon. Sec. or the hockey club changes the fixtures secretary.

Entering dates and period of subscription

If you expect all subscriptions to be renewed annually, for example in February, you only really need to record the year in which the subscription was last paid or will next be due. If you have a publication and start the subscription at varying times in the year, you need to record the year and month or the starting (or finishing) issue for the subscription.

Things are relatively easy if you are recording expiry years, or if you are dealing with subscriptions to a publication which numbers its issues sequentially. You can record 1993 or issue 35, in each case just as a simple number. You will be able to produce reports and renewal notices using greater than (>) and less than (<) numeric comparisons to identify the correct subscriptions for the report. However, if you use the format 92/4 then this is not a "number" to the computer and it will not be able to tell if 92/3 is greater or less. There are ways around this, which we explain further in chapter 5, and in chapter 9 you will find a program for producing reports for a range of dates.

Another decision is needed if all subscriptions are renewed at the same time annually. What are you going to do about those who join late in the previous year? If there is no publication, are you going to say – as does the National Trust for instance – that all those joining in the latter part of the year do not need to renew for the next year? If so, a mark is needed to differentiate them from those who will need renewal notices, or they could be entered as already paid for the next year.

Where do you get your information ?

If you are starting from scratch, you need to design a form which will give you the information – preferably in the order in which you intend to enter it on the computer. You can take this duplicated (or printed) form to the first meeting and ask people to complete it and hand it in to you. If you are sending details out by post, either make the form the last page of your leaflet or, better still, put it in as a separate sheet. Put your name and address for returning the form in *two* places – on the form itself *and* on the leaflet. How many times have you had to re-open an envelope to find where to send a form because the address was *only* on the form and nowhere else?

Taking over an existing membership list has both benefits and disadvantages. Transferring a computerised list is dealt with in a later section of this book (chapter 24). If the list has previously been handled manually, much depends on the quality of the information you are given. If you are lucky, a register has been maintained in legible handwriting and details of names and addresses are clear and in full. Also, if you are lucky, a list has been kept with details of subscriptions paid showing amount, when paid, and in what way the payment was made.

If you are less lucky, some or many of the details will be missing. If the organisation is small, people may well know more about the members than is written down. We would suggest that as a first step, you get what you can onto the computer and print out a list of members showing what information you have. Even if you only have a name and no clear address, put this on. Go through your list and highlight the names where information is needed and then go to the previous organisers and committee members and ask for their help. The details can be written onto your list and then put onto the computer later.

One of the things we have found is that people express interest when a society is first suggested, and their names are listed. They are not then actively chased up to see if they are interested enough to contribute or even attend meetings. They stay on the list and soon no-one knows if they ever paid anything.

If you have this problem then you will need to make a list of all the people in this limbo state. Chapters 7 and 8 have some suitable programs, or you can use the "marker" technique we describe for Christmas cards in chapter 20. Ask any previous officers of the society if they know anything about the people on the list. Then use a "renewal" program like those we give in chapter 16 to write to them politely suggesting that unless you receive their subscription, you will have to delete them from the mailing list. A charity we know of did this recently, and out of 230 "non-payers", well over a hundred paid up immediately.

We've spent this chapter giving you long checklists, discussing all the details you might need, and asking you to make decisions. You should not be unduly worried about this. Get what information you can and start out. The reasons for our remarks may only become clear as you progress. In any case, you *can* change your mind later. We have only been trying to direct you towards decisions which will help limit the number of times you need to make changes!

3
Designing the LocoFile card

This chapter is about how to design the LocoFile "card" which is used to hold information about the people on your list. On a PCW LocoFile is a separate piece of software used to extend the LocoScript system. On a PC LocoFile is a standard part of LocoScript and the word LocoFile is avoided in the manuals, but this part of the program is still quite recognisable as "LocoFile".

Computer people call information **data** (some classically educated ones know that this is the plural of "datum") and the files containing information **datafiles**. Because big systems can be built of many inter-linked files they call the entire stock of information about a particular subject a **database**. In this book we tend to use the term **datafile** because it is unlikely that your database consists of more than one file.

Within the datafiles each card (in computer jargon each **record**) contains details about one member (or if you have joint membership, one couple or family). Sometimes you will hear media people calling an individual's record a "computer file". This usage of file is incorrect. In the computer world a **file** is a collection of records held together under a single filename, which you can see on your Disc Manager screen as ADDRESS.DAT or similar.

The reason for using the term **card** is to reinforce the analogy with little plastic boxes holding 5x3 (or 8x5) cards, which were one of the standard ways of holding information about people before computers came along.

If you are using real 5x3 cards you can write information anywhere, at any size and at any angle. You can even write on the back if there is too much information to fit on the front! Sadly, computers are not yet this versatile. The information has to be held in little boxes called **items** by LocoScript (the usual computer jargon is **fields**). However, you do get to choose the size and position of these items; and this chapter guides you through the process of setting them up.

Designing the card

Start by making a brand-new datafile.

On a PCW press [F1] and select Create LocoFile data. On a PC you press [F9] and select Create datafile. Give the datafile a suitable name such as MEMBERS.DAT. Press [ENTER] and you will see an outline of your card which is 60 characters wide and 15 characters deep. Check that you are in "Datafile set-up" mode.

> Although we give brief instructions throughout this chapter and the rest of the book as to which keys to press, these are really intended to be reminders, and not your first introduction to the subject. So, if you are not familiar with your machine, please have a look at the section on datafiles in your tutorial and work through it. It will all make much more sense after that.

Unlike many programs, LocoScript makes it extremely easy to change your mind at a later stage, but you can save a lot of time by making some fundamental decisions now. The first of these is whether the standard 60 x 15 size is right for you. So look at the list we suggested in the last chapter that you should make of all the things you wish to record about your members. Think about the logical order to place them onto the card, perhaps making a quick sketch on paper of the sort of layout you want.

If you decide to change the size of the LocoFile card, then press [F5]. This will show you the current size and you can change the card height and/or width. The menus differ slightly on the PCW and PC:

Designing the LocoFile card

If you get some other menu (such as a Goto menu) then you didn't follow the instructions we gave above and you are not currently in "Datafile set-up".

If you are not sure about the card size, try some plausible numbers and see what the resulting shape looks like. You are likely to need at least the original width of 60 but almost certainly need to make it taller.

There is no "cost" in making the card as big as possible (78 x 99) or reducing it to the absolute minimum area into which you can cram your items. The way that LocoScript stores and displays information means that it always uses exactly the same amount of disc space no matter what size or shape of card you use.

We would suggest you widen your card to 65 characters wide and make it 20 lines deep. You can make the card longer than your screen – the fact that it extends below the screen will be shown by arrows at the side of the "box". More will come into view as you progress down the screen. However, it makes sense to put your most used pieces of information on the top part of the card so they are readily visible, perhaps saving the off-screen area for your free form general comments item.

Having decided on the card size you can start to place the items onto it. If you run out of space you can always come back and change the card size later. You can also move the items around if you get some better ideas. There is much more about this in chapter 20.

For most of the items on your card, you will wish to know what they are for, and where they are positioned, so you will want the "boxes" to be named. You can call your boxes anything, but later actions will be easier if they are single words or a word and number with no space between them, as we suggest for the lines of the address below. You don't need to worry about whether the box names are made of upper or lower case letters (or with just the first letter a capital), but you will find that your screen looks much neater if you are reasonably consistent.

You have a choice of where you place the name of each item. You can have the name above each box (or some of them) or you can place it at the left hand side, and there are other choices. The positions for the name are defined as if they were the numbers on a clock face. Since you need space for the name, you have to decide where it will go at the same time that you decide where to position the item.

TIP: For one line "boxes" on the screen there is no visible difference between using the 9 o'clock and 10 o'clock positions – both are left of the box. However if your box has two or more lines, then 9 will put the name centrally left of the box, and 10 will put it at the top left corner.

We would expect your first requirement will be to record names and addresses, so we will start with creating the items to hold these.

We prefer the names of boxes on the left, so leave room by moving the cursor (using the cursor keys) to line 2, column 15. The current line and column is shown at top right of the screen. Once in place, press [F3] and select the command to Create new item.

The first box will be for the first part of the member's name, which might be a forename like Jane, or something more formal like Mrs J. We will call this first box Name, so fill this in. To have the name placed left of the item move down and change 11 o'clock to 10 o'clock and press [ENTER]. Enter the width of the box as 15 and press [ENTER]. Set the height in lines to 1 and press [ENTER]. The menu will now look rather like this:

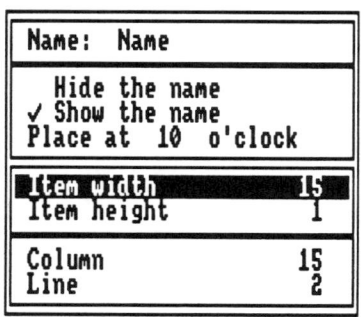
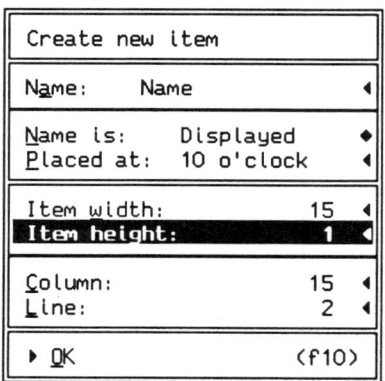

When everything is correct press [ENTER] ([F10] if using a PC). If at any point you don't like what you see on screen, or if you press [ENTER] at the wrong time, just go back in by [F3] and use Change item (PC Amend item) to correct the numbers.

Now move the cursor across to column 40 of line 2, press [F3] and create the box for Surname. This should be a box 20 characters long (by one line high). Surnames can vary greatly in length, but by giving the first name 15 characters, you can really only "afford" 20 characters to be able to print them all on the 36 characters which make one line of a normal label. You can spread your names over two lines, but this will be inconvenient later when you start producing lists and labels automatically.

Instead of one box called Name you may prefer to split it into Title and Initials. If so then you should allocate 9 characters to Title (which is enough for Rev & Mrs), and 5 for the initials (which will allow for 3 letters, since it is not worthwhile to "waste" the space on full stops). This will still leave you 20 characters for Surname.

Designing the LocoFile card　　　　　　　　　　　　　　　　　　　　　*15*

How you choose to split up your names will depend on the sort of members that you have and whether you generally use titles, or know their first names. The main deciding factor will probably be whether you expect to extract these items into automatically created letters. There is no problem if you avoid titles and record their first names, but it is more correct to write `Dear Mr Smith` than `Dear Mr R Smith`, and to get this right you will need the `Mr` and `R` in separate items. We have seen several datafiles which avoided these difficulties altogether by having a completely separate `Salutation` entry, which for Mr Smith might conceivably just have `Bobby` in it!

TIP:　Now move down two lines before starting the address. You could move down only one line, but it is much easier on your eyes if items are not too crowded on your screen. Also, you are less likely to copy down the wrong line, should you need to note down something from the screen.

Create the item for the first line of the address in column 15, two lines below the Surname. Call this item `Address` and make it 36 wide by just one line deep.

You could make the address 5 or 6 lines deep but this has disadvantages in later uses. If you use a PCW and want to print labels more than one across the page (or to use sheets of labels on a BJ-10e inkjet printer) you need the address split into separate lines. On either a PC or a PCW, if you want a list with the addresses in a line across the page, you need each line as an individual item. In any event, you will certainly find it useful to have the town and the postcode on separate lines from the rest of the address.

The second line of the address should be given a title such as `Addr2` and made 36 wide by one line again. This item can be positioned just one line down, but in order to keep the screen tidy the name should be hidden by selecting the hide option in the menu. Do *not* leave the name of the item blank as this will make it impossible to use in the programs in later chapters.

```
┌─────────────────────────────┐   ┌──────────────────────────────────┐
│ Name:  Addr2                │   │ Create new item                  │
├─────────────────────────────┤   ├──────────────────────────────────┤
│ ✓ Hide the name             │   │ N‍ame:     Addr2              ◄  │
│   Show the name             │   ├──────────────────────────────────┤
├─────────────────────────────┤   │ Name is:      Hidden             │
│ Item width           36     │   ├──────────────────────────────────┤
│ Item height           1     │   │ Item width:.            36    ◄  │
├─────────────────────────────┤   │ Item height:             1    ◄  │
│ Column               15     │   ├──────────────────────────────────┤
│ Line                  5     │   │ Column:                 15    ◄  │
└─────────────────────────────┘   │ Line:                    5    ◄  │
                                  ├──────────────────────────────────┤
                                  │ ► OK                       (f10) │
                                  └──────────────────────────────────┘
```

The third line of the address should be called `Addr3` and it is set up in the same way as `Addr2`, but on line 6.

Your next line is called `Town` and this item name should be shown (at 10 o'clock). Your line can be 36 characters long, even though in Britain, you will seldom need more than 25 characters.

The next item is for `County`. The box can be 36 characters long, but you are unlikely to need more than 20. If you feel strongly about putting the county immediately after the town on the same line, it is as well to decide this now. Given the maximum of 36 characters on a normal label, we'd suggest 25 characters for the town, leaving 10 spaces for the county. Most counties will fit or can be abbreviated to this.

The address finishes with the `Postcode` item. The box should be 9 wide and one high.

If you are recording telephone numbers, it makes sense to put this item on the same line as the postcode, making the box 14 wide by one high. Remember to leave space for the item name `Tel` before starting your box.

Making entries

Before proceeding to think about the rest of the card, we will digress a little, to say a little about using the card for entries.

When your card is complete and you start to type in the data, the screen will show just the names of the boxes. You move from box to box by using either [ENTER] to move down the card and [RELAY] to move back up (or [TAB] and [SHIFT][TAB] on a PC). As you move to each box, so the size of the box is shown. When you have completed filling in a box, it is important that you move on by pressing [ENTER]([TAB]). If you press carriage return [↵] (or [ENTER] on a PC!), you will not move to the next box but will put a ↵ into the item, and you are storing up trouble for yourself when you start to make lists. Non-typists will have no trouble with this, but competent typists will have to make a special effort to discipline themselves to press [ENTER]([TAB]) at the end of the line!

The progression through the card so far has been logical and in the same order as you will receive the data in most instances. However, the rest of the information you have will depend on your sort of club, charity, working group or whatever. So, while remembering that you want to be able to move easily down the card from the information you have in front of you, you need to lay out the remainder of the boxes you need.

Designing the LocoFile card 17

Pressing [ENTER] ([TAB] on a PC) moves the cursor left to right down the screen, so this will be the "natural" order of entering data. Thus you should lay out the card so that this makes sense. Don't be tempted to put in a box on the right hand side of the screen "out of order" – it will prove a constant annoyance if you have to keep casting around for the information to go into it. You will also find it easy to enter the wrong information into such a box when you are in a hurry.

The rest of the card

The further information on your card might be, for example:

Class	Type of membership or method of payment;
Joined	Date of joining, or perhaps where and why;
Expiry	Date/issue renewal is due;
Paid	Date paid, and possibly the amount as well;
Reference	Membership number;
Interests (or skills)	These can be coded, and you could have several small boxes which can be indexed as alternative items (see chapter 18);
Comments	A free-form note space for anything and everything else.

Thus the whole screen might look like:

```
         Name ...............  Surname ....................
      Address ......................................
               ......................................
         Town ......................................
       County ......................................
     Postcode .........      Tel ..............
       Expiry .........    Class ..............
         Paid .........   Joined ..............
       Amount .........  Reference ..............
    Interests ......................................
     Comments ......................................
              ......................................
              ......................................
```

Don't forget you can lengthen your card if you need to, up to a maximum of 99 lines.

Having completed making up your screen layout, before you do anything else, sit back for a minute and look at it. Does it look right? Have you forgotten anything from the list you decided on before you even looked at the computer? If possible, leave it for another day and look at it again. If not, have a cup of coffee or a beer and then come back to it.

If you are still happy then you can return to the Disc Manager which will save your new datafile for you. On a PCW you press [EXIT] twice; on a PC, press [F10], select Exit datafile and press [ENTER].

Although it can be helpful on a PC, on a PCW it is **MOST IMPORTANT** that having completed your card design, you then exit to the Disc Manager and copy the empty datafile to a safe place. Call it something which will identify it as your standard layout like CLUB.STD or STANDARD. It *must* be recognisable as your standard layout, so that you won't use it by mistake. It has just taken you quite a while to set it out and you don't want to have to count everything out when you need this basic layout again.

In later chapters we will be explaining procedures which will need empty datafiles with this layout. The problem is that once you have started entering information into the file it will no longer be empty. On a PC there is a procedure called Select template for copying just the layout from an existing datafile. On a PCW there is no such scheme, so your only option would be to erase every single record, which would take a long time. You avoid this by keeping a copy of an "empty" file.

SO COPY IT NOW AND NAME IT. For extra safety, on a matrix printer PCW you could use [EXTRA][PTR] to make a screen dump which shows the shapes of the boxes. If your card is longer than the screen, remember to move down and do it a second time.

TIP: Either do the screen dump whilst in Datafile set-up mode or tick Blanks in the [F8] menu so that the box shapes are visible as dots.

4
Entering the data

You are now ready to start entering your data. As we explained at the end of the last chapter, if you are using a PCW it is important that you keep a pristine copy of your datafile with no data entered into it. So, if you haven't already made a copy of the empty file, do it now!

To enter the data you must first open the datafile. On a PCW you move the Disc Manager cursor to the datafile and press [F1], then R to select Run LocoFile and then [ENTER]. On a PC you just cursor to the datafile, then press E and [ENTER] (just as if you were starting to edit a document).

You can now start at the top of the card to fill in the boxes. As we mentioned before, it is most important that you press [ENTER] ([TAB] on a PC) to move to the next box, and never carriage return [↵] (or [ENTER] on a PC!).

It is essential that you have one box (the same box on every card) that always contains some text. For societies etc., the most obvious choice is Surname; for subscriptions to a periodical it might be that the company name is the item which most easily satisfies this condition. Something must go into this box – where you use company name and an individual subscribes, even a full stop can be put in. This will be unnoticed when you print out labels, but makes all the difference when you are using mailmerge to produce lists (using the techniques we cover later in the book). If the "guaranteed non-empty" item is in fact empty then you will find that your lists and labels can turn out to be incomplete.

With this one exception, if you have not got the information for a particular box, or do not need every line for the address, you just press [ENTER] ([TAB]) again and move on to the next box.

IT IS MOST IMPORTANT that you put the right things in the right boxes! This may sound obvious, but it is true. You will not be able to list by Postcode if the postcode is entered in the box labelled Town. Nor will you be able to list by Town if that is put on the third line of the address!

If what you wish to enter is too long to fit in the box, you may type on, but only up to the end of the line will be entered. (The PC helpfully beeps at this point, but the PCW does not.) So, look before you move on to the next card that you have not omitted something in this way.

WARNING: You may look at the card and see that you have made some mistakes as you typed in the text. As you make corrections, watch that you do not extend your text so that it no longer fits within the box. If this happens you will see that the last word disappears and that there are some dots at the end of the line. You haven't actually lost anything, because the last word is still recorded in the datafile. If you leave it like this, then the missing word will reappear in your lists and labels, where it will probably upset your tabulation of columns! You should retrieve the position by abbreviating the line as necessary.

The same thing can happen if you have a trailing space at the end of the item. When you add characters the last word may disappear whilst there is still apparently room for it. The reason is that LocoScript insists on having room for both the last word *and* the space. This can be especially puzzling if you completely fail to notice that the little dot for "nothing" has been replaced by a space. You can remove any confusion by pressing [F8] and selecting the option to show Spaces as "little piles of cannonballs"!

When you have completed the card, move on to the next by pressing [F1] ([F6] on a PC). The Create new record command is at the top, so press [ENTER].

You can start typing away on the next card before it appears, but this is not recommended for trained typists on a PCW – they will beat the machine and find some letters missing more often than not! It can speed things slightly though, for the one finger typists.

If you have a great number of identical entries to make – perhaps of a date, or even a town, it is worth setting them up as phrases or blocks and then pasting them in on successive cards. This can speed up entry quite considerably. (See your manual if you are not familiar with cutting and pasting.)

On a PC you also have the option of Create duplicate record ([F6]). This can sometimes be helpful (if an entire family joins, for example). However, be warned, that if you use this command it is remarkably easy to forget to change the things which *do* need to be changed between one record and the next.

Entering the data 21

In chapter 2 we suggested that you think about what you need to record and in what form. Remember what you decided! If necessary think again, but then stick to it!

If you change your mind or are inconsistent you will have problems when you wish to generate reports. For example, if you are recording membership classes you will have to decide if you will type the words in full (`Life`, `Social` etc.) or if you will use just the first letter (`L`, `S` and so on). It is important to keep to the same scheme because the computer will treat `L` as a completely different class from `Life`.

Addresses

We have recommended that you make your addresses up as several single-line items, calling these `Address`, `Addr2` and so on. The purpose will be apparent when you want to produce reports with addresses written across the line, or to produce "n-across" or sheets of labels. Even if you decide not to do this, and make your address three lines high, do, however, make separate items for Town and Postcode as you may wish to index on these.

TIP: Hide the names of `Addr2`, `Addr3` because they just clutter your card. Do not hide `Town` and `Postcode` because the text acts as a reminder, so that you put the details on the right line.

Whether the lines have hidden names or not, you must still move from line to line by `ENTER` (`TAB` on the PC) and not by `⏎`. If an address only has a few lines then just leave the relevant items blank. When we start producing labels and reports we will show you how to "close up" the blank lines automatically.

To change an entry

When you have your system up and running, you will start to get changes of address, changes of name, not to mention corrections. You need to find the original entry and put in the new details. Use the appropriate index (see chapter 5) to find the entry, then move to the item (or items) to be changed, delete as necessary and re-enter the information.

If it is a change of address you are entering, don't forget to change the postcode item (very few people move within the same postcode!) And what about the telephone number – has that changed too?

Check the screen before moving to the next record or leaving the datafile. If you have made a (new) mistake, correct it now. If you decide you want the entry as it was before you started on the changes, press [F1] ([F6] on a PC), select Undo alterations and press [ENTER]. You have only this one chance to do this!

When you move onward to another record or return to the Disc Manager, the previous card contents are deleted. They are help temporarily as a **limbo** record (in a similar way to deleted LocoScript PCW files). You can retrieve the previous record from limbo if necessary. However, there is only one limbo record, so you can only undo the changes to a single record.

Unlike documents where the entire previous contents of the file are preserved "in limbo" (or as a PC .BAK file) there is very little opportunity to undo what you have just done to your datafile. For this reason, amongst others, we've devoted a whole chapter (chapter 6) to the subject of keeping safety copies of your data.

Dealing with the disappeared

Unfortunately, despite their interest in your club, some people will fail to tell you that they have moved. If whatever you are mailing has a return address on it, you are reasonably likely to have it returned by the Post Office. It will come back marked "Gone Away" or "Unknown at this address". First, check that what you have on the label looks right, also that you have not received a change of address and failed to enter it. (Or was it one you failed to re-enter after having to return to a backup disc?).

Your second line of enquiry is the telephone book – is the old address in there or a new one? Either way, if it is a local call, ring the number and see if you can find out the new address. You can also try Directory Enquiries but this is now (1992) charged at 40p (+VAT) a time – but this will be worth it to keep a paying member.

If it is really important to get the new address, you can take the letter addressed with your out of date address to the Post Office and pay for "proof of delivery". If they really cannot deliver it you are no better off, and you have to delete that name from your records. But if they do deliver it to another address, then the slip will come back to you showing where the letter was delivered.

Another problem occurs when you receive a cheque out of the blue and have no means of identifying the address of the sender. Take two photocopies of the cheque (one of which you will keep), and then bank the cheque. Meanwhile, write a letter to the cheque signatory (or company) asking for their address and other details. Send this letter and

Entering the data 23

the second photocopy to the manager of the branch of the bank where the cheque was drawn, with a note asking for the enclosed letter to be forwarded to the customer. The manager won't tell you the address because it is confidential, but your letter will be forwarded and your member will, you hope, then get in touch with you.

Changing your mind

No matter how carefully you thought out your card layout and worked out what you wanted, there will often be a time when you wish you could change your mind. Do not despair! It is remarkably easy to change your mind when using LocoFile.

If it is a simple case of adding extra information, then a new item can be added at any time. Of course all your earlier entries will have no information in that box, but this is not a major task to sort out. You can also delete items if you realise that you have no use for the information. There is a lot more about this in chapter 20.

You can also change your card layout around, moving items to better positions or changing their size. However, do *not* delete an item and then just put it back somewhere else. *If you delete the item you also lose all the information in it from every record.* Again, see chapter 20 for the full story.

If you need more drastic changes then chapters 21 and 22 explain how to extract all the information out of your datafile and how then to put it back into a brand-new file. This is time-consuming but worthwhile (and faster than retyping) if your first attempt was not what you really needed.

TIP: If you are entering data on a PCW, then copy your file to drive M and work on the copy as it will be faster. **HOWEVER – DO NOT FORGET TO COPY IT BACK WHEN YOU HAVE FINISHED!** After you turn the power off, drive M is empty just twenty thousandths of a second later!

5
Indexing

Having entered all your data, you need to be able to find information from the datafile. You do not need to work laboriously through the cards, paging backwards or forwards. You can go straight to the information you need. This chapter explains how to add extra information to the datafile which allows LocoScript to go straight to the records you want. In computer jargon we call this an **index** because it is rather like the index in a book. You supply the reference to look up and LocoScript goes straight to the first record with that reference. Adding indexes increases the size of your datafile but they are invaluable tools.

When you set up your entries each page or card was given a record number by LocoScript. If you know this number you can go straight to the record by pressing [F5] ([Ctrl][F5] on a PC) and putting in the number. This will be used to look up the card in the **record number index**, and the card will be displayed, almost immediately, on the screen.

However, numbers are more suitable for computers than humans, so it is much more useful to construct indexes based on the contents of the items (boxes) you have set up. The item containing the surnames is the most obvious example. To construct an index for this, press [F1] (PC [F9]) and select Datafile set-up. Once in Datafile set-up mode, press [F2] and select Create new index. You will be offered a list showing all of the items which you have constructed – move the cursor to Surname and put a tick next to it using the [+] key and press [ENTER]. (On a PC you need only move the ⇒ to Surname and press [ENTER]).

Now that you have said which item is to be used for the index, you also have to say which type of ordering you require. LocoScript will put up a menu from which you make your selection. The exact form of the menu differs slightly between the PC and the PCW, so we have illustrated both (with the PCW on the left hand side and the PC on the right). If you are using a PC but your menus look like the PCW menus you are still using LocoScript PC rather than *LocoScript* Professional! Whichever machine you are using, the options available are similar – they are just presented differently.

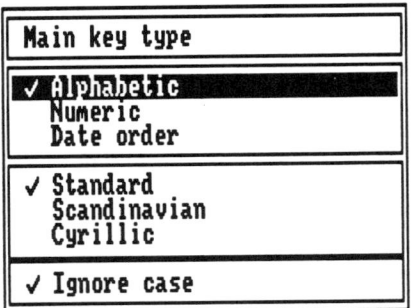 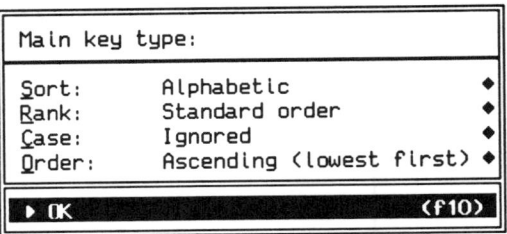

For surnames it is obvious to choose Alphabetic order. This is already selected (as it is the most likely option). We assume that you will not want it ordered by the Scandinavian or Cyrillic alphabets – though you may choose these rather than Standard order if they are relevant. Since you don't want to remember exactly how you've capitalised the surnames, you should leave Ignore case selected.

When you accept the ordering by pressing [ENTER] LocoScript will put up a menu which lets you check what you have chosen so far. You may then make some further changes if you wish.

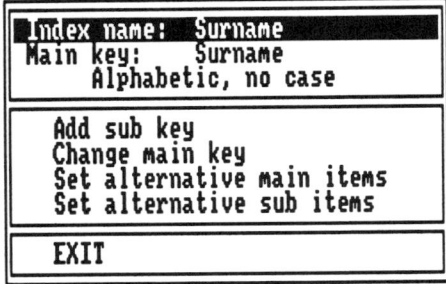 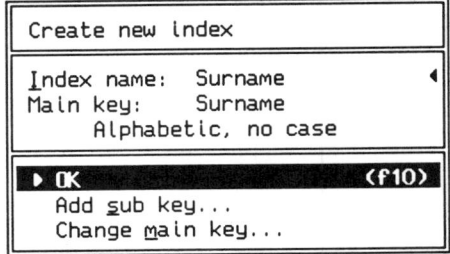

You can change the name of the index. Although your records will be indexed by what you have put in the surname item, you need not necessarily call the index Surname. Most of the time using the same name makes a lot of sense, so the index name will have been filled in for you. If you want some other name for the index then you change this by using the [←] key and then typing in the name you want.

For most purposes a single (**main**) key is sufficient, but if you have a large number of Smith's or Jones's among your members, you may wish to add a **sub key** such as Name (or possibly Town or Postcode).

Indexing 27

Key is the computer jargon for "the item you are indexing on", or (in the right context) "the contents of the item you are indexing on". You can see why computer people use nice short words for ideas like this!

The role of a sub key is that when the main keys are identical, then, and only then, the records will be ordered upon the sub key. If the main keys differ, then the sub keys are irrelevant. You will be used to this from the phone book where people are placed in surname order, and in order of their initials if, and only if, their surnames are the same.

If you wish to add a sub key then move the cursor to this command and press [ENTER]. You are offered the full list of your items, so select the one you want. Again you are offered a choice of alphabetical or other ordering. The selection will be preset to be the same as the main key, but you can alter this if you wish.

You return to a summary menu so that you can check that your choices were correct:

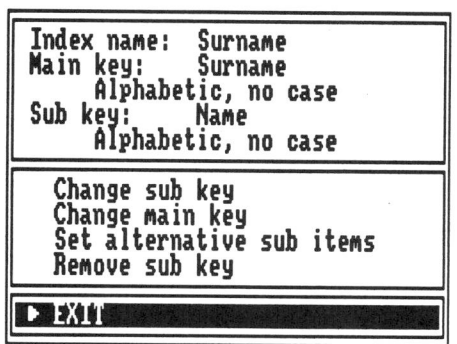 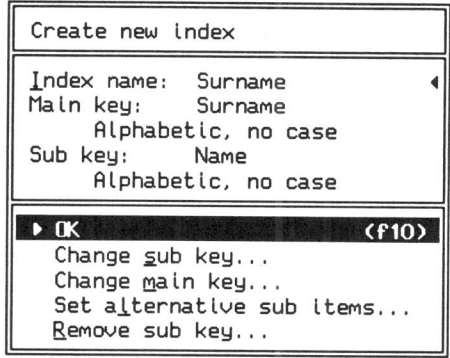

You can change the main key or the sub key if you have made an error.

We would not recommend, at this stage, that you set up any indexes with Alternative main items or Alternative sub items. Indexes with alternative items can have one record appearing more than once in the index. Their uses are rather specialised, so we have delayed discussing them until much later in chapters 18 and 19.

When you are certain all the index details are correct, press [EXIT][ENTER] ([F10] on a PC).

Besides setting up a surname index, it may also be helpful to set up separate indexes for town and postcode. Look at your card and decide what else you will need to search on; the most obvious being the renewal/expiry date and the type of membership.

If you decide to index telephone numbers, then choose alphabetic ordering (or possibly section number order on a PC). A numeric sort will put them in a very odd order!

If you index upon the same item twice (perhaps using a different way of sorting each time) then LocoScript will preset the index name to the item name in its usual helpful fashion. However, you cannot have two indexes with the same name, so you must change the name, because otherwise you will a complaint like this:

Once you have set up the indexes you think you will need, press [EXIT] ([F10][ENTER]) on a PC). Until this point, you have just been specifying your indexes and they are only created now as you leave Datafile Set-up. It will take the system some time to construct all the indexes but the screen will show you a progress menu, and the top left of the screen shows the number of entries to be processed; so you will have an idea of how long you will need to wait.

You can set up the indexes you want before you type in any data. However, particularly on a PCW, this can slow down data entry as the extra work in constructing the index entries means that it will take a little time to move to the next card. We would suggest that if you have a fairly large number of entries to put on by the time you first start to use your PCW, then you put on the entries first, and only then go into Datafile set-up to specify the indexes. These can be left chugging away while you have a cup of coffee or are ringing someone up to proudly announce that you've completed the first stage.

Date indexes

If you wish to index on your expiry item, then you will have to think a little about the form that entries should take, and the type of ordering to be used.

If you are recording the expiry year (1993, 1994 etc.) then you just type it in and use a numeric index. If your expiry is linked to a magazine issue number (such as issue 35) then again you can just use numbers, and everything is easy. However, you will still need to be consistent. For example, you can use either 93 or 1993 but not both, because LocoScript will consider these to be totally different years.

If you need to record an expiry month then things become a little more complex. Using the month name may look attractive, but you will find that `January` sorts a long way after `April`. If you only want to generate lists which relate to a single month then this will not matter. If you need the months to be sorted correctly then you must use numbers (1 to 12) instead of month names.

At first you might think that date ordering was an appropriate choice. Unfortunately, neither month/year nor year/month are options which LocoScript supports. You could type `1/12/93` or `1 7 93` and use day/month/year ordering, but this involves extra typing to provide LocoScript with a totally specious day number.

The best format to use is `93/04`, `93/12` etc. It is important to have the year first because otherwise `01/94` will sort before `12/93`.

If you are using a PCW then you will need to select `alphabetic` ordering. You will have to be consistent, and always use the same character (such as /) between the year and the month. You will also need a zero in front of single digit months, i.e. you will have to type in `01` to `09` for the months 1 to 9.

On a PC you should select `section number` ordering. This is more flexible, in that LocoScript will not insist upon the zero, and you need not remember to always use the same separator. Thus a PC can correctly order `93/2` before `93:12` and `93/12`, whereas the PCW cannot.

What indexes do you need ?

You should not over-index. Put in only the most important indexes. If you index everything you might ever possibly need, you slow down future entries and you use up space on the disc. There is also a limit of eight indexes, so you may have to pick and choose a bit. You can always add indexes at a later stage. You can even create one-off indexes for a special purpose which you remove after use. On a PCW, whenever you make an index you will usually find it much faster to make a copy of the file on drive M and index that. **BUT DO REMEMBER TO COPY IT BACK AFTERWARDS!**

You will certainly need a surname index. If you use membership numbers (and your members remember to use them as well!) then a membership number index will be helpful. In later chapters we give program examples which assume that as well as a `surname` index, you have also set up indexes on `town`, membership `class` and the `expiry` item.

How to look up an entry

To look up an entry you start by entering the datafile by [F1] Run LocoFile (E on the PC). The first thing to do is to see which index the datafile is currently set to use. This is shown in the top left hand corner of the screen. If you wish to search on a different index (e.g. town or surname), press [F2] and select the index you want by using [+] or [Space]. Now you can search using [F5] ([Ctrl][F5] on a PC). For successive searches you will have to delete the text of the previous entry in the menu. If you don't do this then you will get an unexpected answer! Delete your previous search by using the [←] key. If you search on the wrong index, then change to the right one and your previous search text will still be there to be tried again.

If the computer finds only one card which corresponds to your search entry, it will show this at the top of the screen as Unique. If there is more than one record with the same key then there will be a blank. Press [PAGE] ([PgDn] on a PC) to see the next entry.

If there is no card which corresponds to your search, you will get a message saying that you have been placed on the next entry in the index. (If the main key does not match, then the sub key is completely ignored). If you are sure that the card must be there, try going back a record with [ALT][PAGE] ([PgUp] on a PC) and/or forward a record with [PAGE] ([PgDn] on a PC). Also press [F5] and check your request again – did you put it in right?

If it still "not there" – can you search for it on another index? Did you put it in at about the same time as another entry – can you find that one? If so, change your index ([F2]) to Record Number and go backwards and forwards for a few either side of the one you have found.

When you do find it – work out why it wasn't found the first time. Did you put a space at the beginning of the box? On a PCW leading or trailing spaces will prevent an entry from being found (or it even being in the same part of the index as you might expect). Is there a trailing dot or comma? LocoScript does not think that Jones is the same as Jones. and so although it will put you nearby in the index, possibly even on the card you want, it will still warn you that the match was not exact. Did you spell the text right? Maybe your member has the wrong name in your datafile. If so, you'd better correct it. Did you put the entry in the *right* box? LocoScript just indexes on the contents of the item, it won't take any notice of surnames put in some other item altogether.

If you have still not found the record and you are certain that it must be there, then you can use [F6] ([Ctrl][F6] on a PC) to locate some text on the card. This will find a piece of text anywhere on the card on any record in the whole datafile, but it is *slow*.

6
Backing up your data

A **backup** is computer jargon for a security copy of your data. Should your original data be lost then you would still have the backup to use instead. This chapter describes the sort of things that can happen to your data and how you can make backup copies to minimise your loss.

Now, don't misunderstand. Data stored on computer discs is pretty reliable. You can leave discs on a high shelf out of harm's way for years on end and you will still be able to access the data. However, discs you use every day can get lost, eaten by the dog, covered with coffee or they can just plain wear out. More subtly, if your computer isn't working properly then a lot of your data can be altered before you realise it. You might even be unlucky enough to encounter a software "bug" which damages your data. So, if you ever take your discs down from that high shelf you ought to make regular backups.

You have two choices for backing up your data. You can keep copies of whole discs or just single files. We can't tell you which is best because it depends how much data you have and the sort of changes you make to it. Supposing you have a datafile for your hundred members, and you've typed in a dozen programs from later chapters of this book to provide you with lists and labels in various formats. You'd probably do best to make a copy of the whole disc to backup the little programs. Thereafter you need only copy the file with all the member details in. If your membership was a couple of thousand and almost filled the disc then it would be just as simple and as quick to backup the whole disc as to copy the single file. Alternatively, if you were always altering and improving the little programs it might be easier to copy the whole disc than to remember what you changed recently.

Your next decision is how often to backup. Again, we can't really tell you the answer. What you do when you backup is to expend a little extra time and effort as a form of insurance, so that if the worst happens you won't have to repeat everything you've done since the last backup. If you're a one finger hunt and peck typist you might begrudge having to type a single line in again, but if it only took you twenty minutes to type in your entire membership, then you might feel that spending an extra five minutes a session making a backup was a waste of your time. But, beware! If you do not make a backup at the end of the session and the dog does eat your disc then you will have to repeat everything you've just done – which will be most unfortunate if you have thrown away the scraps of paper with the address amendments you have just typed in! For this reason alone, we will stop saying that it is "up to you" and "your choice" : **YOU SHOULD BACKUP YOUR MAIN DATAFILE AT THE END OF EVERY SINGLE SESSION.** However well intentioned you won't always manage this because, like us, you take risks. But, we don't want to have your disaster on our conscience – so we've given you the best advice we could!

The final decision is how many backups you need to keep. The answer to this one is easy – as many as you can afford discs for; but **NEVER** just one. If you only keep one backup disc and religiously copy your data onto it every evening then one awful night you will find that you cannot read all the data on your disc. And where is the backup? That's right. Half copied onto and totally useless for recovering your data. You **MUST** keep at least two backup copies, so that there is one copy of your data which is not involved when the unthinkable happens.

One way of working is to copy to backup disc 1 this time, to backup disc 2 next time, then 1 again and so forth. This is fine and lets you label your backup discs neatly. Better though, (if you're copying whole discs) is to use the **grandfather, father, son** system. After making your backup from your original disc (the grandfather) onto the first backup disc (the father) you put grandfather away and use the father for your work. Next time you backup from the father onto the third disc (the son) and put father away. The third time you backup from the son onto the grandfather and put the son away, and so on and so on, in an indefinite cycle. One advantage of this system, which is rather like rotating tyres on a car, is that you aren't using the same disc all the time, so it is less likely to wear out! You will also know for sure that the duplicate copy is complete and usable, rather than just trusting that this will be the case when the backup is needed.

Whatever system you use, from time to time you should make an extra backup and store it somewhere else. In computer jargon this is an **off-site backup**. There are two reasons for this. First, your house might burn down. Admittedly, after such a catastrophe the safety of your membership list isn't likely to be high on your list of concerns, but even a membership list you backed up months ago will be of assistance when you get around to worrying about your computer again. The second reason is pragmatic. If your machine does start going wrong (supposing it suddenly decides to scratch every disc put into it), then by the time you stop and think and realise why you don't seem to be able to read your original disc, nor any of the backups, you've probably damaged everything in sight. At least, if you have to drive across town to collect the off-site backup, that will give you a few more minutes in which to think!

How to copy entire discs:

Before you start to copy a disc, there is one very important thing to do. You should **WRITE-PROTECT** the source disc which you're going to make a copy of. You do this to avoid accidents when you put the discs into the drives or swap them. If you put in the wrong disc (or the cat walks across the keyboard and presses [ENTER] before you've swapped anything at all) then the information on the write-protected source disc cannot be altered. If you're using grandfather-father-son backups then there is a second thing to check. The destination disc is probably still write-protected from when you last copied it. Write-enable it now, not half-way through the copying operation when you might make a mistake.

If you're using a PCW: LocoScript 2 has a disc copying function built into the [F2] Disc Manager menu. Select Copy disc and press [ENTER]. You will then be asked what sort of copy you want to make. The options you are offered depend upon the model of PCW you own and how many drives it has. Select the appropriate option and press [ENTER]. The next menu then warns you that all the existing information on the destination disc will be destroyed. It makes you press [ENTER] one last time to ensure you really mean it. LocoScript now copies the disc by alternately reading and writing large chunks of data. If both reading and writing occur in the same drive then you will need to swap the source and destination disc in and out as you are asked.

TIP: The number of swaps is reduced if you have more spare space on drive M. So before starting, erase any big files from drive M. In particular you should erase the LocoSpell dictionary LOCOSPEL.DCT. Even if you don't go straight to bed after doing your backup, you can easily copy the dictionary to drive M again if you need it.

If you're using a PC: Unfortunately PC disc drives are not as standardised as those on a PCW so it was not feasible to build a disc copying function into LocoScript. Instead you will need to exit to DOS. Then type DISKCOPY A: A: (or if you have two drives DISKCOPY A: B:). DISKCOPY is the standard copying program which comes as part of DOS. The first parameter (A:) is the source drive, the second parameter (A: or B:) is the "target" or destination drive. Just as on a PCW, you'll find that if you only have one drive, and the size of your disc is bigger than the memory in your machine, then the copy will proceed in several chunks, and you will need to swap discs in and out when you are prompted.

How to copy single files:

As we discussed earlier, you might adequately insure yourself against disaster by just copying your main membership file.

If you're using a PCW: The `Copy file` function is in the Disc Manager [F3] menu. If you have more than one drive then copying from disc to disc is easy. If you have only one drive then you'll actually have to do two copies. First copy the file to drive M, then change the disc, press [F7] to register the change, then perform the second copy. If your datafile will not fit on drive M then you'll either have to expand your machine or give up doing file copies and copy whole discs instead.

> **TIP:** If the file already exists at the destination (because you regularly backup this way) then you don't need to erase it first. LocoScript will notice the clash and ask you what to do. Select the option to `Replace with the new file` and LocoScript will overwrite it for you.

If you're using a PC: The best way to do copies is to "tag" the file to be copied by pressing the space bar. You will see a little tick appear, and the end of the Disc Manager cursor flashes to remind you of the tag. If you want to copy more than one file at the same time then you can tag the other files too. Now move to the destination, press [F3] and use the `Copy tagged file` function.

If you only have one drive on your PC then you proceed just as above. However, unlike the PCW, you may not have a RAM disc to hold a temporary copy whilst you swap discs. Instead, you can get LocoScript to handle two discs in the one drive. Having tagged all your files on drive A you use [Ctrl][PgUp] to display the drive list on the screen. Move to drive B. Press [Ins]. LocoScript will ask you to remove the "drive A" floppy and insert the "drive B" floppy. You can then proceed as normal, except that during the copy operation LocoScript will ask you for the floppies as it needs them. You should take care, however, to only swap floppies when LocoScript asks you because otherwise you run a serious risk of corrupting the data.

> **TIP:** When you're swapping discs on a PC, LocoScript asks for them by name. So always give all your floppies unique names (using `Set volume label` in the Disc Manager [F2] menu). Also, write this name onto the cover of the disc, so you (as well as the computer) will know which one is which.

We've suggested that PC users tag a file, then move to the destination, and only then invoke the copy command. There are two reasons for this. The first is that tagging

Backing up your data 35

allows you to copy several files in one go. The second reason is that you can use other Disc Manager functions whilst you find the destination, such as Search drive, Goto quick path, or even Make Directory. However, a word of warning is necessary. If you find that the destination is full you might decide to erase some files before proceeding with the copy. If so, then you should first use the Clear all tags option from the [F3] menu. Otherwise when you select Erase file LocoScript will erase *all* your tagged files, rather than just the one you're pointing at! That's why the file cursor is flashing at you. It is trying to remind you that you've got some tagged files selected.

If your PC has a hard disc then you will find it much more reliable than floppies. However, when hard discs do fail they often fail completely, so that you lose absolutely everything on them. For this reason, people often prefer to backup their entire hard disc, not just the few files concerned with their membership lists. DOS comes with a utility program called BACKUP which will do this for you. There are also far better third party programs which will do the same job faster, which are much easier to use, and require fewer floppies because they compress the data before saving it.

Using backups

One day you will find to your dismay that LocoScript will not read your file, and you will actually have to use one of the backups which you've been making for just this occasion. When this day comes you have to be extra careful for a few minutes because you have one less copy of your data than is usually the case. You may also be rather more flustered than is usually the case. Therefore, the first thing you must do is to **WRITE-PROTECT THE BACKUP DISC** before you put it into the computer. This will protect the data on the disc from anything except physical damage. Now make a new copy of the backup disc and put the backup disc back in its safe place. Only now, when you have the normal number of backups again, should you start using the copy to get your system running.

Alternatively, despite our good advice, one day you might find that LocoScript will not read your file and you have *not* got a backup. Though this is pretty bad news it may not be a complete disaster. In the PCW world the "Disc Doctor" David Smith will try to recover your data in return for a donation to the cancer charity BACUP. In the PC world Dr. Alan Solomon runs a Data Recovery service, which can even recover data from dead or re-formatted hard discs. You will find the details in chapter 27. Neither service is cheap – and you may find it more economic to type in your membership list again from a printed copy.

TIP: From time to time use one of the listing programs we give in chapter 7 to produce a complete membership list onto some continuous paper. If everything else fails to get you back your membership list then at least you will have a neat record from which to type it back in again. You might also sleep better for knowing that you aren't trusting the computer with absolutely everything!

Human nature being what it is, you probably won't start doing regular backups until you have a disaster or near disaster. Please, though, be more sensible than this and learn from other peoples' misfortune.

7
Simple lists

This chapter explains how to get a list of your members. This is done by creating a document and merging it with the membership datafile. The document you merge is just an ordinary LocoScript document like any other, except that it contains some special commands written in the mailmerge language. LocoScript can tell which bits of the document are just text (headings perhaps) and which bits are commands because the commands are introduced by a (+Mail) code and finish with a (–Mail) code. These mailmerge codes are entered by using the "Set" and "Clear" menus, i.e. by pressing [+] then M or [–] then M. ([+] and [–] are the special keys marked + and –, not the normal typewriter keys on the top row.)

The commands in the document will tell LocoScript:

- which order to list the members in;
- what details we want.

We'll start with one of the simplest possible lists; a complete list of all the members in surname order along with their membership class.

The "program" to do this is:

```
(+Mail)
$= "surname"
space = " "
tab = " → "
cr = "
"
loop = "
name : space : surname : tab : class : cr
$+
"
%loop @ surname
(-Mail)
```

Program 7A

NOTE: In our program examples we have assumed that the datafile contains an item called Name. If you have set up your datafile with Title and Initials then you will need to replace name :... by title : space : initials :...

To run this program you will first have to type it in. Start by creating a new document, calling it, say, MEMBERS.LST. Type in the text exactly as shown and save it onto disc. Besides typing in the program itself, you will need to edit the tabs in Layout 1 so as to have just one tab stop, 40 columns across from the left margin.

TIP: When typing in mailmerge programs use the [F8] menu Codes option so that you can see where all the codes are.

When the program is complete, finish the edit, then point at your new document with the Disc Manager cursor and press M (for merge). LocoScript will ask what you want to merge with. Move the cursor to the membership datafile and press [ENTER]. If you intend to print your list, decide at this point if you wish to use Draft or High Quality print and select accordingly. Press [ENTER] again to the confirmation menu and LocoScript should now produce a list of your members on the screen looking rather like this:

```
Mr & Mrs Abson            Family
Mr & Mrs C E Allingham    Family
E Anderson                Life
Mrs M Anderson            Full
Mr & Mrs Andrews          Life
Mrs G Appleby             Full
Mr J Arthurson            Junior
J Bloggs                  Social
Andrew Church             Junior
Major D Claxton           Full
D W Hill                  Full
Mrs R Johnson             Full
Mrs M Perry               Full
J Smith                   Social
Ainsley Smythe            Full
```

If you are a compulsive viewer of the screen then sit there with pen in hand as the merge proceeds. Make a note of any horrible mistakes you see. You can't do anything at the time, but you will be able to correct the membership list later.

If the screen is rolling past too fast then press [STOP] ([Esc] on a PC). To continue the merge you press [ENTER] on either machine. If you want to give up the merge altogether then press [STOP] (or [Esc]) for a second time. Select the Abandon option from the menu to return to the Disc Manager.

Simple lists 39

If your merge does not work, or produces the wrong sort of information, then you could now turn onward and read chapter 25 which is all about "Troubleshooting". However, there are only three things likely to go wrong.

First, LocoScript may have objected when you typed M. This means that you are a PCW owner who hasn't installed LocoMail onto your machine! Turn back to chapter 1 and check you have the software you need.

Second, your merge program may have started, but then some sort of message like Syntax error appeared. This means you didn't type the document in correctly. Check it and fix it. Make sure the carriage returns (↵) and double quotes (") are exactly as shown. Make sure you typed in the (+Mail) and (−Mail) codes correctly (and that you used the [+] and [−] menus : typing + M a i l is not the same thing at all).

TIP: You can usually tell when you get the (+Mail) and (−Mail) codes wrong because you will not get the same pattern of highlighted (inverse) areas as on the illustrations, which are exact electronic "screen dumps" of our programs.

The third possibility is that you get an error message saying Name does not exist. This doesn't mean one of your members has evaporated! One of the words in the program, such as surname or class does not correspond with the items in your datafile (or one of the spellings is wrong). Perhaps you typed name as shown in our program but you called your item initials. However, if you get Name does not exist immediately after the $= command, then that means that your datafile does not have an index called surname.

Let us be positive and assume that you have made the program work. Now we'll explain what it does so that you can write your own variations to produce the sort of lists that you want. But first, what shall we do with the list on the screen?

When the program reached the end of the members it will have put up a menu looking like this:

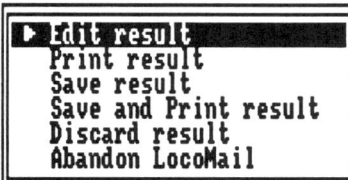

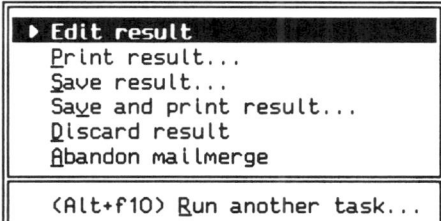

The options are:

`Edit result`

> Selecting this command allows you to edit the list of members, just as if you'd typed it in yourself. You might for example wish to adjust some of the page breaks "by hand". You could fix spelling mistakes, but you'd be better off fixing them in the original datafile – or else they'll still be wrong next time.

`Print result`

> The list of members is printed. This will be the most common choice you make. The list is not kept after printing is finished. It will print as Draft or High Quality as you selected at the beginning.

`Save result`

> The list of members is saved to disc. This sounds attractive because a document containing all your members' names sounds useful. But since it is so easy to make an up-to-date version, there is usually no point in saving your list.

`Save and Print result`

> The list is saved on disc and then printed. It will print in Draft or High Quality as you specified at the beginning of the merge.

`Discard result`

> This discards the list. Because you've already gone through all of the members, there is nothing further for LocoScript to do, so it will then return to the Disc Manager screen. If the program does restart, it is because there is a record in the datafile with a blank `surname` item.

`Abandon LocoMail` (or on the PC: `Abandon Mailmerge`)

> This option also discards the list, but then unconditionally returns you to the Disc Manager screen.

TIP: When you've forgotten to pick the right Quality for printing (or you can't remember whether you did or not) then use the `Save result` option. You can then use a normal `P` command to print the document from the Disc Manager.

If you want to print the list, then be our guest, otherwise select the `Abandon` option. In all cases the original document that contains the program will be unaltered, as indeed will be the membership datafile.

Simple lists 41

TIP: Instead of abandoning, select Discard Result instead. If the merge restarts then you will know that you have some records with blank surnames, which will need correcting. As we stress elsewhere, it is important that surname contains text on every card.

Paper types

Before we look at the program in detail we will briefly discuss paper types and related subjects.

Whenever you create a new document in LocoScript it is assumed to use a particular sort of paper. You can change this using the [F5] menu in Document set-up. The paper which is used for the results of merges is that set in the document containing the merge program.

Therefore, if you want your lists printed out on A4 paper you should select A4 in the program document. If you want your lists printed out on 11 inch continuous paper then you should select this. Similarly, you should set the correct printer, character set and font details into the program document, because this is what will be used to decide the "intended" printer for your results.

You may be aware that there is also printer and paper information recorded in the datafile itself. These are for use by the datafile [F4] print commands and are ignored when merging. In fact, they are ignored in this book altogether, because the printing options in the datafile are inferior to the techniques we use.

How the program works

Returning now to the program we were using, we will start to explain what all these strange mailmerge commands are:

$-"surname" is a mailmerge command which determines the order in which the datafile is produced. You could change this to $-"town", save the document and do another merge. You would now get the same list, but in the order of the town. You don't have to actually print out the town in order to get the list ordered this way (which may make it hard to believe the order is correct!) You should take careful note that although the word surname turns up three times in the program it is doing different things each time, so if all you want to do is change the order of your list, then you should only change this one command and leave the other occurrences of surname alone.

What the command is actually doing is selecting the datafile index to be used. So if you try to change it to `$="address"` then you may get an error message (`Name does not exist`). This doesn't mean that `address` is not an item name (which it is), but rather that you haven't got an index in your datafile called `address`. In such a case you need only create the index you require and your program will then generate the list you want.

The next part of the program sets up some useful constants; a space, a tab and a carriage return (↵). We call this part of the program the **definitions section**, and you will see it again and again. The constants are used in the list to arrange the items which come from the datafile; putting a space between the name and surname, for example. If you want to arrange things differently, then you can change these definitions, putting more spaces, or other characters and codes between the double quotes. It is important that all the names you use in your program (which are not items in your datafile) are defined here. If you try to use an undefined item then you will get a `Name does not exist` error message.

When you define an item with a tab (→) in it (such as `tab`) then it does not matter which tab stop it moves to in the definition. LocoScript just remembers you want a tab. When it is used (just before the membership class item) it will move to the next tab stop from wherever LocoScript is then positioned. You will need to put a tab stop into the current layout so that your details come out looking tidy.

The next part of the program sets out the information which is required.

> `name : space : surname : tab : class : cr`

This says that we want the item `name` from the datafile, a `space` (which we just told LocoScript about), the `surname` item, a `tab`, the `class` item and finally `cr` (carriage return) to provide a ↵ to the left margin. Of course you don't *have* to request spaces, tabs and ↵s between the datafile items; but if you don't ask for something to be put there then your list will be very hard to read. Whatever items you have, the colons are essential to separate them. If the colons are missing LocoScript will not accept the program and you will get a `Syntax error` or a `Name does not exist` error.

It does not matter whether the item names are in upper or lower case, because LocoMail takes no notice. It does matter that the names are spelt correctly! However, if the names in your datafile start with digits, contain spaces, or include characters which are not letters or digits (such as colons or other punctuation), then you will need to use slightly different names within mailmerge programs. The details of this are in chapter 25.

Do remember, because we won't say it again, we have used `Name` but if you have laid out your datafile card with `Title` and `Initials` you must change this accordingly!

Simple lists 43

TIP: The names of items in the datafile are fixed (at least for the moment), but you can use any name you want for separators like space or tab. Use names which are easy to spell and mean something; writing `space="→"` and `tab=" "`, though it will work, is likely to confuse you in the future.

Remember that you cannot use things which LocoScript does not know about. If you want to use a comma separator:

```
name : comma : surname : tab : class : cr
```

then you must put what `comma` is in the definitions section. If you do not then you will get the error message `Name does not exist`. It will not matter if you have extra definitions which you never use, but it is rather untidy, and you'll notice that we only ever define just the things we need for each program.

Finally there are the commands which tell LocoScript to list all the members details.

Effectively we have:

```
loop = "↵
    {{ details required }} ↵
$+↵
"↵
%loop @ surname↵
```

What is happening here is that the item `loop` is set up, rather like we set up `space` and `tab`. Then the special command `%loop @ surname` tells LocoScript to perform commands from the item `loop` until the item `surname` is blank. When you reach the end of the datafile there are no more records and all the items are set to be blank. Therefore this command causes LocoScript to "loop" round and round, executing the same commands until the end of the datafile. You may recall that in chapter 4 we made a point of telling you never to leave `surname` blank – if you do not follow our advice then you will get incomplete lists – because `surname` will become blank before you run out of members to process.

The {{ **details required** }} part we've just discussed, leaving only the `$+` command to explain, which is quite simple. The `$+` command is the one which tells LocoScript to move on to the next record.

And that is all there is to listing people!

You now know enough to produce any list of all your members, with any details and in any order you desire. For example, supposing you want to list your members' names in order of the town they live in. This is easy (provided you have indexed on town!):

```
⌐⌐......... 1.........?.........?.........?.........?......
(+Mail)
$= "town"
space = " "
tab = "→"
cr = "
"
loop = "
"
name : space : surname : tab : town : cr
$+
"
"
%loop @ surname
(-Mail)
```
Program 7B

In changing Program 7A to 7B, all we have done is to change the $= command to select another order, and, so that we can that the program is indeed producing this order, the {{details required}} part now produces the town rather than the membership class.

The result of the merge will be a document like this:

```
⌐⌐......... 1.........?.........?.........?.........?......
       Mr J Arthurson→               Beccles
       E Anderson→                   Cromer
       Andrew Church→                Cromer
       Mrs G Appleby→                Great Yarmouth
       Mrs M Perry→                  Ipswich
       J Bloggs→                     London
       Mrs R Johnson→                Lowestoft
       Ainsley Smythe→               Lowestoft
       Mrs M Anderson→               Lowestoft
       J Smith→                      Manchester
       Mr & Mrs C E Allingham→       Norwich
       Mr & Mrs Andrews→             Norwich
       Major D Claxton→              Norwich
       D W Hill→                     Norwich
       Mr & Mrs Abson→               Saxmundham
```

Note especially that although we are producing different information in a different order we have not changed the %loop @ surname line. This is because surname is still the special item guaranteed to be non-blank (i.e. always to contain some information) and this does not change whatever order we want, or whatever {{ details required }} we may ask for.

Simple lists 45

The next program produces telephone numbers, in surname order:

```
(+Mail)
$= "surname"
comma = ","
tab = "    "
cr = "
"
loop = "
surname : comma : name : tab : town : tab : tel : cr
$+
"
%loop @ surname
(-Mail)
```
Program 7C

Note here how we've rearranged the details line to give information like:

```
Arthurson,Mr J        Beccles         0502 12345
Bloggs,J              London          081 873 4567
Church,Andrew         Cromer          0263 34567
Claxton,Major D       Norwich
Hill,D W              Norwich         050 88 9999
Johnson,Mrs R         Lowestoft       0502 65432
```

and so we've removed the space=" " command (because we don't need it) and introduced a comma="," command to set up a comma for us to use. We've also changed the tab positions so that the results will look neat.

Once the initial novelty of producing these lists wears off, you'll realise that you need more than just the information from the datafile. You probably want the pages numbered, and you may want some titles at the top of the list or some explanatory text at the end. All of these are straightforward to do. If you want some header/footer text such as page numbers then you just enter it into the relevant sections of the program document. Just like the printer and paper details, anything you set in the program document will be transferred into the results document. If you want some text of your own in the results document then this too will be transferred if you put it either at the very start of the program document, before the (+Mail) code; or at the end, after the (-Mail) code.

In fact, we've only put the (-Mail) code into these programs to show you where the commands stop and your own extra text can begin, so if you don't have any extra text then you could leave this code out. However, **DO NOT** leave out the ↵ which follows the %loop @ surname command. It is vital that this is here and that any (-Mail) appears on the next line.

If you want to add some extra emphasis to the data, perhaps to underline the surname or put it into a different pitch or font, then this is also easy. You just add suitable codes to the definitions for the various separators you want to use. For example, you can underline the surnames by using this program:

```
(+Mail)
$= "surname"
tab = "     "
intro =" (+UL) "
outro =" (-UL) "
cr="
"
loop = "
name : intro : surname : outro : class : cr
$+
"
%loop @ surname
(-Mail)
```

Program 7D

Do not worry that some strange bits of the definitions section appear to be underlined. This will sort itself out when you run the merge.

The next program produces a list with all the details of all the members:

```
(+Mail)
$= "surname"
comma=","
space = " "
cr = "
"
tab = "    "
etext = "                              expires: "
ctext = "         class = "
loop = "
name : space : surname : cr
tab : address : comma : addr2 : comma : addr3 : cr
tab : town : comma : county : comma : postcode : cr
etext : expiry : ctext : class : cr
              ;add any other items here
cr : cr : cr
$+
"
%loop @ surname
(-Mail)
```

Program 7E

Simple lists

You may remember that we commended this sort of list to you at the end of chapter 6. You can use it as a last ditch backup when all else fails.

You will find it useful for other things too, especially to answer telephone queries when your phone is some distance from your computer. You can of course lay out the information as you wish, but our program produces output like this:

```
Mr & Mrs C E Allingham↵
↵       Campion Meadow,Framingham Pigot,↵
↵       Norwich,Norfolk,NR14 7QR↵
↵           ↵  expires: 93/05↵          class = Family↵
↵
↵
↵
E Anderson↵
↵       Garden Cottage,Mill St,↵
↵       Cromer,Norfolk,NR28 9QZ↵
↵           ↵  expires: 93/05↵          class = Life↵
↵
↵
↵
```

TIP: To avoid page breaks in the middle of a set of details select Do not break paragraphs in the PCW Document Set-up [F5] menu (PC Layout [F8] menu).

The line ;add any other items here is a mailmerge comment (because it starts with a semicolon) – LocoScript will ignore it, so it will not matter if you type it in or not. However, as should be clear, it is really there as a reminder that you should add any further items from your datafile card which you need in your listing.

TIP: You will find it easier to predict how your output will look if you lay out your programs like this one. You can freely add spaces, tabs and carriage returns because LocoScript ignores them when it is executing mailmerge commands (except those inside double quotes of course). We have put a lot of spaces in our programs so that the screen dumps are easier for you to read. We have also put commands which generate a particular line of text in the results document onto a single line in the program. This makes it much quicker to get the resulting lists to look neat.

BUT, beware!, although you can add or miss out tabs and spaces with impunity, you cannot take out carriage returns (↵) as easily as you can put them in. In general you have to type either a carriage return or a colon to separate items and commands from each other.

It is especially important in adapting all of our programs that you do not remove the ↵ just before the closing double quote for the loop definition. You should also leave in the ↵ which follows immediately after loop=". We would recommend that you always put in carriage returns where we have done so, though you can add more if you wish.

If you have dabbled with mailmerge before, you might have encountered a rather different way of constructing programs and loops from the one we use. The alternative way uses lots of (+Mail) and (−Mail) codes within the loop to distinguish between the items and the separating spaces, tabs and so on. Although this way is not "wrong" we don't recommend it because it is all too easy to make a mistake and mismatch the codes. Then, when you *have* made a mistake the screen is so cluttered it is remarkably easy to miss it. However, if you come across a useful program which adopts the alternative approach then do not let a slight difference in style dissuade you from using it.

You can find a full (and quite lucid) explanation of the way in which mailmerge commands are executed in the PCW LocoMail manual (chapter 9) or the PC Database and Mailmerge book (chapter 12).

Try it yourself !

Even if you feel experienced and confident, we strongly recommend that you try out the programs in this chapter before you move on to the more interesting programs that await you later in the book. Although we have tried to emphasise how simple lists are (because it is the truth!) you will only really believe it if you try some out for yourself.

We would also recommend that you try out the programs *before* your need for them actually arises. If you are not an accurate typist, or you haven't fully understood just by reading the chapter, then you could be in for a fraught time if you leave it until your deadline is upon you.

Besides the benefit of the lists themselves, you will also get some valuable experience in typing in our programs and then adapting them to cater for your own needs. In particular, if the item names in your datafiles differ, even slightly, from ours then you'll find you have to substitute your names for ours. If your program does not work then don't give up. Turn to chapter 25 on "troubleshooting" and work through that.

8
Selective lists I

This chapter explains how to make selective lists of your members. All of the lists in chapter 7 included absolutely everyone in the datafile. This chapter shows you how to arrange to list only a particular type of member, or just the members who meet a particular set of criteria. Naturally, you can only get LocoScript to filter lists in this way if the datafile holds the information you want to filter upon. You can only pick out the people with red hair if your datafile includes an item for hair colour! However, your datafile will hold quite a lot of information about your members, and you have recorded some of it precisely so that you are able to produce selective lists of your members.

In order to produce a selective list we must test the value of an item (or items) to see if the record should or should not be listed. To do this we use the mailmerge language test command #. This tests whether a condition is true, in which case it executes some commands. If the condition is false then the commands are skipped over. The format of the # command can be expressed as: # {{ condition }} :<: {{ commands }} :>:.

You will recall that at the heart of a listing program we always have a section like this:

```
loop - "↵
    {{ details required }} ↵
$+↵
"↵
%loop @ surname↵
```

We are now going to modify this section to read:

```
loop - "↵
# {{ condition true }} :<: ↵
    {{ details required }} ↵
:>:↵
$+↵
"↵
%loop @ surname↵
```

An example will help to make this clear. Suppose we want a list of all of our Life Members. The program we require is:

```
(+Mail)
$= "surname"
life = "Life"
space = " "
tab = "	"
cr = "
"

loop = "
# class = life :<:
name : space : surname : tab : class : cr
:>:
$+
"
%loop @ surname
(-Mail)
```

Program 8A

If you looked back to chapter 7 you would see that the only difference between this program (8A) and the first program in chapter 7 (7A) is that we've added the three lines:

```
        life = "Life"
        # class = life :<:
and     :>:
```

The first line is part of the definitions section. It sets up an item to contain the word `Life`. The second line is a command to test "is this a Life member?", which it does by comparing `class` in the current record with the item holding the word `Life`. The third additional line marks the end of the commands which are for Life members only.

The program will produce a list which contains just Life members. Of course the program is assuming that Life members are indeed distinguished by the word `Life` in the class item. If you marked your Life members with just `L` then you should alter the definition to `Life="L"`.

The best way to read the curious symbols `#`, `:<:` and `:>:` is as **IF**, **THEN** and **ENDofIF**. What is happening is that LocoScript is still stepping through every record in your datafile, just as it was in chapter 7. However, instead of just unconditionally putting the details of that record into the results document it performs the commands:

  IF this is a Life member **THEN** (and only then) display the details **ENDofIF**

Selective lists I   51

The **ENDofIF** is essential. If you miss it out you'll find that the listing program doesn't work (it will in fact only process the first record).

The other thing to note is that **ENDofIF** occurs *before* the **$+** command. You always want to step on to the next record, no matter whether the details were listed or not!

The test we are making is completely independent of the order you work through the file (i.e. which index you select with the **$=** command). It is also totally independent of the {{ **details required** }} which you choose to extract. This means that you can modify any, or all, of your programs from chapter 7 in the same way. You will get exactly the same details as before, in exactly the same order as before. The only differences will be those introduced by your **IF THEN ENDofIF** statement which will exclude some members from the list.

As an example, to demonstrate how simple this really is, we present a modified version of program 7C; the one which produced the list of members which looked like this:

    Bloggs, J.   London   081 873 4567

This is the same as 7C, with just three extra lines added to it, in exactly the same way as in the previous program. This program will produce the same list of information as 7C did, but for the Social members only:

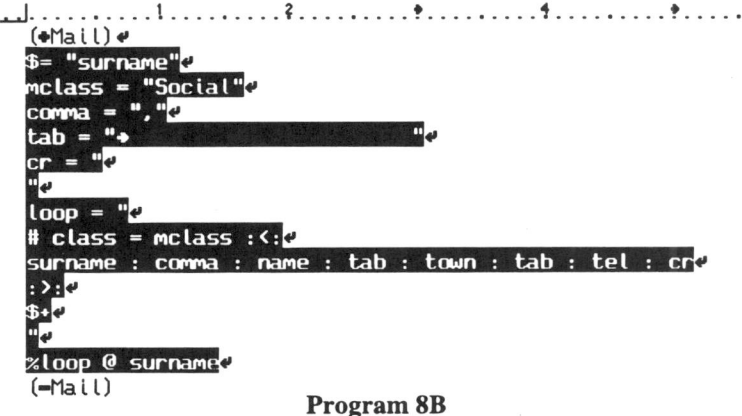

Program 8B

Prompting for information

You might be wondering why we've called the constant `mclass`, instead of `Social`, when we said earlier it was a good idea to give constants "obvious" names. The reason is that we're about to make program 8B far, far, more useful.

You could, if you wished, type in a separate listing program for every membership class which you have recorded in your datafile, but this would be rather tedious. Instead, you can write just one program and tell it the membership class which you want this time. You do this by replacing the line:

```
mclass = "Social"↵
```

by the line:

```
mclass = ? ;Which membership class↵
```

When you run the amended program you'll find that when LocoScript reaches this command it stops and prompts you with a screen looking like this:

```
⌐┘.........|.........?.........•.....█...
    (+Mail)│Which membership class│(-Mail)
                                 ↵
```

You should now type in `social`, or `life`, or whatever it is that you want today. Press `ENTER` on a PCW (or `F10` on a PC) and LocoScript will close up the prompt and proceed to produce a list for the required class. If you make a mistake as you are typing in the response then, provided that you notice before you press `ENTER`(`F10`), it can be corrected by using `←DEL`, or indeed by cursoring back and pressing `DEL→`.

TIP: Once you have typed in the program, use the `F8` menu to hide the intrusive (+Mail) and (–Mail) codes. You can tidy up the prompt in other ways too. Add a question mark and, if you feel you are typing your response too close to the prompt, put some spaces between the text and the ↵.

Although it does not matter whether your response is upper or lower case (or some mixture of the two), you must ensure that you type in a correct class name. If you misspell `Social` as `Socail` then LocoScript will obediently traipse through the entire file looking for "Socail" members and produce an entirely empty list – although of course the list will not be empty if you have similarly misspelt the class of any members in the datafile!

Selective lists I 53

TIP: Since you can have any prompt you might like by altering the text which follows the semi-colon (;) you can avoid problems by having the prompt indicate valid responses, such as:

```
mclass=? ;Which class (Life, Full, Family or Social)↵
```

If you have a lot of trouble with spelling, or you've got some rather exotic categories then you could use some LocoMail commands to help you.

For example, instead of just:

```
mclass = ? ;Which class↵
..etc.
```

you could have:

```
classx = ? ;Which class?↵
# classx = 1 :<: mclass = "Life"   :>:↵
# classx = 2 :<: mclass = "Full"   :>:↵
# classx = 3 :<: mclass = "Family" :>:↵
# classx = 4 :<: mclass = "Social" :>:↵
..etc.
```

When you're prompted, all the valid responses will be visible on the screen (amidst the clutter of the mailmerge commands). You just type a number 1..4 and this is stored away into `classx`. Then a series of **IF THEN ENDofIF** statements arrange to set `mclass` to a suitable value. We'd recommend this scheme if there are only a few possible responses, but it wouldn't be sensible for items like prompting for a town name, where there might be hundreds of possible responses.

Prompting to decide what to do

If you need to produce many lists with different details in each, then you could take this general purpose approach even further. You could, for example, prompt at the beginning of the program as to what information should be listed and then write **IF THEN ENDofIF** statements in the {{ **details required** }} section.

For example, a listing program for potential coffee morning attendees would need you to specify the town. You might then generate a list of the members' names, town and telephone number.

A suitable program would look like this:

```
(+Mail)
$= "surname"
reqtown = ? ;Which town
comma = ","
tab = "	"
cr = "
"
loop = "
# town = reqtown :<:
surname : comma : name : tab : town : tab : tel : cr
:>:
$+
"
%loop @ surname
(-Mail)
```

Program 8C

This program will work perfectly well. But, sometimes you might want a slightly different list. You might not need the town details, or you might want to add the membership class. We can provide this flexibility within just one program by adding some extra prompts:

```
qtown  = ? ;Include town details (Y/N)
qclass = ? ;Include membership class details (Y/N)
```

and an extra definition for comparing the answers against:

```
Yes = "Y"
```

When prompted you must type Y (upper or lower case will do equally well) to indicate "yes" or something else to indicate "no" (preferably N, but the program does not actually check for this).

The next step is to change the {{ details required }} part of the loop to actually check your responses and conditionally generate some of the details:

```
surname : comma : name
# qtown  = yes :<: tab : town  :>:
# qclass = yes :<: tab : class :>:
tab : tel : cr
```

These commands will always generate the surname, a comma and then the name. If you replied "yes" to the first prompt you will get a tab (to space it out) and then the town

Selective lists I

name. Similarly, if you replied "yes" to the second prompt you will get a tab and the membership class. Finally you will always get a tab, the phone number and a carriage return (↵) to move you to a new line.

After adding an extra tab stop to the layout, the entire program should look like this:

```
(+Mail)
$= "surname"
reqtown = ? ;Which town
qtown   = ? ;Include town details (Y/N)
qclass  = ? ;Include membership class details (Y/N)
yes = "Y"
comma = ","
tab = "    "
cr = "
"
loop = "
# town = reqtown :<:
surname : comma : name
# qtown  = yes :<: tab : town  :>:
# qclass = yes :<: tab : class :>:
tab : tel : cr
:>:
$+
"
%loop @ surname
(-Mail)
```

Program 8D

When you run this program it will prompt you for the town and the details you want in the resulting list. When your wishes are known your customised list will be created and you can save or print it as you require.

TIP: Instead of the command `yes="Y"` use the command `yes="Y*"`. The `*` is a wildcard character which matches anything. This means that you can type `Yes` as well as `Y`. (Indeed you could type `Yashmak`, but this is less useful.)

Remember, you don't *have* to set up complicated documents like this one: it is merely a useful technique for you to know about. There is nothing wrong with having dozens of different listing programs and choosing the one you need today. There is also nothing wrong with doing what many people do, and creating a new listing program each time by making alterations to a copy of another program.

Anyway, as the old joke has it, provided the raw information is in your datafile, you will now find it easy to produce a list of your members broken down by age and sex – and another list of the healthy ones.

Comparisons

So far, we've said very little about the sort of things you can test for. The only condition we've used is equality, and we have only been testing for one thing at a time. LocoScript can do rather more for you than this.

The comparisons which can be made are:

=	equals
≠	not equals
< >	not equals
>	greater than
>=	greater than or equal
≥	greater than or equal
<	less than
<=	less than or equal
≤	less than or equal

You can use any or all of these tests with items which are numbers. If the item contains any text you can only test for equality or inequality (= or ≠).

TIP: ≠ is a bit tricky to type. On a PCW you have to press [EXTRA] and #. On a PC you need to press [Alt][F4] then [Ctrl][Shift]= then [Alt][F1]. It is usually much simpler to type < > instead, which works just the same. Similarly, it is usually best to avoid ≤ and ≥ which are again only to be found in the further reaches of the keyboard layout. We'd recommend using the <= and >= versions instead.

These extra conditions are all very well, but more important in practice is the ability to combine two or more tests using **AND** and **OR**:

    # town = reqtown AND class = mclass :<:

or:

    # class = class1 OR class = class2 OR class = class3 :<:

or even both at the same time:

    # town = reqtown AND (class = class1 OR class = class2) :<:

Each side of the AND or OR is a condition in its own right, which is evaluated by LocoScript and then combined with the result of the other test.

TIP: If you are using AND and OR together then the order of combining the tests can affect the result. Use round brackets to force LocoScript to group the tests the way you want them grouped, just as we did in the example above.

There is a further way of using comparisons like > and < which does two tests in one. Instead of writing:

```
(a < b) AND (b < c)
```

you can combine these as:

```
(a < b < c)
```

This is occasionally useful for things like:

```
# 20 <= donation < 100 :<: ...commands for £20-£100 donations... :>:
```

However, since you can always do this another way (using AND) you can instantly forget about this if you wish!

Finally, you can negate a condition:

```
# NOT (class = mclass) :<:
```

Note that in this case the round brackets are required by LocoScript. Missing them out will produce a syntax error. This particular example is obviously the same as:

```
# class <> mclass :<:
```

but NOT( ) can be very useful in making complicated things look much simpler, for example:

```
# town = reqtown AND NOT (class=class1 OR class=class2):<:
...
```

which will list all your members from the requested town provided that they are not in two particular categories (Junior or Social, perhaps).

As you can see, there is a great deal of power available in the conditions for when you need it, but we'll finish with just a simple example, the exact reverse of the first program in the chapter (8A). All of the members *except* the Life members:

```
(+Mail)
$= "surname"
life = "Life"
space = " "
tab = "	"
cr = "
"
loop = "
# class <> life :<:
name : space : surname : tab : class : cr
:>:
$+
"
%loop @ surname
(-Mail)
```

Program 8E

where you can see the only difference is that we've put:

```
# class <> life :<:
```

rather than:

```
# class = life :<:
```

Before moving on, we want to stress again how simple it is to produce exactly the lists you want. The programs we give are just a few examples from the many possibilities. You can make your own by adapting the {{ **details required** }} or the condition to be tested.

9
Selective lists II

In the previous chapter we worked through the records in the datafile in a requested order and tested each and every one of them to see if particular criteria had been met. This chapter is concerned with a different way of making a list which contains only a selection of members.

But, by means of introduction, let us first consider what happens if you run one of the programs from chapter 7 or chapter 8 and for any reason it fails to finish properly. Perhaps the paper wrecks in the printer, or the ribbon fades, or it was just far too late and you had to switch off and go to bed. It would obviously be a good idea to be able to restart the merge from the middle so that you did not have to repeat the successful part.

The command you need is the $$ command which moves directly to a particular record, just like the Goto menu does when you are in the datafile itself. For example we could alter program 7A to list only the members from C onwards:

```
(+Mail)
$= "surname"
$$ "C"
space = " "
tab = "    "
cr = "
"

loop = "
name : space : surname : tab : class : cr
$+
"
%loop @ surname
(-Mail)
```

Program 9A

This is exactly the same program as 7A except for the addition of the one line:

```
$$"C"
```

You can alter any of the programs we have written so far in the same way. You need only add a suitable $$ command after the $= command. If the index you are using has a sub key (and you wish to specify it) then you need a command like:

   $$"Smith"$"J"↵   to start at the first J Smith.

Just as when you are using the Goto menu in the datafile, the sub key will only be considered when there is a complete match to the main key. Furthermore, you do not *have* to give a sub key; $$"Smith" would start at the first Smith, and $$"S" would start at the first surname beginning with S.

The double quote (") marks are only required because we have been writing the keys as text, rather than getting the key from an item. You could prompt for the restart position and store the response in an item. In this case the commands to be added would be:

   mainkey = ? ;surname for restart↵
   subkey = ? ;forename for restart↵
   $$ mainkey $ subkey↵

Selective lists

Let us now suppose that you want a list containing *only* the members whose names began with C. The following program will do this:

```
(+Mail)
$= "surname"
$$ "C"
cstar = "C*"
space = " "
tab = "        "
cr = "
"
loop = "
# surname = cstar :<:
name : space : surname : tab : class : cr
:><: stop = 0 :>:
$+
"
stop = 1
%loop @ stop
$= "" : $$ "9999999"
(-Mail)
```

Program 9B

Selective lists II

The first command of this program is quite familiar; `$="surname"` arranges to step through the datafile in surname order. The `$$` command which we've just met will position the merge onto the record containing the first surname beginning with C, instantly leaping over all the As and Bs.

The next command `cstar="C*"` is setting up a constant for the test we are going to make. The test will be: "Are we still in the part of the file where surnames begin with C?" The asterisk `*` is a "wild-card" character, which will match any number of characters. Thus `#surname=cstar` will be a test to determine whether the surname starts with a C, but we don't care how many characters follow the C, nor what they are.

The rest of the definitions section is standard, setting up items like `space`, `tab` and `cr` as necessary. Inside the definition of `loop` you will see a test rather like the ones we dealt with in the previous chapter. However, this time we have:

`# condition :<: action1 :><: action2 :>:`

which you should read as:

IF `condition` **THEN** `action1` **ELSE** `action2` **ENDofIF**.

In this particular case our program executes the command:

IF	the surname starts with a C
THEN	produce the {{ **details required** }}
ELSE	set `stop` to zero
ENDofIF	

The program works as follows: First the `$$` command moves us directly to the surnames starting C. A list of all the C surnames is then generated. Instead of performing the loop for all non-blank surnames (`%loop@surname`), as we have before, in this case we perform the loop only whilst `stop` is non-zero by using the command `%loop@stop`. We start with `stop` non-zero (by setting it to 1), but as soon as we reach the D surnames (or whatever letter is used next after C), `stop` is set to zero by the **IF** command and so the loop stops, and the list is complete.

A final frill is necessary. The list is complete, but you are not at the end of the datafile (you are currently positioned on a surname starting with D). Thus when you print your list (or save it, or whatever) LocoScript will notice that there are more records to be processed. It will therefore restart the merge from the current position in the datafile. You will then get *another* list of C surnames and another and another *ad infinitum* until you press [STOP] (or [Esc]) and abandon. The commands $="":$$"9999999" avoid this. The first command changes to the record number index. The second tries to move to (nearly) record ten million – which will not be in your datafile, so it moves to the end of the datafile instead. (You could probably get away with far fewer 9s!) At the end of the datafile there are no more records to be processed, so the merge will not be restarted, and you will return to the Disc Manager in the normal way.

TIP: On a PC you can use the single command $* instead of $="":$$"9999999". We have chosen to use the other form because it works equally well on all versions of LocoScript.

We *could* have written program 9B using the techniques of chapter 8, testing each and every record to see whether the surname began with C, and only listing those members who passed this test. If most of the records fail the test (so that no information is produced) this can take rather a long time to produce rather a short list. Program 9B is so much faster because we have arranged to look only at the records which satisfy our test (the C people).

This technique of only looking at the interesting records can be used for any selective list – provided that you have an appropriate index to group these records together. As another example, here is a variant on the "coffee morning" program (8C) from the last chapter, but organised in this new way so as to run faster:

```
(+Mail)
$= "town"
reqtown = ? ;Which town do you want a listing for
$$ reqtown
mclass = "Junior"
comma = ", "
tab = " → "
cr = "
"
loop = "
# town = reqtown :<:
    # class <> mclass :<:
        surname : comma : name : tab : town : tab : tel : cr
    :>:
:><: stop = 0 :>:
$+
"
stop = 1
%loop @ stop
$= ""  :  $$ "9999999"
(-Mail)
```

Program 9C

Selective lists II

You will see that we prompt for the town (using a ? command). Therefore we use the command $$reqtown. We miss out the double quotation marks to show that reqtown is the name of the item which contains the name of the town we are interested in. If we wrote $$"reqtown" then this would select the people who lived in REQTOWN, much as $$"Norwich" will select the people who live in NORWICH! This distinction between name and contents is a little subtle, so you might want to read this paragraph again!

We have also shown you how you might apply a secondary condition; in this case we have excluded all the Junior members from our list. The command for this was:

    # class <> mclass :<: {{ details required }} :>:

TIP: We have indented this secondary **IF THEN ENDofIF** command with tabs. It doesn't matter at all to LocoScript whether it is indented or not, but you will find it much easier to check your program if you lay it out neatly this way.

Drawbacks

If you run this program, you'll find that it works fine, but it may well produce a different list than the earlier program, and not just because the Juniors are excluded. The first program produced a list in surname order whereas this program produces a list in the order of the town index. However, the town is the same for every record and so the list will in fact be generated in record number order.

The reason for this is that when LocoScript creates an index it puts records into order using the main key (town in this case) first. If the main key is the same then any sub key is consulted (in this case there is no sub key). Finally, if the records still cannot be distinguished they are placed into record number order.

This sounds reasonably obvious, but in practice it can be rather confusing, especially when you have recently created your list from scratch. If your source material was in surname order (a common situation) then record number order will be almost the same as surname order. You'll find that most of the list is apparently in surname order, with a few "mistakes" at the end where record number order and surname order start to diverge.

This problem with ordering is a fundamental restriction of the type of listing program we are dealing with in this chapter. You are using the order in which you work through the cards to avoid having to look at all of them. This means that you cannot have the list which the program produces come out in a different order!

However, all is not lost. You *can* list in surname order within each town if you have a suitable index. Remove your simple one item town index from the datafile and then create a new town index, with a main key of town, and a sub key of surname. viz:

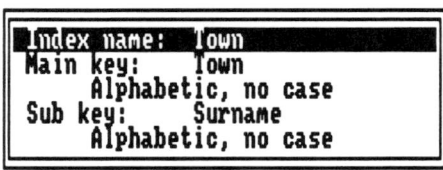

Now your datafile is still arranged in town order, but when you work through all the records for a particular town they will appear in surname order.

Besides the ordering, there are other difficulties with this technique of using indexes to only process the "interesting" records – which is really why we bothered to mention the simple "test every record" scheme in the previous chapter, even though it is invariably slower than this second method. You will find, for example, that it can be rather tricky to write the condition which stops the loop.

The basic layout of a program which uses this "interesting records" technique is:

```
(+Mail)↵
{{ set the order }} ↵
{{ find first wanted record }} ↵
loop - "↵
# {{ still a wanted record }} :<:↵
     {{ details required }} ↵
:><: stop - 0 :>:↵
$+↵
"↵
stop - 1↵
%loop @ stop↵
$-"" : $$"9999999"↵
(-Mail)
```

In the cases so far we have tested if this is {{ still a wanted record }} by using an equality; surname=cstar or town=reqtown. But, suppose you wanted to produce a list of your members with surnames A...M. You cannot use > and < because these items are text. You could, if you were patient, write

```
# surname - astar OR surname - bstar OR ...
```

Selective lists II 65

A better idea would be to turn the test around and spot the first record you do not want:

```
nstar = "N*"
# surname <> nstar :<:
..etc.
```

This works fine, provided that you have some N surnames in your datafile. If no-one with an N surname has joined you yet, then you have a slight problem; you will have to test for the first O (or P or Q...) surname and then remember to fix up your program when Mr. Nabisco joins. However, you can avoid this difficulty altogether by using a little trick, as this program illustrates:

```
(+Mail)
$= "surname"
letter1 = ? ;First letter required       (type nothing for start of file)
letter2 = ? ;First letter not required (type nothing for rest of file)
# letter2 <> "" :<: $$ letter2 : endname = surname :><: endname = "" :>:
$$ letter1
space = " "
tab = "→"
cr = "
"
loop = "
# surname <> endname :<:
name : space : surname : tab : tel : cr
:><: stop = 0 :>:
$+
"
stop = 1
%loop @ stop
$= "" : $$ "9999999"
(-Mail)
```

Program 9D

We use letter1 in a $$ command to move to the first required record, much as we did with reqtown in program 9C. If you type nothing (i.e. you just press ENTER or F10) then the $$ command moves to the very first record in the file (Mr. Aardvark).

However, before this we use letter2 in another $$ command to find the first record which we do *not* want. For example, if you type N and there are no N records then the $$ command will position you on the next available record (O, P etc.). We then record something unique about the record so that we will recognise it again when we see it. In this case we have recorded surname. The test inside the loop is whether we have reached this unwanted record yet. If you type nothing for letter2 we explicitly set enddate blank and the program then gives the right results.

TIP: On a PC we recommend using $# (the record number) as the unique information to identify a record. On a PCW this facility is not available, so you should use the field which forms the basis of your index (in this case surname).

This trick of moving to the first unwanted record, making a note of it and then stepping through until it is encountered is the easiest way of handling dates (indeed on a PCW it is the only practical way). Suppose you want a list of your members who need to renew in March 93. That's pretty easy, we just check for equality:

```
renew = "93/03"
....
# expiry = renew :<:
```

But, supposing we wanted *everyone* who has not paid yet. i.e. their renewal date is less than 93/04. You cannot write expiry < 93/04 because 93/04 is not a number and you can only use < comparisons with numbers. We solve this by once again using the trick of moving to the first unwanted record (93/04), recording the expiry date of this record, and then producing the list, stopping when we recognise that we have reached the first unwanted record.

```
(+Mail)
$= "expiry"
start = ? ;first date to consider  (eg 93/01) type nothing for start
done  = ? ;first date not required (eg 93/04) type nothing for end
# done <> "" :<: $$ done : enddate = expiry :><: enddate = "" :>:
$$ start
space = " "
tab = "    "
cr = "
"
loop = "
# expiry <> enddate :<:
name : space : surname : tab : expiry : cr
:><: stop = 0 :>:
$+
"
stop = 1
%loop @ stop
$= ""  : $$ "9999999"
(-Mail)
```

Program 9E

Note that this program assumes you have set up your expiry dates in a suitable form (like 93/03) so that you can set up an index on them. You can find more about this in chapters 2 and 5.

10
Splitting lists into sections

In chapter 8 we introduced the "test every record" technique of producing lists. This can be very slow when only a minority of records match, so in chapter 9 we showed you how to use indexes to process only the "interesting" records. However, if a great many records match, you may find that your results document becomes too big; or, for reasons of your own, you may want a list in several documents, or on several individual printouts. This chapter shows you how both techniques can be adapted to produce your results in suitable sized batches.

Splitting into batches

The way to split up lists into several pieces was hinted at earlier when we discussed why the `$="":$$"9999999"` command was in some of our programs. If you leave out this command, we said, you will not be at the end of your datafile when the merge finishes and LocoScript will not return you to the Disc Manager. Thus, we can split a list into sections by deliberately stopping before the end of the datafile. For example:

```
(+Mail)
$= "surname"
space = " "
tab = "→"
cr = "
"
null = ""
loop = "
name : space : surname : tab : class : cr
batch = [batch - 1]
# batch <> 0 :<: $+ :>:
# surname = null :<: batch = 0 :>:
"
batch = 50
%loop @ batch
(-Mail)
```

Program 10A

When you merge this program with your datafile, only the first fifty members' details are produced. You will need to dispose of this document by selecting Save, Print, etc. from the exit menu in the normal way. However, instead of returning to the Disc Manager the merge will immediately be repeated, producing the details of the next fifty members. We call each of these merges a **pass**. At the end of the second pass you should again dispose of the document and the merge will then make further passes to produce further groups of members. Only when all the members have been processed will LocoScript return to the Disc Manager screen.

If all you want to do with the individual lists is to print them, you can get LocoScript to do this for you automatically. Point the Disc Manager cursor at the program and press M in the usual way. Now pick out the datafile with your members and press [ENTER]. Set the printing options as you require. Move down to the Automatic line (use [TAB][TAB] to move down quickly) and only then press [ENTER]. LocoScript will now perform an "Automatic" merge, in which the result of each pass will be immediately printed without your further intervention. If the merging process gets ahead of the printer then you will see the menu:

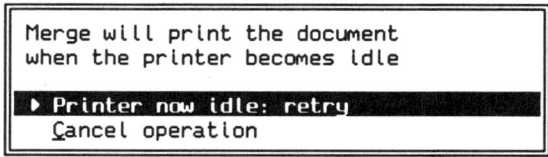

You don't need to do anything, LocoScript will move on by itself once the printer has caught up.

The program itself is quite simple to understand, since it is just program 7A with yet another modification. We move through the datafile in surname order ($="surname"). The loop contains the {{ **details required** }}, in this case name:space:surname:tab: class:cr. The $+ command inside the loop has been replaced by:

```
batch = [batch - 1]↵
# batch <> 0 :<: $+ :>:↵
# surname = null :<: batch = 0 :>:↵
```

The first of these commands reduces the value of batch by one. The second command ensures that, provided batch is non-zero, we execute the usual $+ command to move on to the next record. The third command is there to deal with the situation at the end of the datafile when the surname item is blank. In this case we immediately set batch to zero.

Splitting lists into sections 69

Having defined `loop` the program then sets `batch` to 50 and then executes the commands within `loop` repeatedly until `batch` becomes zero, which happens after fifty members or when the end of the datafile is reached. Once the loop is finished, there is no more program, so the pass is complete. However, LocoScript will notice that there are still records to be processed so it will move on to the next record and run the program again for another pass. It is because LocoScript moves on to the next record before the next pass that we have to skip over the `$+` when `batch` is exhausted.

Obviously there is nothing special about 50, you can set the batch size to anything which you find convenient. However, you should note that each batch is produced as a separate document, so if you are printing the results it is best to choose values which conveniently fill up sheets of paper.

Splitting into classes

Instead of splitting your output up into equal sized chunks you may wish to divide it into logical sections. The following program produces separate documents, each containing the members who belong to particular membership classes:

```
(+Mail)
$ = "class"
space = " "
tab = "→"
cr = "
"
same = class
class : cr : cr
loop = "
name : space : surname : tab : tel : cr
$+
# class <> same :<: stop = 0 :>:
"
stop = 1
%loop @ stop
# surname <> "" :<: $- :>:
(-Mail)
```
Program 10B

When you merge this program with your datafile the first pass will generate a list of all your members in the first membership class (`Family` perhaps). Dispose of this document and the second pass will produce the next membership class (`Full`). Subsequent passes will then produce the `Junior`, `Life` etc. members. Only when all classes have been processed will LocoScript return to the Disc Manager screen.

TIP: If you want the members to come out in surname order within each membership class then you must ensure that the class index has class as the main key, and surname as the sub key.

This is a similar situation to the one we covered when discussing Program 9C. You are using the main key to provide the basic ordering which allows you to split the list into sections. Therefore, if you want a particular order within the sections this must be provided by a sub key.

The program itself is quite simple to understand. We move through the datafile in membership class order ($="class"). After the usual definitions section we record the current class (same=class). We then output the class followed by two crs (↵) as a title for the list.

TIP: You can make the title stand out more by adding LocoScript codes around it. You could define some constants bold="(+Bold)" etc., but you might find it easier to add the codes directly. However, codes are discarded within programs, so you must first stop LocoScript from treating this part of the document as a program. Use a (–Mail) code to signal the end of the program commands. Insert the codes you want, then start treating the document as a program again by means of a (+Mail) code. For example:

```
(-Mail)(Centre)(+Bold)(+Mail)class(-Mail)(-Bold)↵
↵
(+Mail)↵
loop="↵
..etc.
```

Note that we have turned the program off then on again twice (because class is part of the program). Note also that we have put in the ↵s directly, rather than using cr items; there is nothing special about this – it just feels neater.

The loop contains the {{ **details required** }}. These are followed by the usual $+ command to move to the next record.

However, this is not the end of the commands within the loop. We test if the new record is in the same membership class by the command #class = same :<: ... :>. If the new record is for a *new* membership class then we set stop to 0 (i.e. asking to stop). We run the loop repeatedly until stop is set to zero (%loop @ stop). When we have finished looping we will have generated the details for all the records for one particular membership class.

Splitting lists into sections 71

Finally, we have to deal with the fact that we have already read the first record in the new membership class. When LocoScript starts the next pass its default action is to automatically move on to the next record. This was not a problem for program 10A because we could avoid the $+ command at the end of the batch. In this case we will only realise that we have completed the class list when the $+ command has already been issued. If we do not do anything about it then the automatic move to the next record will mean that the first record of the next class will not appear in the result documents at all.

We can prevent LocoScript from automatically moving on to the next record by means of a $- command. This command does not move backwards (nice though this might sometimes be); it just prevents the automatic move forwards. However, we must put the $- inside an **IF THEN ENDofIF** command so that at the end of the datafile (when surname is blank) the $- is not executed. If we did not do this then the merge would continue forever at the end of the datafile.

Creating programs which split up lists

The structure of this type of program is:

```
(+Mail)↵
{{ set the order }} ↵
{{ definitions section }} ↵
same = {{ item value }} ↵
loop = "↵
{{ details required }} ↵
$+↵
# {{ item value }} <> same :<: stop = 0 :>:↵
"↵
stop = 1↵
%loop @ stop↵
# surname <> "" :<: $- :>:↵
(-Mail)
```

It is important that {{ item value }} is the value of the main key item for the index in the {{ set the order }} part of the program. Apart from making sure of that, you will find it easy to adapt any of your other programs to work in this way. There are, however, a few snags for the unwary, which we will now discuss so that you can avoid them.

The first problem is that if your program asks for data then it will ask you each and every pass. This can be avoided by changing the form of the command you use from:

    item_name = ? ; prompt↵

to:

    ! item_name = ? ; prompt↵

The addition of the ! to the command will ensure you are only asked on the first pass. (Strictly, you are only asked if the item is unset, but unless you've got some very fancy conditional statements around these commands then the only time your items will be unset is on the very first pass.)

The next problem occurs with $$ commands. $= commands do not cause problems on a second or subsequent pass (because if the index is already selected they do nothing). However, $$ commands are always acted upon, whenever they are met. In practice this means that you will always get the same part of your list, whichever pass it is. The solution is to use an **IF THEN ENDofIF** command to skip over the $$ command on the second and subsequent passes.

For example, suppose we wanted to generate lists of membership renewals, one month per file, starting at some given date:

```
(+Mail)
$= "expiry"
! start = ? ;first date to consider (eg 93/01) type nothing for start
! pass = 1 ; # pass = 1 :<: $$ start : pass = 2 :>:
same = expiry
space = " "
tab = "    "
cr = "
"
loop = "
name : space : surname : tab : expiry : cr
$+
# expiry <> same :<: stop = 0 :>:
"
stop = 1
%loop @ stop
# surname <> "" :<: $- :>:
(-Mail)
```

                                      Program 10C

Splitting lists into sections   73

We have placed a ! before the request for the start date so that we are only asked on the first pass. We have also dealt specially with the $$ command so that it will not cause difficulties on later passes:

   !pass=1 : # pass=1 :<: $$ start : pass=2 :>:↵

The first command sets pass to 1, but only if it was unset beforehand (the ! can be read as **IF unset THEN**) which will indeed be the case on the first pass. If pass is 1 the $$ command is executed, and pass is set to 2. Thus, on the first pass of the merge we execute the $$ command. On the next pass the ! prevents pass from being altered (from 2), and so the **IF THEN ENDofIF** skips over the $$ command.

Program 10C starts at a particular place, but then continues all the way to the end of the datafile. If we also wanted to stop the merge at a given place then this too is reasonably straightforward to achieve:

```
⌐⌐|....•....1.........?........•........4.........5.........6.........7
(+Mail)↵
$= "expiry"↵
! start = ? ;first date to consider (eg 93/01) type nothing for start↵
! done  = ? ;first date not required (eg 93/04) type nothing for end↵
! pass = 1 : # pass = 1 :<:↵
    # done <> "" :<: $$ done : enddate = expiry :><: enddate = "" :>:↵
    $$ start↵
    pass = 2↵
:>:↵
same = expiry↵
space = " "↵
tab = "    "↵
cr = "
"↵
loop = "↵
name : space : surname : tab : expiry : cr↵
$+↵
# expiry <> same :<: stop = 0 :>:↵
"↵
# expiry <> enddate :<:↵
    stop = 1↵
    %loop @ stop↵
:>:↵
# expiry <> enddate :<: $- :><: $= "" : $$ "9999999" :>:↵
(-Mail)
```
                           Program 10D

This program looks a little more complex than usual, and you might be beginning to feel a little daunted. However, it is in fact very similar to program 9E, as you can see by comparing the two programs.

First we have placed a ! in front of the prompt commands so that you will be asked only once. Next the #done="":<: ... commands have been placed inside a #pass=1:<: test, just as in program 10C. These are exactly the sort of changes we have just been discussing.

Thereafter, we have the structure for the "splitting into classes" style of program we are using in this chapter, rather than style we used for 9E. In order to make the program work properly we need two slight enhancements. The first is to make the execution of the loop conditional by using an **IF THEN ENDofIF** command:

```
# expiry = enddate :<:↵
     stop = 1↵
     %loop @ stop↵
:>:↵
```

This is the most straightforward way of dealing with the case where there are no records at all within the requested range.

The second enhancement is that after the loop has been executed (or even if not) there is an **IF THEN ELSE ENDofIF** command which arranges to do either a $- command (if we will want the next pass) or to do the same "trick" as program 9E and execute a $="":$$"9999999" command if we want to stop.

TIP: Indent the commands which lie within the IF commands as we have done. This makes it much easier to see how the program is intended to work, and a bit easier to check that it is correct.

Splitting lists by surname

Before we leave this topic, to avoid you wasting a lot of time, we will deal with something you cannot do (at least not very neatly). You might decide that you want to split up your list of members by surname, putting all the As into one document, Bs in the next and so on.

The problem here is the one we touched upon earlier; the need to construct a stopping condition. We got round this before (though so subtly you might not have noticed!) by prompting for the letter, and that is the only practical way to solve this problem.

Splitting lists into sections 75

You can construct the As by testing for equality with "A*" (the * acts as a wildcard and matches anything). But then you need to test for equality with "B*", and so on. Unfortunately, you cannot get these comparison strings generated automatically for you.

The only possibility is to get the program to prompt you for the letters, and for you to type them in one at a time. The command which does this is letter=?. Note that we avoid using !letter=? because in this case it is essential to prompt on every pass.

So, the best we can offer is:

```
(+Mail)
$ = "surname"
letter = ? ; Next letter
$$ letter
letterstar = letter & "*"
space = " "
tab = "→         "
cr = "
"
loop = "
# surname = letterstar :<:
name : space : surname : tab : tel : cr
:><: stop = 0 :>:
$+
"
stop = 1
%loop @ stop
# surname <> "" :<: $- :>:
(-Mail)
```

Program 10E

There is one command in this program we have not used before:

    letterstar = letter & "*"

where we've used the **concatenate** operator & which glues together two separate pieces of text to make a single piece of text. Thus if letter is A then letterstar is set to A*; which is exactly what we need for the test inside the loop.

Stopping with the [STOP] key

The last thing we shall mention about stopping loops in the right place to produce a section of a list is that there is also a rather inelegant (but highly practical way) of doing this. You can always sit there and watch the output scroll past on the screen. When sufficient has been produced for your needs then you just press [STOP] then [STOP] again (on a PC use [Esc][Esc]).

From the menu:

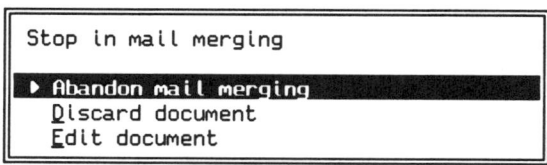

choose the option to Edit document. Now use the normal editor functions to remove any text you do not require, then press [EXIT] ([F10] on a PC) to finish the merge with a Print or Save in the usual way. However, since you stopped the merge in the middle it will then automatically restart with the next record. Stop the new pass of the merge again just as you did before, but this time take the Abandon mail merging option to return to the Disc Manager.

If, later on, you want to restart the merge then you can use a suitable $$ command (just as in program 9A) to start from wherever you wish.

11
Counting records

This chapter uses the techniques we've just been developing for selective lists to count how many records you have in particular categories. There are several reasons why you might want to count your records – you might actually be interested in how many Social Members you have, how many Life Members, and so on. Much more to the point, is that you may find that besides 117 Social members you have 3 Socail members. As we said right at the beginning of this book, computers are not particularly clever. If your datafile has misspellings in it then the misspelt records have a most unfortunate tendency to "disappear". This is because the computer insists upon treating Social and Socail members differently! Whenever you have been updating your datafile you should run some counting programs and check the output for any evidence of your typing errors.

A typical program (which you run in the usual way by merging it with your datafile) is:

```
(+Mail)
$= "class"
tab = "→        "
cr = "
"
same = ""
count = 0
loop = "
# class = same :<: count = [ count + 1 ]
:><:
# count <> 0 :<: same : tab : count : cr :>:
same = class
count = 1
:>:
$+
"
% loop @ surname
same : tab : count : cr
(-Mail)
```

Program 11A

We work through in class order ($="class"). After the usual definitions section we start by setting same to null ("") and the count to zero. Inside the loop we test if the next record has the same membership class as the last (#class=same). If it is the same class then we just increase the count by one (count=[count+1]). If the class does not match then we output the details of the membership class which has just finished (same:tab:count:cr), unless the count was zero (which happens the first time through). Having output the details of the previous class we then record the new class (same=class) and reset the counter (count=1). This loop is executed for every record in the file (%loop @ surname). Finally, we output the details for the very last class (same:tab:count:cr).

Typical output would be:

```
_J..........1..........?..........3...
    Family→           22↵
    Full→             37↵
    Junior→           12↵
    Junoir→            2↵
    Life→              2↵
    Social→           22↵
    →                  3↵
```

TIP: You can make the counts look neater than this by changing the tab position into a decimal tab.

Obviously, you have two Junoir members whose records need correcting, and three members whose membership class item is blank. In order to fix these records you need to edit the records in the datafile. First use the [F2] menu to select the class index. Now use the [F5] (PC [Alt][F5]) menu to move directly to the first Junoir member. Correct the entry and press [PAGE] ([PgDn] on a PC) to move to the next entry (the next Junoir member). You will get a prompt like this:

Select the Step from old value command and press [ENTER] because you want to move to the next Junoir member. If you select Step from new value you will step on from where the record has been correctly repositioned, which is not what you want at all.

Counting records 79

To locate the records with blank class items you cannot get there by making the search string in the Goto menu blank (because that moves you to the start of the index). Instead, press [DOC] ([Ctrl][End] on a PC) to move to the very end of the index where all the null items are collected. Correct the record then use [ALT][PAGE] ([Ctrl][PgUp] on a PC) to move backwards through the file (stepping from the old key value) until all the records with a blank item have been corrected.

Sometimes you may find that the program gives you output like this:

```
⌐┘........... 1........... ?........... ?..
       Life→           1↵
       Family→         2↵
       Full→           6↵
       Junior→         1↵
       Junior↵
       →               1↵
       Junior→         1↵
       Life→           1↵
       Social→         2↵
```

The problems here are that there is one Life member with a leading space on the class name (this is not usually a problem on the PC version of LocoScript, but this will certainly cause difficulties on a PCW). There is also one Junior member with an item which has a ↵ added on the end. This has caused the counting program to think a new class has started (even though a PC will consider them to be identical keys within the index). When the next record contains a further (correct) Junior member the counting program again thinks another class has started. So just one error has apparently given you three separate Junior classes! You should correct the real problems by finding the appropriate records and editing them, and then the other, imaginary, problems will disappear.

You should have one variant of this program for every item in your datafile which you are going to use for producing lists. You modify program 11A by changing the $= command to select the appropriate index and then changing the item class to the item you want to check out. It is of course vital that the index matches the item, i.e. that the index has the item as its main key. It will not matter if the index has a sub key – but if the item is not the main key then stepping through in index order will not have collected all of the items with the same value together, so the output will be useless.

Occasionally you will want to validate an item which is not usually indexed. For example, you might have an item which indicates why people joined your club. You are collecting this information "just in case", and you dutifully fill in advert, friend, article, sheer chance or whatever. In order to count these categories you need an index. So make one! Run the datafile, and go into Datafile set-up. Press [F2] and create a new index. Set the main key to be your item and pick a suitable ordering (probably Alphabetic, Ignore case). Exit the menu and exit from Datafile set-up. The new index will be created. Now exit from the datafile. Run the counting program. If the output is a real mess then you can correct the item contents as required, but you may feel it is just as simple to edit the results document.

Once you have the information you need, the index you've just created will no longer be useful (until next year when you get interested in this topic again). You might as well discard it. Go into Datafile set-up again and press [F2]. Select Remove index and press [ENTER]. Select the index you no longer require and press [ENTER] again. (On a PC you need to select the index first and then press [ENTER]. Remove index is then at the bottom of the next menu). On both machines LocoScript will warn you before removing the index, telling you that it might take some time to recreate the index. (In fact, since you've just done it you know exactly how long!) Once you give a final confirmation the index is discarded.

TIP: On a PCW always create or remove indexes with your datafile on Drive M if at all possible. You'll find it a great deal faster. Of course, you must remember to copy the datafile back to a real disc before you switch the machine off.

You could always create temporary indexes in a temporary copy of the datafile. That way you don't have to remove the index when you've finished, you just discard the copy. However, having the index is useful for finding and correcting any incorrect entries and removing an index is a very rapid operation (much faster than creating it in the first place).

TIP: If you do remove an index then the datafile may or may not return to its original size; depending how the free space within the datafile is distributed. If you have the time then you should use the [F1] (PC [F9]) command to Squash the datafile. This will return it to the minimum possible size. See chapter 20 for more about Squash.

12
Introducing envelopes and labels

This is the first of three chapters about envelopes and labels. One of the most useful things you can do with your computerised membership list is to print out the members' names and addresses onto sticky labels and place these on envelopes containing your newsletter, yearbook, or even just a charity appeal.

But, before you rush to create programs to produce labels you should remember that they aren't always the best way of doing things! They are fine when the contents of every envelope is the same, but a nightmare if the contents of the envelopes differ and the right label must go with the right contents.

Window envelopes

When you get to the point of sending out renewals you should seriously consider using window envelopes for this. Some people don't like window envelopes because they don't feel that window envelopes are terribly posh, or because they think they're associated with bills. Well indeed! That's because they're an excellent solution to sending out bills, renewals and reminders.

In order to use window envelopes successfully you need the address to remain visible through the window. That means that you have to arrange for it to be printed at the correct height on the page, and you must fold the paper in the right place. If you're sending out a magazine you can get A4 sized window envelopes (or even transparent mailers) which avoid all the folding. Failing that you'll either need a good eye, or a couple of measured out marks on your desk to show you where the first fold goes.

TIP: If you are doing a mass mailing you can score the edge of a pile of paper to show where to fold. If you use headed paper then ask the printer who makes it for you to add a little horizontal black line at the right place on one side of the paper. No-one you write to will ever notice it, but it will be invaluable to you. (Locomotive headed paper has just such a little line!)

Arranging for the address to print out in the correct place is reasonably straightforward. You merely have to do a few quick experiments and set up your templates to correspond. However, you must remember that the position on A4 single sheet paper will not necessarily have the same line number as the correct position on continuous stationery because the various top gaps and header zones may differ.

If you put the address at the top of your letter you should have few problems in keeping the position correct. If you put it at the bottom then you will have to take more care because any edit to the body of the document has the potential to cause the text to be laid out differently and thereby move the address up or down. In particular, you will find it difficult to put the address at the bottom if the text of your letter varies depending on the contents of your datafile (as we discuss in chapter 15). On the PC there is a command ($!) which tells you the "height" of items, but this is only a partial solution.

TIP: *LocoScript* Professional will put your address at a constant position at the bottom of a letter if you put a (Height) code at the start of the letter and an (EndCol) just before the start of the address.

Labels

We've done our best to persuade you that there are alternatives to labels (remember that the next time one wraps itself around your platen and takes half the night to remove), but they are often required. The best way of producing them is so different on a PCW and on a PC that we've decided to split the discussion into two separate chapters.

So, if you are using a PCW read chapter 13 and then skip 14. If you are using *LocoScript* Professional on a PC then skip 13 and read chapter 14.

If you are still using LocoScript PC on a PC then you really should upgrade to Professional before starting to produce any labels. The features of the newer program are so much better that we see little point in explaining how to do it on the old software. If you insist on trying then you should pretend you have a PCW and read 13 (the PCW chapter), but you'll obviously need to use PC keystrokes ([F9], [F10] rather than [F1], [EXIT] etc.).

Introducing envelopes and labels

Using the Post Office

Before we split and go our separate ways, there is a practical point to be made about labels, and indeed window envelopes. If you post one letter then you write it, put it into an envelope, address the envelope, stick on a stamp and you put it into the pillar box. If you are sending out your renewals then you must write 700 letters, put 700 letters into envelopes, stick on 700 labels but then you *should not* stick on 700 stamps! Well you could, but unless your members live abroad and are keen philatelists then you'd be wasting your time.

If you are posting over 130 items at any one time then stamps are unnecessary. You can take your letters to the Post Office made up in bundles of fifty or one hundred, all faced the same way, and they will be franked for you. You have to pay for them at the counter.

If you are going to be bulk posting as a regular thing then it is worth applying for the "authority card" which allows you to pay by cheque. This is particularly useful if you can pay with a cheque drawn on your Society's bank account. It takes about a week from applying for this facility to receiving your card. You then show the card whenever you pay.

It may be that you wish to post a large number of issues of your publication and they are too substantial to carry into the Post Office. You still need to prepay at the Post Office counter, but the issues can then be delivered to the sorting office, which usually has space to take them in by car. If you are posting a number of items monthly, you can get a book from the Post Office into which you enter the number of items, the postage rate, and the cost. The counter clerk stamps the top sheet to go with the items and you have a carbon in the book to keep as your own copy.

If you have over a thousand items to post at any one time then, provided they are prepaid, the Post Office will come by van and collect them from you. They like at least 24 hours notice of such a collection. You can ring up your local head office or arrange it when you pay the day before.

If you get into the big league and have thousands of items to post, ring up your local Head Post Office and ask for someone to come and tell you what discounts and services are available. One of the first requirements the Post Office will want is to have the mail sorted by postcode. If you have followed our instructions, you will already be able to do this with ease.

If you get really serious about such things and start considering Mailsort (which is the system used for most of the junk mail that comes through your front door) then you may find that you need a more powerful way of processing your datafile than is provided by LocoMail. The extract programs in chapter 22 will enable you to transfer your data to your new system.

If your membership list is getting this big then you will almost certainly be using, or thinking about using, the information in your datafiles in such a way that you have to register under the Data Protection Act. This is discussed in chapter 26.

13
Labels on a PCW

This chapter is about producing labels on a PCW. If you are using *LocoScript* Professional then you should skip this chapter and read the next one instead!

If you've being reading the chapters about lists then you may be wondering why we are treating labels specially, because you can probably work out that a labels program is going to look something like this:

```
(+Mail)
$ = "surname"
space = " "
cr = "
"
loop = "
name : space : surname : cr
address    : cr
addr2      : cr
addr3      : cr
town       : cr
county     : cr
postcode : cr : cr : cr
$+
"
%loop @ surname
(-Mail)
```
Program 13A

Don't type this program in, because it won't actually work very well! (which is why labels get a chapter to themselves). But before we get to that, and for the benefit of the people who skipped some of the earlier chapters (because this one looked more interesting) we'll examine carefully what the program is actually doing. First of all the $="surname" is arranging for the labels to come out in alphabetical order. This is useful because after you've run off a full set of labels you often want to find one or two specially.

TIP: Remove the label for yourself, and anyone else who needs special treatment, before you, and any members of the family you've persuaded to help, switch on the television and start automatically peeling off labels and sticking them onto envelopes. Besides not wasting an envelope, searching through labels is easier!

We then have a definitions section where the commands `space="  "` and `cr="↵"` set up some values for later use. Then `loop="  {{ details required }}  :  $+"` sets up a loop to produce the details that we want and finally `%loop@surname` causes the labels to be produced for everyone in your datafile (provided they have a surname!). The `{{ details required }}` in this case are the person's name and address. At the end of each line is a `cr` to add in a carriage return (↵). At the end of the label are some extra `cr`s to make the total height of the label right.

All fairly simple, and just like our previous listing programs, so you might be wondering why we said it wouldn't work very well. There are four main reasons:

- Unless you tell LocoScript otherwise, it will think you're using A4 paper and will split your labels into pages on this basis. Furthermore, when it prints the document LocoScript needs to know that you are using continuous rolls of labels, otherwise it will wait for new paper to be fed in, or it will skip paper gaps and pagination zones in a most inappropriate manner.

- You might not have your addresses as single lines (`address`, `addr2` etc.). The problem then is that you don't know how high each address is, so you don't know how long to make the `cr:cr:cr:` you need at the end of each label to move to the next one. If they are single lines, they may be blank.

- You might not be using rolls of labels which are just one label wide; there may be two or three across the page, or the labels may come in single sheets of A4 paper. You need to lay out the names and addresses to deal with this.

- You may have so many members that your PCW runs out of disc space whilst LocoScript is generating the names and addresses, so it never gets round to printing them. In other words, you may need to produce many small output documents rather than one long one.

The first step towards solving these problems is to tell LocoScript what is going on so that it can help you. You do this by setting up a **paper type** which describes the paper you are going to use (i.e. the labels). The way to proceed is slightly different if you are using labels on a continuous roll, continuous fan-fold sheets of labels, or if you are using individual flat sheets.

Labels on a roll

If your labels come on a roll with two or three (or more) labels across the paper then this chapter contains all the instructions you need to use them. However, the programs are invariably more complex than the programs for "1-across" labels. Given a free choice we recommend that you always purchase labels which are "1-across", because you will find things a great deal simpler.

However many labels there may be horizontally, the first step is to measure your labels vertically down the paper. You need to know how far it is from the top of one label to the top of the next. This will be the paper height. **DO NOT** measure the height of the label itself. What you have to set is how far to move downward to get to the same place on the next label.

You should now put your Start-of-day (SOD) disc back into drive A, so that you can permanently record the changes you make to the Settings file. Press [F6] at the Disc Manager screen to start editing your Settings. Select New Paper Type and press [ENTER]. If you do not get offered this option then you have set up ten paper types already and you will have to change one of the ones you do not need any more.

```
┌─────────────────────────────────┐
│ Paper: 2Inch labels             │
├─────────────────────────────────┤
│   Single sheet                  │
│ ✓ Continuous stationery         │
├─────────────────────────────────┤
│ Height              12          │
│ Left offset          0          │
├─────────────────────────────────┤
│ Top gap              0          │
│ Bottom gap           0          │
├─────────────────────────────────┤
│ Ignore paper sensor             │
├─────────────────────────────────┤
│ ▶ Create new Paper Type         │
└─────────────────────────────────┘
```

Give your new paper type a name which you will recognise, like 2Inch labels or Label roll. You can remove any existing name by pressing [←]. Ensure you have Continuous stationery ticked rather than Single sheet paper.

Type in the height of your labels, measured in lines, which are 1/6th of an inch high. So if you measured your labels as 1½ inches then this is 9 lines, 2 inches is 12 lines etc.

Set the top gap to be zero. Set the bottom gap to be zero.

Set a suitable left offset (possibly zero). The left offset allows you to put the labels in the middle of your printer, without having to adjust the position of your margins. The value you set specifies where the zero position is placed. Remember that LocoScript will add onto this the size of your document's left margin. The left offset is measured in 1/10th inch characters, i.e. the value 20 means two inches.

Once all the details are filled in, press [ENTER] and then close up the Settings menu and return to the Disc Manager. You will be offered the chance to write the changed Settings to your Start-of-day disc. You should do this, otherwise your nice new paper type will not be there tomorrow.

Fan-fold sheets of labels

If you are using continuous sheets of labels (which usually come in a "fan-fold" style) then you will find that the individual labels are a fixed distance apart, even over the perforations at the end of the sheet. This is not accidental!

We strongly recommend that you treat fan-fold sheets as if they were a continuous roll of "1-high" labels and use the instructions we gave in the previous section. You could, in principle, use these fan-fold sheets as "n-high" and treat them in the same way as the individual sheets of labels we are about to discuss. However, you will find that the programs you need are significantly more complicated than they would otherwise be.

TIP: When using fan-fold labels, especially on the PCW matrix printer, do not line up the print-head on the topmost label, but pick a label two or three down the first page. You will find it much easier to get the labels to feed properly. If you don't use them immediately you can use the top couple of labels to note what they are.

Individual sheets of labels

If your labels come on individual sheets then this chapter contains all the instructions you need. However, these instructions are invariably more complex than those for continuous labels. Sadly, the BJ-10e printer sold with the 9512+ will not handle continuous stationery, nor indeed will laser printers or DeskJets. For printers where you have the choice, we recommend that you avoid single sheets of labels if you can.

To use sheets of labels you need to tell LocoScript the dimensions of the sheet of paper, not of the individual labels. The chances are that the labels come on a standard size of paper such as A4. However, it is still worthwhile setting up a special paper type. This is

Labels on a PCW

for two reasons. First, you will want to check that the dimensions of the paper called A4 on your system are correct (just because it is called A4 doesn't mean that it is 70 lines long if you've altered it in the past!). Second, and more practically, if you have a separate paper type then LocoScript will prompt you to change the paper in your printer both before you print the labels and afterwards when you print something else.

You should now put your Start-of-day (SOD) disc back into drive A, so that you can permanently record the changes you make to the Settings file. Press [F6] at the Disc Manager screen to start editing your Settings. Select New Paper Type and press [ENTER]. If you do not get offered this option then you have set up ten paper types already and you will have to change one of the ones you do not need any more.

```
┌─────────────────────────────┐
│ Paper: Label sheets         │
├─────────────────────────────┤
│ ✓ Single sheet              │
│   Continuous stationery     │
├─────────────────────────────┤
│ Height               70     │
│ Width                50     │
├─────────────────────────────┤
│ Top gap               6     │
│ Bottom gap            3     │
├─────────────────────────────┤
│ ✓ Ignore paper sensor       │
├─────────────────────────────┤
│ ▶ Create new Paper Type     │
└─────────────────────────────┘
```

Give your new paper type a name which you will recognise, like Label sheets. You can remove any existing name by pressing [←]. Ensure you have Single sheet ticked rather than Continuous stationery.

Type in the height of your paper. This height is measured in lines, and is the height of the entire piece of paper. If you measured your A4 paper as 11⅔ inches then this is 70 lines, 11 inches is 66 lines etc.

Set the top and bottom gaps to the usual values for the unprintable areas of single sheet paper. If you are using the 8256/8512/9256+ matrix printer or a 9000 series daisywheel then the top gap should be 6 lines and the bottom gap 3 lines. If you are using a BJ-10e then these values reduce to 1 line and 2 lines respectively, because this printer can print nearer to the edges of the paper. In all cases, if the first label is within this unprintable zone then you will not be able to print on it, and it will be wasted.

Set a suitable left offset (possibly zero). The left offset allows you to put the labels in the middle of your printer, without having to adjust the position of your margins. The value you set specifies where the zero position is placed. Remember that LocoScript will add onto this the size of your document's left margin. The left offset is measured in 1/10th inch characters, i.e. the value 20 means two inches.

Once all the details are filled in, press [ENTER] and then close up the Settings menu and return to the Disc Manager. You will be offered the chance to write the changed Settings to your Start-of-day disc. You should do this, otherwise your nice new paper type will not be there tomorrow.

Creating the program document

Now that you have set up your standard paper type in Settings you can use it in your documents. Create a new document and from the editing screen press [F1] and select Document setup. Press [F5] in Document set-up and select Paper type. Your new paper type will be in the list. Tick it and press [ENTER]. Now move down the [F5] menu to Page layout and press [ENTER]. Set the header and footer zones to zero.

If you are using continuous labels then you should now see that the Paper length and Page body are both the same (because everything else is zero). If you are using individual sheets then you will have a Page body of 61 or so. If the first or last labels turned out to be unprintable (because of the way your printer feeds single sheet paper) then you can adjust the header and footer zones so that your page body will cover just the printable areas. Strictly, you ought to adjust the top and bottom gaps in the paper definition to reserve these areas. In practice this adjustment works just as well.

Close up the menus with [ENTER][EXIT][ENTER]. Check that you do not have any header/footer text to mess up your labels. You can clear any extraneous text by using the Delete header/footer option in the [F1] menu. Now [EXIT] from Document set-up.

If you are using rolls of labels or fan-fold continuous then following the instructions above will have meant that you have set the page length to be suitable for just one label. This means that when you return to the document you'll see in the top right of the screen that you now have far fewer lines per page than normal – probably just 9 or 12. This means that when you type in your label listing program you may find it is spread out over several pages. Do not let this worry you, because it will all be sorted out when you do the merge.

Labels on a PCW 91

Of course, you can use your labels paper type for other purposes than the programs we are about to discuss. It might be useful to produce some one-off labels for prospective members. You only need to type in the addresses, following each one by a form feed ↓ (ALT RETURN) and then print the document.

If you start using your labels paper type for other things besides the programs in this chapter we must caution you about one thing. In order to make things simpler we've ignored the gaps between labels, setting the bottom gap to zero. This means that for a typical 1½ inch label you will apparently get 9 lines per label. In fact, if you use 6 lines per inch you can't really get more than 7 lines onto a 1½ inch label.

If some of your text is too long to fit on single labels then you should set the bottom gap to allow for the space between the individual labels. This will cause LocoScript to automatically skip the backing paper and print only on the labels. For the programs in this chapter we have not done this because it just makes setting things up more complicated. There is no need to skip the gaps because your labels cannot be more than 7 lines high anyway! You know this, because the addresses fit in the boxes on the datafile card, and you've carefully designed the boxes to avoid overfilling the labels!

TIP: If you use the labels paper type for other purposes then set the page break rule in the Document set-up [F5] menu to be Allow any page break rather than the usual Prevent widows and orphans. If you don't do this you may get only 6 lines per label rather than 7!

Now that you have made your paper type, and created a new document which uses it, the next step is to return to the main editing screen and type in the appropriate program.

Which program you need depends upon what sort of labels stationery you have. The simplest case is 1-across continuous labels, which we discuss first in program 13B and improve slightly in 13C. We adapt this for sheets of labels 1-across in 13D. The more complicated programs (13E & 13F) are for use when you have 2 or more labels across each row. This is handled by building up each horizontal line of printing from 2 or more datafile records. When the line is complete it is printed.

Each program is discussed individually, so it is only necessary to read whichever section is appropriate to you, and then continue the rest of the chapter, starting with the general discussion of **Generating groups of labels** on page 100.

1-across continuous labels

The basic program for 1-across continuous labels is:

```
⌐┘.........1.........2.........3.........4.........5.........6..
(+Mail)↵
$= "surname"↵
space = " "↵
cr = "
"↵
ff = "
"↵
----------
"↵
loop = "↵
name     : space : surname : cr↵
address  : cr↵
addr2    : cr↵
addr3    : cr↵
town     : cr↵
county   : cr↵
postcode : ff↵
$+↵
"↵
%loop @ surname↵
(-Mail)
```

Program 13B

Note: You will get a page separator line after the ↧ character, and you may also get another further down, depending upon the height of your labels. Do not worry; when the program is merged with the datafile this will all come out right!

The first line of the program is the usual $="surname" which determines the index used to create the labels. You can change this if you want your labels in another order. Just remember that the name inside the quote marks must be an index in your datafile.

The rest of the program will be familiar. After the definitions section we set up the loop which produces the labels themselves. Note that after the last item, instead of cr, there is an ff to insert the form feed ↧ to move to the next label (on the next page).

You run the labels program in the usual way, by merging the program with the datafile containing your data. At the end of the merge select Save and Print, and your labels will be printed. The reason for advising you to choose Save and Print, rather than Print, is that you may get a paper wreck or problems with the ribbon. You don't have to be a rocket scientist to see that you can abandon printing and then use Print part of document to reprint the labels you are missing. Once the labels are all successfully printed you can erase the saved document.

Labels on a PCW 93

However, there is a minor problem with program 13B. Unless all your members have seven line addresses you will find you get blank lines on some labels. Of course the Post Office will cope, but it is certainly more conventional to close up the gaps.

To fix this you need to change the central part of the loop to have lines like:

```
# addr2 <> null :<: addr2 : cr :>:↵
```

What we have done is to use the # condition :<: action :>: command (read as **IF** condition **THEN** action **ENDofIF**) to suppress lines which would otherwise be blank. The comparison we are making is <> or "not equal to".

Thus, changing 13B appropriately we get:

```
(+Mail)↵
$= "surname"↵
space = " "↵
cr = ""↵
""↵
ff = ""↵
----------
""↵
null = ""↵
loop = ""↵
name : space : surname : cr↵
# address  <> null :<: address  : cr :>:↵
# addr2    <> null :<: addr2    : cr :>:↵
# addr3    <> null :<: addr3    : cr :>:↵
# town     <> null :<: town     : cr :>:↵
# county   <> null :<: county   : cr :>:↵
# postcode <> null :<: postcode :>: ff↵
$+↵
""↵
%loop @ surname↵
(-Mail)
```

Program 13C

Note that although the cr items are conditional the final ff item is not because you always need to move on to the next label.

If you do not in fact have separate items for your address lines but one monolithic item containing ↵s at the end of each line then you have to use program 13B (or 13C). **No other program in this chapter is suitable**; *or to put it another way* **you have to use continuous 1-across labels.** To adapt 13B (or 13C), all you do is to remove the addr2 etc. items from the {{details required}} section, and of course the cr items. Be careful to leave the ff so that the ↓ will move you on to the next label.

Individual sheets of 1-across labels

If you are using individual sheets of labels then you need to make two changes to program 13B. Firstly, you need to repeat the details *n* times (where *n* is the number of labels down the page). You could do this by just copying and pasting the relevant lines, but it is neater to do it with a loop within the main loop. The second change is that you cannot separate the labels by a ⏎ because this will move to the next sheet of paper, so you need to issue just the right number of ↵s. A final frill is to adjust the number of ↵s to allow for the suppression of blank lines. Putting this all together gives:

```
⌐⌐⌐.........1.........2.........3.........4.........5.........6.........
(+Mail)↵
$= "surname"↵
space = " "↵
cr = "
"↵
ff = "
"↵
────────────────────────────────────────────────────────────────────
"↵
null = ""↵
xcr = "h = [h-1] : cr : "↵
label = "↵
h = 9                                            ;height of each label↵
name : space : surname : %xcr↵
address : %xcr↵
# addr2    <> null :<: addr2    : %xcr :>:↵
# addr3    <> null :<: addr3    : %xcr :>:↵
# town     <> null :<: town     : %xcr :>:↵
# county   <> null :<: county   : %xcr :>:↵
# postcode <> null :<: postcode :>:↵
%xcr @ h↵
$+↵
# surname = null :<: c = 0 :><: c = [c-1] :>:↵
"↵
loop = "↵
c = 6                                            ;labels per page↵
%label @ c↵
ff↵
"↵
%loop @ surname↵
(-Mail)
```

Program 13D

When you type in this program, you must alter the definitions of c and h (from 9 and 6) to be appropriate for your own stationery. The text on these lines after the ; is just a comment for humans to read, so you can omit it if you wish. However, note particularly the extra : at the end of the definition of xcr. This must not be omitted.

Labels on a PCW 95

Following our usual practice we will now explain briefly how the program works, but since this is rather more complicated than usual we would not be surprised if you decided to use the program first and worry about quite how it worked later!

You will see that the program has a slightly unusual form. The normal loop contains a command to execute another "program unit", called label, 6 times (or however many times is appropriate for the number of labels per page). When the page is full an ff command will move to the next sheet.

Within label we find the usual {{ **details required** }} section. After the $+ command to move to the next record we reduce c by one unless we have reached the end of the datafile when we set c to zero, thus leaving the last sheet with some blank labels.

Instead of the usual cr items we have a program unit called xcr which we invoke by the command %xcr. This puts a ↵ into the document as is usual, but also keeps count (in the variable h) of how many ↵s have been inserted. At the end of each label %xcr@h will bring the total count up to 9 (or whatever you have filled in for the label height). The extra colon at the end of xcr is there as a command separator because the colon after the % command has already been used up.

You cannot use program 13D with monolithic, multiple line address items which contain ↵ characters. It is vital to keep count of the number of carriage returns which have been issued so that the appropriate movement can be made to the next label. *If your address item is not made of individual lines then it is not possible to use sheets of labels on a PCW.* If you turn to chapter 22 you will find how to restructure your file to fix this.

"N-across" continuous labels

This section contains the programs you need for 2-across, 3-across etc. labels. These programs work by gathering up the text for 2, 3 etc. labels and then printing them all together. The text for the individual labels is separated by means of tabs.

You cannot use any of the programs here if you do not have the addresses split up into individual lines. If your address items are monolithic blocks with ↵s inside them you will need to convert your data into single line items. Chapter 22 contains the details of how to do this.

We have incorporated suitable tests into the program to "close up" addresses so that you do not get blank lines in labels which do not have a full 7 lines of address.

The program you require for n-across continuous labels is:

```
(•Mail)
$= "surname"
space = " "
cr = "
"
ff = "
"
tab = "	"
null = ""
k1 = "a"
k2 = "= a"
k3 = "& text :"
k4 = "& tab :"
line = "# text <> null :<: %k1&[n]&k2&[n]&k3 : n = [n-1] :>: :"
atab = "%k1&[n]&k2&[n]&k4 : n = [n-1] :"
label = "
n = 7
text = name & space & surname : %line
text = address         : %line
text = addr2           : %line
text = addr3           : %line
text = town            : %line
text = county          : %line
text = postcode        : %line
$+
# surname = null :<: r = 0 :><: r = [r-1] :>:
# r <> 0 :<: n = 7 : %atab @ n :>:
"
loop="
a7=null : a6=null : a5=null : a4=null : a3=null : a2=null : a1=null
r = 2                                    ;number of labels across
%label @ r
a7 : cr
a6 : cr
a5 : cr
a4 : cr
a3 : cr
a2 : cr
a1 : ff
"
%loop @ surname
(-Mail)
```

Program 13E

Note: You will get a page separator line after the ↓ character, and you may also get more further down, depending upon the height of your labels. Do not worry; when the program is merged with the datafile this will all come out right!

Labels on a PCW 97

When typing in program 13E be sure to put in the extra : characters which occur at the end of the definitions of `k3`, `k4`, `line` and `atab`. The definitions `k1 .. k4` are part of the program and should be input exactly as shown. You should change the definition of `r` to be the number of labels across each row on your stationery. The text after the semicolon on this line is a comment for humans only. It may be omitted.

If your datafile has different items then you will need to alter the lines starting `text =` to correspond. Note that if you are putting more than one item per line (as with `name` and `surname`) then you need to combine the items by `&` commands.

As well as typing in the program you will also need to set up tab stops at appropriate positions. Measure your labels with a ruler then convert the label positions into character positions at the appropriate scale pitch for your document (usually 10 or 12 characters per inch). If you have two labels across then you will probably need one tab stop at column 40. With three labels you will need two tab stops, and since the paper is usually wider you should adjust your margins to suit.

If you are using more or less than 7 lines per label then you will need to add or remove from the set of `a1..a7` items within which the labels are built up. Note that besides the line which sets all the items to `null` and the `a7:cr..a1:ff` lines which actually generate the text there are also two places that set `n=7` which must also be changed.

We will now explain briefly how the program works, but the techniques it uses are quite complicated, so we will not go into great detail. If you type it in as shown then it will work for you whether you understand it or not! The typing may look hard but remember you only need to do it once and it is there for use ever after!

The first line of the program is the usual `$="surname"` which determines the index used to create the labels. You can change this if you want your labels in another order. Just remember that the name inside the quote marks must be an index in your datafile.

As normal, `%loop@surname` is used to generate labels for every person in the file. However, instead of `loop` containing the {{ **details required** }} it sets some working variables `a1..a7` to null. It then runs another program unit called `label` once for each label across the paper. This generates the {{ **details required** }} placing them into the items `a1..a7`. Then the actual labels are generated, with a `cr` at the end of each line and an `ff` at the end of the `a1` line to move to the next row of labels.

That was all fairly straightforward. Within `label` things are a little more complex. Here the details of the current record are placed into `text` and then the program unit called `line` is used to add text to the next variable `a7`, `a6`, `a5` etc. `Line` is very complicated indeed! It is defined as a series of fragments of commands (k1, k2 etc.) which & operators combine together with digits made by [n] to generate commands of the form a7-a7 & text, a6-a6 & text etc.

Once all the new text is added to the working variables the program moves on to the next record by a $+ command. A check is then made for reaching the end of the datafile, and if so, r is set to zero immediately, otherwise it is just reduced by one to count along the current row. Unless this is the last label in the row then a → is added to the end of every line by repeatedly running the program unit atab; yet another horribly complicated combination of command fragments.

You run the labels program in the usual way, by merging the program with the datafile containing your data. At the end of the merge select Save and Print, and your labels will be printed. The reason for advising you to choose Save and Print is that you will be able to restart the printing from any point if you get a paper wreck or problems with the ribbon. Once the labels are successfully printed you can erase the saved document.

Sheets of n-across labels

If you are using sheets of labels which are 2-across, 3-across etc. then you need program 13F (see opposite). When you type in this program, you must alter the definitions of c and r to be appropriate for your own stationery. The text on these lines after the semicolon is just a comment for humans to read, so you can omit it if you wish. You also need the correct number of cr items on the a1 line to pad each label out to the correct height. In our example we have assumed each label is 9 lines high, so having already had six crs, we need another three.

This program is in fact almost the same as the previous one (13E). All we have altered is the a1 line from a1:ff to a1:cr:cr:cr. We have also changed the name of the program unit we called loop before to be row in this program. We then made a new loop unit which runs row once for each row of labels until the bottom of the page where we issue a ff (↓) to move to the next sheet. Since the program is so similar you should read the section about 13E for an explanation of how this program works.

You might be wondering what would happen if you set r or c (the number of labels across or down) to one. The answer is that the program would continue to work, so you could in principle ignore all the other programs in this chapter and just use this one, even for simple 1-across rolls of labels. However, this would be needlessly complicated. If you can use one of the other simpler programs, then we strongly recommend that you do so.

Labels on a PCW

```
(+Mail)
$= "surname"
space = " "
cr = "
"
ff = "
"
tab = "                                        "
null = ""
k1 = "a"
k2 = "= a"
k3 = "& text :"
k4 = "& tab :"
line = "# text <> null :<: %k1&[n]&k2&[n]&k3 : n = [n-1] :>: :"
atab = "%k1&[n]&k2&[n]&k4 : n = [n-1] :"
label = "
"
n = 7
text = name & space & surname : %line
text = address     : %line
text = addr2       : %line
text = addr3       : %line
text = town        : %line
text = county      : %line
text = postcode    : %line
$+
# surname = null :<: r = 0 :><: r = [r-1] :>:
# r <> 0 :<: n = 7 : %atab @ n :>:
"
row="
a7=null : a6=null : a5=null : a4=null : a3=null : a2=null : a1=null
r = 2                              ;labels across the page
%label @ n
a7 : cr
a6 : cr
a5 : cr
a4 : cr
a3 : cr
a2 : cr
a1 : cr : cr : cr    ;this line needs enough <cr>s to fill the label
# surname = null :<: c = 0 :><: c = [c-1] :>:
"
loop = "
c = 6                              ;labels down the page
%row @ c
ff
"
%loop @ surname
(-Mail)
```

Program 13F

Generating groups of labels (for any paper type)

Now that you have a program for your particular type of labels stationery, we will now turn our attention to the various issues which arise with *all* of these programs.

The first difficulty you may meet is that you do not have space on drive M to store the document holding the labels before it is printed. If drive M fills up then you will get a message telling you that it is full:

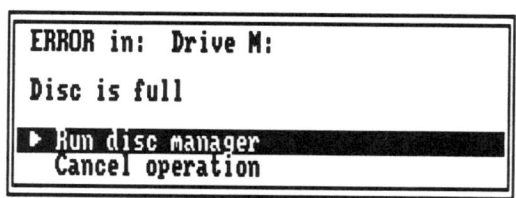

You may be able to get around this by erasing LOCOSPEL.DCT or any other files which can be reloaded onto drive M later. You could even buy a RAM expansion and make drive M bigger. However, even this may not create sufficient space to help in all cases. The solution is to create your labels in batches just like we did in program 10A.

In the definitions section add the line:

```
batch - 60↵
```

Also, if your program does not have such a definition already, add:

```
null - ""↵
```

You don't need to use a batch size of 60. In fact, if you use "n-across" labels or sheets of labels, you should set the batch size to be a multiple of the number of labels across, or the number of labels per sheet. Otherwise you will waste labels at the end of each batch.

Change any tests in the program which read #surname=null... to read #batch=0... instead (this does not apply to 13B & 13C which have no such tests).

Next you must replace the $+ by the following three lines:

```
batch - [batch-1]↵
# batch <> 0 :<: $+ :>↵
# surname - null :<: batch - 0 :>↵
```

Labels on a PCW 101

The first of these lines decreases the value of batch by one. The square brackets make this an arithmetic command. The next line tests if batch is zero; if not then the $+ command will move on to the next record in the datafile. The third line is there to deal with the situation at the end of the datafile, when all the labels have been produced. If you reach the end of the datafile then surname will become blank. If so then we set batch to zero immediately. This means that there is no need to pick the batch size so that it divides neatly into the total number of labels you are producing.

Finally, change the %loop @ surname command to read %loop @ batch.

Thus (as an example) Program 13D becomes:

```
(+Mail)
$= "surname"
space = " "
cr = "
"
ff = "

"
null = ""
batch = 60
xcr = "h = [h-1] : cr : "
label = "
h = 9                              ;height of each label
name : space : surname : %xcr
address : %xcr
# addr2    <> null :<: addr2    : %xcr :>:
# addr3    <> null :<: addr3    : %xcr :>:
# town     <> null :<: town     : %xcr :>:
# county   <> null :<: county   : %xcr :>:
# postcode <> null :<: postcode :>:
%xcr @ h
batch = [batch - 1]
# batch <> 0 :<: $+ :>:
# surname = null :<: batch = 0 :>:
# batch = 0 :<: c = 0 :><: c = [c-1] :>:
"
loop = "
c = 6                              ;labels per page
%label @ c
ff
"
%loop @ batch
(-Mail)
```

Program 13G

The modified program will now generate labels until batch becomes zero, i.e. until you reach the end of the group of labels, or until you reach the end of the datafile. If there are more labels to be generated then LocoScript will not return to the Disc Manager at the end of the batch. Instead, the program will be automatically run again to make the next batch of labels whilst the first batch are printed.

It is best to run this variant of the program in a slightly different way. As usual you start by pointing the Disc Manager cursor at the program, press M, pick out the datafile and press [ENTER]. Set the number of copies you require (usually one), and whether you want Draft or High Quality printing. Now, instead of pressing [ENTER] move down to the Automatic line ([SHIFT][↓] does this quickly!) and then press [ENTER] to invoke the Automatic merge option.

```
┌─────────────────────────────┐
│ Merge documents             │
├─────────────────────────────┤
│ Data:    MEMBERS  .DAT      │
│ Group:     group 0          │
│ Drive:   A                  │
├─────────────────────────────┤
│ Name:    PROG     .13G      │
│ Group:     group 0          │
│ Drive:   A                  │
├─────────────────────────────┤
│ ✓ High quality              │
│   Draft quality             │
│ Number of copies:     1     │
├─────────────────────────────┤
│   Manual                    │
│ ▶ Automatic                 │
└─────────────────────────────┘
```

In an automatic merge each batch of labels will be immediately printed without you having to pick out Print result from the exit menu. If the merging process gets ahead of the printer then you will temporarily see the menu:

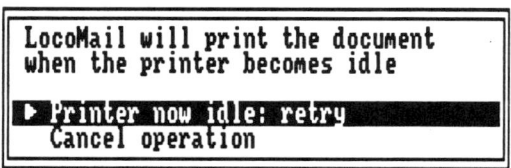

```
┌─────────────────────────────────┐
│ LocoMail will print the document│
│ when the printer becomes idle   │
├─────────────────────────────────┤
│ ▶ Printer now idle: retry       │
│   Cancel operation              │
└─────────────────────────────────┘
```

Strictly, our commands batch up the records you process rather than the labels you produce. Up to now we have been producing one label per record, so this distinction has not been important. We mention it only because the next section is going to show you how to produce labels for only some of your records. If you are producing only some labels then you will have to ensure that when you skip a record you also skip the command which reduces the batch file count. If you cannot see how to do this, you could just be ultra-pragmatic and increase your batch size to reflect the fact that only a proportion of records will produce labels!

Printing only some labels

Label programs can become rather complicated if you fail to stick with 1-across rolls of labels. You also have to remember to set up their paper types correctly. Apart from this, they are not in fact very different to the other programs in this book which generate lists. Therefore all of the techniques which we explored in chapters 8 and 9 to generate selective lists can be adapted quite straightforwardly to label programs.

To illustrate this we will give a couple of examples. These will be for rolls of labels only, but the same sort of changes could equally well be made for sheets of labels.

If you want to produce labels for just your life members then you could use the technique from program 8A within our labels program (13C) to give you:

```
(+Mail)
$= "surname"
mclass = "Life"
space = " "
cr = "
"
ff = "
```

```
"
null = ""
loop = "
# class = mclass :<:
name : space : surname : cr
# address  <> null :<: address  : cr :>:
# addr2    <> null :<: addr2    : cr :>:
# addr3    <> null :<: addr3    : cr :>:
# town     <> null :<: town     : cr :>:
# county   <> null :<: county   : cr :>:
# postcode <> null :<: postcode :>: ff
:>:
$+
"
%loop @ surname
(-Mail)
```

Program 13H

You would adapt the n-across program (13E) in much the same way:

```
(+Mail)
$= "surname"
mclass = "Life"
space = " "
cr = "
"
ff = "
"

"
tab = "        "
null = ""
k1 = "a"
k2 = "= a"
k3 = "& text :"
k4 = "& tab :"
line = "# text <> null :<: %k1&[n]&k2&[n]&k3 : n = [n-1] :>: :"
atab = "%k1&[n]&k2&[n]&k4 : n = [n-1] :"
label = "
# class = mclass :<:
n = 7
text = name & space & surname : %line
text = address      : %line
text = addr2        : %line
text = addr3        : %line
text = town         : %line
text = county       : %line
text = postcode     : %line
$+
# surname = null :<: r = 0 :><: r = [r-1] :>:
# r <> 0 :<: n = 7 : %atab @ n :>:
:><:
$+
# surname = null :<: r = 0 :>:
:>:
"
loop="
a7=null : a6=null : a5=null : a4=null : a3=null : a2=null : a1=null
r = 2                             ;number of labels across
%label @ n
a7 : cr
a6 : cr
a5 : cr
a4 : cr
a3 : cr
a2 : cr
a1 : ff
"
%loop @ surname
(-Mail)
```

Program 13I

Labels on a PCW 105

If you examine 13H and 13I closely you will see that they are identical to 13C and 13E except for the definition mclass = "Life" and some changes within the innermost program unit.

In 13H we test the condition which interested us (class = mclass) and then only generate a label if the condition was met. In both cases we want to move on to the next record by $+, so we just put an **ENDofIF** just before the it.

In 13I we have done much the same thing. If the condition is met then we execute exactly the same commands as in 13E. If the condition is not met we have an **ELSE** section to step on to the next record ($+). We can then check for the end of the datafile (# surname = 0...). This is more complex than the changes made to 13H only because of the need to conditionally execute not only some commands which are before the $+ (the {{ details required }}) but also some which follow the $+ (the counting commands).

Similarly, you would change the innermost loop of 13D to read:

```
# class = mclass :<:↵
h = 9 ....
# surname = null :<: c = 0 :><: c=[c-1] :>:↵
:><:↵
      $+↵
      # surname = null :<: c = 0 :>:↵
:>:↵
```

and the innermost loop of 13F to:

```
# class = mclass :<:↵
n = 7 ....
# r <> 0 :<: n=7 : %atab @ n :>:↵
:><:↵
      $+↵
      # surname = null :<: r=0 :>:↵
:>:↵
```

If you want to develop other selective label programs then the changes you make will be very similar to these. Any of the techniques of chapter 8 can be applied to these label programs in just the same way as we have shown you for 8A.

If you want to apply a "process the interesting records" technique from chapter 9 then this is a straightforward change as well. As an example we shall adapt what we did in program 9E (which listed all the members who had not yet paid). We shall alter program 13C (for 1-across continuous labels), and this will give us labels to stick onto the reminder notices we are about to send out:

```
_|.........1.........?.........?.........4.........5.........6.........
(+Mail)
$= "expiry"
start = ? ;first date to consider  (eg 93/01) type nothing for start
done  = ? ;first date not required (eg 93/04) type nothing for end
# done <> ""  :<: $$ done : enddate = expiry :><: enddate = "" :>:
$$ start
space = " "
cr = "
"
ff = "
```

```
"
null = ""
loop = "
# expiry <> enddate :<:
name : space : surname : cr
# address  <> null :<: address  : cr :>:
# addr2    <> null :<: addr2    : cr :>:
# addr3    <> null :<: addr3    : cr :>:
# town     <> null :<: town     : cr :>:
# county   <> null :<: county   : cr :>:
# postcode <> null :<: postcode :>: ff
:><: stop = 0 :>:
$+
"
stop = 1
%loop @ stop
$= "" : $$ "9999999"
(-Mail)
```

Program 13J

In the way of all good textbooks, we shall leave the equivalent changes to 13D, 13E and 13F as an exercise for the interested reader. As you are probably aware this is usually a way of saying that such changes are not as trivial as they might be. However, in this case the changes *are* quite straightforward. You should start from program 13I (or the fragments which follow it) and then make the same changes as we made in converting program 13H into 13J.

Having reached the end of the chapter, we shall now leave the entire subject of labels to the interested reader. Do not be daunted by the label programs we have shown you. All the programs in this chapter will work if you type them in exactly as we have written them. Your PCW won't care whether you could have written them yourself from scratch; it just gets on with what it has been told to do!

14
Labels on a PC

This chapter is about producing labels using *LocoScript* Professional. If you are using a PCW then you should read the previous chapter instead. If you are still using LocoScript PC then the programs in this chapter will not work for you because they use new features, not present in LocoScript PC, which make labels especially easy. You ought to upgrade to Professional as soon as practicable. In the meantime you should read chapter 12, and then read chapter 13.

If you've being reading the chapters about lists then you may be wondering why we are treating labels specially, because you can probably work out that a labels program is going to look something like this:

```
(+Mail)
$= "surname"
space = " "
cr = "
"
loop = "
name : space : surname : cr
address  : cr
addr2    : cr
addr3    : cr
town     : cr
county   : cr
postcode : cr : cr : cr
$+
"
%loop @ surname
(-Mail)
```

Program 14A

Do not type this program in, because it won't actually work very well! (which is why labels get a chapter to themselves). But before we get to that, and for the benefit of the people who skipped some of the earlier chapters (because this one looked more interesting) we'll examine carefully what the program is actually doing. First of all the `$="surname"` is arranging for the labels to come out in alphabetical order. This is useful because after you've run off a full set of labels you often want to find one or two specially.

TIP: Remove the label for yourself, and anyone else who needs special treatment, before you, and any members of the family you've persuaded to help, switch on the television and start automatically peeling off labels and sticking them onto envelopes. Besides not wasting an envelope, searching through labels is easier!

We then have a definitions section where the commands space=" " and cr="↵" set up some values for later use. Then loop=" {{ details required }} : $+" sets up a loop to produce the details that we want and finally %loop@surname causes the labels to be produced for everyone in your datafile (provided they have a surname!). The {{ details required }} in this case are the person's name and address. At the end of each line is a cr to add in a carriage return (↵). At the end of the label are some extra crs to make the total height of the label right.

All fairly simple, and just like our previous listing programs, so you might be wondering why we said it wouldn't work very well. There are four main reasons:

- Unless you tell *LocoScript* otherwise, it will think you're using A4 paper and will split your labels into pages on this basis. Furthermore, when it prints the document *LocoScript* needs to know that you are using continuous rolls of labels, otherwise it will wait for new paper to be fed in, or it will skip paper gaps and pagination in a most inappropriate manner.

- You might not have your addresses as single lines (address, addr2 etc.). The problem then is that you don't know how high each address is, so you don't know how long to make the cr:cr:cr: you need at the end of each label to move to the next one. If they are single lines, they may be blank.

- You might not be using rolls of labels which are just one label wide; there may be two or three across the page, or the labels may come in single sheets of A4 paper. You need to lay out the names and addresses to deal with this.

- You may have so many members that your PC runs out of disc space whilst *LocoScript* is generating the names and addresses, so it never gets round to printing them. In other words, you may need to produce many small output documents rather than one long one.

The first step towards solving these problems is to tell *LocoScript* what is going on so that it can help you. You do this by setting up a **paper type** which describes the paper you

Labels on a PC

are going to use (i.e. the labels). The way to proceed is slightly different if you are using labels on a continuous roll, continuous fan-fold sheets of labels, or if you are using individual flat sheets.

Labels on a roll

The first step is to measure your labels. You need to know how far it is from the top of one label to the top of the next. This will be the paper height. **DO NOT** measure the height of the label itself. What you have to set is how far to move downward to get to the same place on the next label.

Display the Disc Manager screen, press [F9] and select Settings. Press [F3] for the Paper menu; cursor down to Create new paper type and press [ENTER]. *LocoScript* allows you to define up to fifty different paper types, so you are pretty unlikely to run out! You are then asked which paper type your new paper will be based on. Picking something similar will save you a little typing, but otherwise it will not matter which paper you choose.

You will now see the paper type menu:

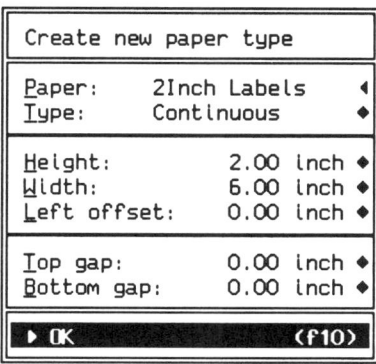

Give your new paper type a name which you will recognise, like 2Inch Labels or Label roll. Ensure you have Continuous selected rather than Single sheet.

Type in the height of your labels. You can either use inches directly, or, if you prefer, you can use **picas**. One pica is 12 points, which is 12/72 of an inch, which is 1/6th inch, i.e. a pica is just the old PCW notion of a **line** under another name! If you measured your label in millimetres then find another ruler! Even on the continent (where they've been using the metric system for hundreds of years) continuous stationery is always made as exact values in inches (or 1/6ths of inches). Setting values in millimetres *will not be precise enough*, always causes trouble, and should be avoided.

Set the paper top gap to be zero. Set the paper bottom gap to be zero.

Set a suitable left offset (possibly zero). The left offset allows you to put the labels in the middle of your printer, without having to adjust the position of your margins. The value you set specifies where the edge of the paper is to be placed. Remember that *^{Loco}Script* will add onto this any page margins which may be set in the document. You can choose any units for the left offset which you feel happy with, inches, mm or picas.

You should also set the paper width to the full distance across the paper. Do not measure any individual labels or columns of labels. The page margins set in the document will be measured from the edges of the paper.

Once all the details are filled in, press [F10] to close the paper menu. Now press [F10] and [ENTER] to return to the Disc Manager and your new paper type is saved away.

Fan-fold sheets of labels

If you are using continuous sheets of labels (which usually come in a "fan-fold" style) then you will find that the individual labels are a fixed distance apart, even over the perforations at the end of the sheet. This is not accidental! We would usually recommend that you treat them as if they were a continuous roll and use the instructions we gave in the previous section.

The alternative is to follow the instructions we give in the next section for individual sheets of labels. However, you will have to set the paper type to be `Continuous` rather than `Single sheet`.

You must also ensure that the paper height you give is in either inches or picas (1/6th inch). You should avoid using mm because no real sheets of continuous paper are ever an exact number of millimetres high (whereas they will *always* be an exact number of picas high – even "continuous A4" is in fact 70 picas not the precise 297mm which real A4 should be). An error of a fraction of a millimetre may not sound a lot, but *^{Loco}Script* will feed sheets as accurately as the printer will allow, so after 10 or 20 sheets the error will mount up and you will find that text is being printed onto the backing paper, or an adjacent label.

Individual sheets of labels

If you are using individual sheets of labels then you need to tell $^{\text{\textit{Loco}}}Script$ the dimensions of the sheet of paper, not of any labels on it. The chances are that the labels come on a standard size of paper such as A4. However, it is still worthwhile setting up a special paper type. This is for two reasons. First you will want to check that the details of the paper called A4 on your system are correct (just because it is called A4 doesn't mean that you haven't altered it in the past!). Second, and more practically, if you have a separate paper type then $^{\text{\textit{Loco}}}Script$ will prompt you to change the paper in your printer both before you print the labels and afterwards when you print something else.

Display the Disc Manager screen, press [F9] and select Settings. Press [F3] for the Paper menu; cursor down to Create new paper type and press [ENTER]. $^{\text{\textit{Loco}}}Script$ allows you to define up to fifty different paper types, so you are pretty unlikely to run out! You are then asked which paper type your new paper will be based on. Picking something similar will save you a little typing, but otherwise it will not matter which paper you choose. You will now see the paper type menu:

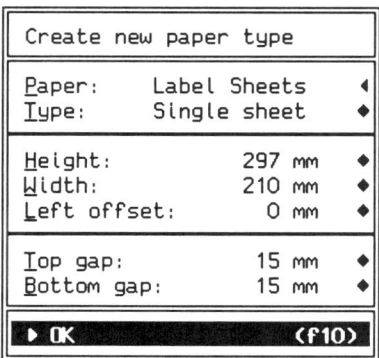

Give the paper type a name which you will recognise, like Label Sheets. Fill in the dimensions of your sheets of labels, remembering to set Single sheet.

You should fill in the size of the non-label areas at the top and bottom of the sheets. The values you put here must not be less than your "Printer top gap" and "Printer bottom gap" for single sheet paper (you can find out what these are set to through the Printer control [F5] menu). What this means in practice is that if your printer always feeds in one inch of paper and the labels start higher than this then you are forced to waste the top label on every sheet.

Set a suitable left offset (possibly zero). The left offset allows you to put the labels in the middle of your printer, without having to adjust the position of your margins. The value you set specifies where the edge of the paper is to be placed. Remember that $^{Loco}Script$ will add onto this any margins which may be set in the document. You can choose any units for the left offset which you feel happy with, inches, mm or picas.

You should also set the paper width to the full distance across the paper. Do not measure any individual labels or columns of labels. The page margins set in the document will be measured from the edges of the paper.

Once all the details are filled in, press [F10] to close up the paper menu. Now press [F10] and [ENTER] to return to the Disc Manager and your new paper type is saved away.

Creating the program document

Now that you have set up your standard paper type in Settings you can use it in your documents. Create a new document and from the editing screen press [F9] to enter Document set-up. Press [F5] and press [ENTER] on the Paper line. Your new paper type will be in the list. Move the ⇒ to your labels paper type and press [ENTER].

Now move down the [F5] menu to Top/bottom page margins and press [ENTER] again. Set the page top and bottom margins to zero.

Set the Left/right page margins to the distance from the paper edge to the edge of the labels. It is important to get these right if you have several labels across the page because we will shortly be setting up columns, and these will be evenly spread across the distance between the page margins.

Set the Header margins and Footer margins all to zero and close up the menu and exit back to the main document. If you have any header/footer text then $^{Loco}Script$ will complain that you have overlapping areas, or that the text will not fit. You will need to Edit header/footer and remove it all using [F9] Delete header/footer, since pagination text is not appropriate for labels!

If you are using rolls of labels or fan-fold continuous then your page length is now suitable for just one label. You will see in the top right of the screen that you now have a far smaller page than normal : with perhaps just 9 or 12 lines per page. When you type in your label listing program you may find it is spread out over several pages. Do not let this worry you, because it will all be sorted out when you do the merge.

Labels on a PC

Of course, you can use your labels paper type for other purposes than the programs we are about to discuss. It might be useful to produce some one-off labels for prospective members. You only need to type in the addresses, following each one by a ↓ (`Ctrl`+`↵`) and then print the document.

If you start using your labels paper type for other things besides the programs in this chapter we must caution you about one thing. In order to make things simpler we've ignored the gaps between labels. This means that for a typical 1½ inch label you will apparently get 9 lines per label. In fact, if you use 6 lines per inch you can't really get more than 7 lines onto a 1½ inch label.

If some of your text is too long to fit on single labels then you should set the paper (or page) margins to allow for the space between the individual labels. This will cause *LocoScript* to skip the gaps and print only on the labels. For the programs in this chapter we have not done this because it this just makes setting things up more complicated. There is no need to skip the gaps because your labels cannot be more than seven lines high anyway! You know this, because all the addresses fit in the boxes on the datafile card, and you've carefully designed the boxes to avoid overfilling the labels!

TIP: If you use the labels paper type for other purposes then alter the Layout `F8` option to be Allow any page break rather the usual Prevent widows and orphans. If you don't do this you may only get 6 lines per label rather than 7!

If you are using 2-across (or 3- or 4- across) labels then you must set up some columns so that *LocoScript* will not put all the labels in the first column. Press `F2` and select Amend layout to alter the layout. (You could, if you wanted, change one of the Stock layouts and use all the fancy inheritance system of the program, but there is little necessity when setting up an individual document like this one).

Use the `F5`-Frame menu to change the number of columns, by typing the value you want into the Columns entry. You may also need to adjust the size of the inter-column gap to correspond to the gap between the labels.

If you've never used columns before you may be surprised by the way in which columns appear on the screen. You may find it helpful to review chapter 20 of the *LocoScript* Reference book before proceeding.

TIP: If you set up the columns before typing in the program then it will be laid out across several columns, and it will be harder to check you've typed it in correctly. It will be easier to type the program in first and check that it seems to be correct, and only then set up the columns.

The basic program you need for labels is:

```
   ┘ . . . . . . . . . 1 . . . . . . . . . 2 . . . . . . . . . 3 . . . . . . . . . 4 . . . . . . . . . 5 . . . . . . . . . 6 . .
   (+Mail)↵
   $= "surname"↵
   ht = "(+Height1.5")▓↵
   ec = "(EndCol)▓↵
   space = " "↵
   cr = "
   "↵
   loop = "↵
   ht↵
   name : space : surname : cr↵
   address    : cr↵
   addr2      : cr↵
   addr3      : cr↵
   town       : cr↵
   county     : cr↵
   postcode : ec : cr↵
   $+↵
   "↵
   %loop @ $#↵
   (-Mail)
```

Program 14B

The first line of the program is the usual `$="surname"` which determines the index used to create the labels. You can change this if you want your labels in another order. Just remember that the name inside the quote marks must be an index in your datafile.

The next line tells the program how high your labels are, and you should change it to correspond with your own labels:

```
ht = "(+Height1.5")"
```

(+Height) is a code which you can put into the document either from the [F5] menu (Height of column) or from the [+] menu. The height of each label will usually be an exact number of 1/6^{ths} of an inch (picas), but you may come across some labels which have some very strange lengths (usually sheets of labels for photocopiers rather than computers).

Measure the size as accurately as possible, but do not worry if you are a little inexact because the accumulated error is discarded when each page is filled. As always when measuring labels, the distance you want is from the top of one to the top of the next. If you are using continuous labels then the height you set here will be exactly the same as the paper height you set earlier.

Labels on a PC

The function of the (Height) code is to ensure that there is room for each label on the current page. If not, *LocoScript* will move on to the next page without any need for a form feed (↓). The next line contains another special code. (EndCol) can also be put in from either the [F5] menu (End of column) or from the [+] menu. The function of this code is to put a marker on the last line of each label to signal that the next label should start in a new column.

The next part of the program will be familiar. After the definitions section we set up the loop which produces the labels themselves. Note that ht precedes any text from the datafile to ensure that the label is put on the right page. Similarly, after the last piece of text there is an ec command to insert the (EndCol) before the final cr.

There is no need for your address to be split into lots of individual lines as in our example. This program will work perfectly well with multiple line address items which contain embedded ↵ codes. However, you still need to add the (EndCol) code and then another cr after the end of the address.

Finally, we have a slightly different command to run the loop:

```
%loop @ $#↵
```

You may recall that we recommended that you always used $# (the record number) to control loops if you were using *LocoScript* on a PC. In this PC-only chapter we are taking our own advice. Of course %loop@surname will still work (just as on a PCW).

You run the labels program in the usual way, by merging the program with the datafile containing your membership. If you are using columns then when the output appears on screen, it will look distinctly odd with the names and addresses being positioned into each column in turn. Have faith, all will be well when they are printed! At the end of the merge select Save and Print. The reason for advising you to choose Save and Print rather than Print, is that you will find it easy to restart the printing from any point if you get a paper wreck or problems with the ribbon. Once the labels are successfully printed you can erase the saved document.

One program suffices for all type of labels stationery because we cope with multiple labels across a row by using columns, and with multiple labels down the page by using (+Height) codes. However, if you use 1-across n-high labels then you may encounter a problem with the very earliest versions of *LocoScript* Professional where the (EndCol) code does not work quite the way we assume. So if you are using version 1.01 or 1.02 **and** you are using 1 x n labels (which are rather unusual) then you will need to contact Locomotive Software with a view to getting your software upgraded.

Generating groups of labels

One of the problems you may find with the labels program is that you do not have space on disc to store the temporary document which holds all the labels before they are printed. This document is created in the directory you nominate as the Temporary path in the Settings [F2] menu. If you've been clever and changed this path to be a RAM disc then you could consider changing it to another (larger) drive in order to run the labels program.

However, even changing the temporary path may not help in all cases. The solution is to create your labels in batches just like we did in program 10A. In the definitions section add the line:

```
batch = 100↵
```

where 100 is the batch size. You do not need to use a batch size of 100. In fact, if you use "n-across" labels or sheets of labels, you should set the batch size to be a multiple of the number of labels across, or the number of labels per sheet. Otherwise you will waste labels at the end of each batch.

Now replace the $+ line by the following three lines:

```
batch = [batch - 1]↵
# batch <> 0 :<: $+ :>↵
# $# = 0 :<: batch = 0 :>↵
```

The first of these lines decreases the value of batch by one. The square brackets make this an arithmetic command. The next line tests if batch is zero; if not then the $+ command will move on to the next record in the datafile. The third line is there to deal with the situation at the end of the datafile, when all the labels have been produced. If you reach the end of the datafile then the record number ($#) will become zero. If so then we set batch to zero immediately. This means you don't have to pick the batch size so that it divides neatly into the number of labels you are producing.

Finally, we have a slightly different command to run the loop:

```
%loop @ batch↵
```

That is, the loop generates labels until batch becomes zero, i.e. until you reach the end of the group of labels, or until you reach the end of the datafile. If there are more labels to be generated then the program will be automatically run again to make the next group whilst the first group are printed.

Labels on a PC 117

It is best to run this variant of the program in a slightly different way. Point the Disc Manager cursor at the program in the usual way and press M. Now pick out the datafile with your members and press [ENTER]. Set the number of copies you require (usually one), and whether you want Draft or High Quality printing. Now, instead of pressing [ENTER] press [Alt][F10] instead to invoke the Automatic merge option.

In an automatic merge each batch of labels will be immediately printed without you having to pick out Print result from the exit menu. If the merging process gets ahead of the printer then while you are waiting you will see the menu:

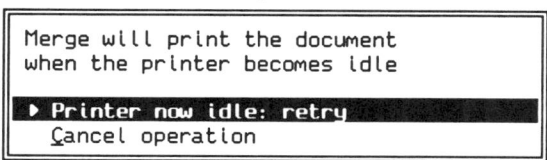

No action is needed from you should this menu appear. *LocoScript* will continue all by itself when the printer has caught up.

There is one final thing to consider when batching up labels. Strictly, our commands batch up the records you process rather than the labels you produce. Up to now we have been producing one label per record, so this distinction has not been important. We mention it only because the next section is going to show you how produce labels for only some of your records. If you are producing only some labels then you will have to ensure that when you skip a record you also skip the command which reduces the batch file count. If you cannot see how to do this, you could just be ultra-pragmatic and increase your batch size to reflect the fact that only a proportion of records will now produce labels!

Printing only some labels

We've spent most of this chapter treating label programs as being special, and not like other lists. However, we can now see that the "specialness" is confined to using a suitable paper type and adding the (Height) and (EndCol) codes. Apart from that, label generating programs are really just the same as any other program.

Therefore everything we've discussed in earlier chapters about selective lists is equally applicable to labels. That being so, we will not repeat every example altered for use with labels, but will restrict ourselves to the most useful.

If you want to produce labels for just your life members then you would use the technique from program 8A within our labels program (14B) to give you:

```
(+Mail)
$= "surname"
mclass = "Life"
ht = "(+Height1.5")"
ec = "(EndCol)"
space = " "
cr = "
"
loop = "
# class = mclass :<:
ht
name : space : surname : cr
address   : cr
addr2     : cr
addr3     : cr
town      : cr
county    : cr
postcode : ec : cr
:>:
$+
"
%loop @ $#
(-Mail)
```

Program 14C

In a similar way we could use the technique of program 9E which listed all the members who had not yet paid to produce a set of labels to go with a reminder notice.

```
(+Mail)
$= "expiry"
start = ? ;first date to consider  (eg 93/01) type nothing for start
done  = ? ;first date not required (eg 93/04) type nothing for end
# done <> "" :<: $$ done : enddate = expiry :><: enddate = "" :>:
$$ start
ht = "(+Height1.5")"
ec = "(EndCol)"
space = " "
cr = "
"
loop = "
# expiry <> enddate :<:
ht
name : space : surname : cr
address   : cr
addr2     : cr
```

Labels on a PC 119

```
addr3    : cr
town     : cr
county   : cr
postcode : ec : cr
:><: stop = 0 :>:
$+
"
stop = 1
%loop @ stop
$= ""  : $$ "9999999"           ;or $* since this is PC
(-Mail)
```
Program 14D

To generate programs 14C and 14D we made the following simple modifications to the original programs they are based upon:

- We changed the document paper type so that it was suitable for labels;
- We changed the columns to be suitable for the labels we are using;
- We added the definitions of `ht` and `ec` to the definitions section;
- We replaced the `{{ details required }}` of the original by the lines for the label, remembering to start with `ht` and end with `ec`.

That's all we did! In other words, when you need labels for a special purpose then all you need do is to find a suitable program elsewhere in the book and make the same modifications as we have done. Labels are easy with *LocoScript* Professional!

Blank lines in labels

Finally, before we finish with labels, a little tidiness is in order. In each of programs the details we have been producing have been:

```
name : space : surname : cr
address   : cr
addr2     : cr
addr3     : cr
town      : cr
county    : cr
postcode  : ec : cr
```

This is all very well, but unless all your members have seven line addresses you will find you get blank lines on some labels. Of course the Post Office will cope, but it is certainly more conventional to close up the gaps.

To avoid the blank lines, you need to add null="" to the definitions section and alter the central part of the loop to have lines like:

```
# addr2 <> null :<: addr2 : cr :>:↵
```

What we have done is to use the # condition :<: action :>: command (read as **IF** condition **THEN** action **ENDofIF**) to suppress lines which would otherwise be blank. The comparison we are making is <> or "not equal to".

Applying this to 14B we get the *LocoScript* Professional Universal Label Listing Program:

```
(+Mail)↵
$= "surname"↵
ht = "(+Height1.5")"↵
ec = "(EndCol)"↵
space = " "↵
cr = "
"↵
null = ""↵
loop = ""↵
ht↵
name : space : surname : cr↵
# address <> null :<: address  : cr :>:↵
# addr2   <> null :<: addr2    : cr :>:↵
# addr3   <> null :<: addr3    : cr :>:↵
# town    <> null :<: town     : cr :>:↵
# county  <> null :<: county   : cr :>:↵
# postcode <> null :<: postcode :>: ec : cr↵
$+↵
"↵
%loop @ $#↵
(-Mail)
```

Program 14E

Note that although the cr items are conditional the final ec:cr commands are not because you always need the (EndCol) at the end of each label!

15
Writing letters to everyone

This chapter tells you how to send a letter to all the people on your lists. The major reason that you'd want to do this is to get these people to renew their membership or subscription. You will find a great deal more about this in the next chapter; here we concentrate on more general aspects of automatic letter writing and are just using "renewals" as a running example. If you ignore the financial aspects, this chapter is equally applicable if you want to write to clients with details of your new services, or family and friends with your yearly round-up of news.

When you produce letters automatically you may want to write to everyone, or to only some of the people on your list. You may even want to send different letters to different groups of people. Up until now we have been producing lists with the details of lots of people on just one sheet of paper. The real difference in this chapter is that we are going to produce one sheet of paper per person, which means that some slightly different techniques are required.

Sending a letter to everyone

Before we get to the details of how to send letters to only some of the people in your datafile we will first consider how to send a letter to everyone. The simplest possible case is when everyone gets exactly the same letter. LocoScript will do this task if you command it, though it might be wiser to walk down the High Street and get some photocopies made.

Start by creating the letter you want to write. Don't put any (+Mail) commands in it at all. Return to the Disc Manager screen. Place the cursor on your letter and press M for Merge. Now move the cursor to your datafile and press [ENTER]. LocoScript will display a confirmation menu showing the two filenames. Before you press [ENTER] to confirm the menu you need to do three things. First, if your printer will do both High and Draft Quality you need to ensure that the correct option is ticked. Second, you should ensure that the number of copies (1) is correct. Third, and finally, you should move the cursor down to the `Automatic` command line before pressing [ENTER].

In an "Automatic merge" LocoScript processes your letter, and when it reaches the end it immediately prints the result without you having to do anything at all. It then moves on one record in the datafile and calls up a fresh copy of the document. You need do nothing, except to make sure that there is paper in the printer. If LocoScript processes the document faster than it can be printed then you'll see this message:

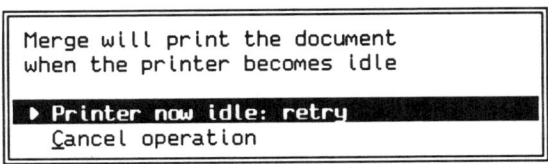

Once LocoScript has produced one copy of the document for every record in the datafile then it will stop and return to the Disc Manager. If you want to stop it before this then you should press [STOP] ([Esc] on a PC), then [STOP] ([Esc]) again. The following message will appear:

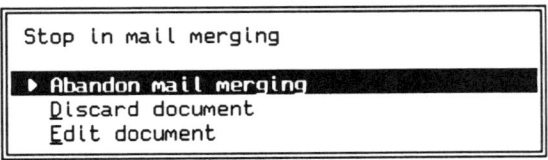

You should select the `Abandon mail merging` command and press [ENTER].

As we warned you, the documents this procedure prints are all the same and you might as well have photocopied them. So now we'll see how to make them all different by inserting information from each record into the document. We insert this information by specifying the items we want surrounded by (+Mail) and (–Mail) codes.

For example:

```
Dear (+Mail)name(-Mail) (+Mail)surname(-Mail),
You are a (+Mail)class(-Mail) member of our club. Pay your dues
immediately!
```

Writing letters to everyone 123

You may feel this is rather abrupt for an actual letter, but the important thing to look at is the way we've used the information from the member's record. We've pulled in the contents of an item by putting the item name. So that LocoScript knows that we want the item inserted (and not just some text) we have put a (+Mail) to introduce the item and a (–Mail) to show where we return to normal text. So that you can easily see which parts of the document are commands LocoScript highlights them on the screen. The final thing to notice is that in order to stop the name and the surname running into each other we've separated them by a space (which is not highlighted).

If you try merging this document with your datafile you will see that besides filling in the information from each record LocoScript is also re-formatting the document so that all the line endings are in the right place. This means that you don't have to work out the longest possible class and leave extra space on the line. LocoScript does all this automatically for you:

```
_.J..........1.........?.........3.........4.........l.........6......
    Dear Mrs Robertson,↵
    ↵
    You are a Provisional member of our club. Pay your
    dues immediately!↵
```

You can even put information into the document which is not in your datafile. For example, you could add the date:

```
    (RAlign)      (+Mail)? ;Date please (-Mail)↵
```

When LocoScript encounters the ? it will prompt you with the text that you put after the semicolon:

```
_.J..........1.........?.........3.........4..▌.....l.........6......
    (RAlign)       (+Mail)|Date please|(-Mail)|-Mail)
```

and you can type in the date. Of course it will ask you again for the next letter, which will be a little boring. So instead of using the ? command, use a !? command instead.

```
    (RAlign)      (+Mail)!?today ;Date please (-Mail)↵
```

Now LocoScript will only prompt you on the first time through, and on subsequent letters it will insert the date automatically from the item today where it has stored whatever you typed. So check what you have typed before proceeding, for otherwise it will be wrong on every letter!

Making parts of the letter optional

We will now think some more about our payment demand. What we'd like to put into the letter is the amount which each member should pay. This value is not an item in our datafile, but we can work out what the amount must be by doing some tests on the membership class (which is recorded for every member). Once surrounded by some suitable text we get:

```
Dear (+Mail) name (-Mail)  (+Mail) surname (-Mail), 
 
(+Mail) 
# class = "Family"  :<: (-Mail)Your family membership of
£20 is now due. (+Mail) :>: 
# class = "Social"  :<: (-Mail)Your social membership of
£10 is now due. (+Mail) :>: 
# class = "Junior"  :<: (-Mail)Your junior membership of
£5 is now due. If you were 16 or over on the 1st
January then your dues now become £15. (+Mail) :>: 
# class = "Full"    :<: (-Mail)Your membership of £15 is
now due. (+Mail) :>: 
(-Mail) Please pay up! 
```

What we have here is a series of **IF** (#) **THEN** (:<:) **ENDofIF** (:>:) commands. If the condition is not true then LocoScript skips the part of the document between the :<: and the :>: and the sentences here are not included in the printed out document. If the condition is true then LocoScript will process this section, encounter the (–Mail) and thus include the correct sentence into the printed document.

For example:

```
Dear Mrs Johnson, 
 
Your membership of £15 is now due. Please pay up! 
```

or:

```
Dear Mr Arthurson, 
 
Your junior membership of £5 is now due. If you
were 16 or over on the 1st January then your dues
now become £15. Please pay up! 
```

Writing letters to everyone

You can include or exclude any amount of text. Half the letter might not be appropriate to social members, or you might just want to add an extra s somewhere for family members only.

You should note carefully which bits of your letter are text and which are commands. You will see that in a letter like this the commands are always highlighted. This isn't something we've made much of before, because we've been dealing with programs which loop and almost everything has been highlighted and so it has not been very useful. Here in automatic letter writing you can see what the highlighting is for.

You can use the full power of LocoScript to write complicated tests like:

```
(+Mail)# town="NORWICH" AND NOT (class = "Junior") :<:
(-Mail)Don't forget our regular pub meet on
Fridays.(+Mail):>:(-Mail)
```

Instead of using **IF THEN ENDofIF** there are two other useful forms of the **IF** command you can use. The first is **IF THEN ELSE ENDofIF**:

```
(+Mail) # class="Junior" :<: (-Mail)Why not ask your
parents if they'd like to join too?(+Mail):><:(-Mail)Why
not let your children join too?(+Mail):>:(-Mail) Family
membership is only £20.
```

IF (#) the condition is true **THEN** (:<:) the first sentence is included **ELSE** (:><:) the second sentence is used. The **ENDofIF** (:>:) shows where LocoScript is to stop skipping and include the next piece of text for everyone.

The other form is **IF THEN ELSEIF ELSEIF ... ELSE ENDofIF**.

```
Please contact (+Mail)
#    town="NORWICH" :<: (-Mail)Mrs Smith 0603-123456(+Mail)
:># town="LOWESTOFT" :<: (-Mail)Ms Brown 0502-123456(+Mail)
:># town="CROMER" :<: (-Mail)Mr Robinson 0263-123456(+Mail)
:><: (-Mail)Mr Jones 0603-654321(+Mail)
:>:(-Mail) for advice.
```

Instead of using **ELSEIF** in this way, we could have written **IF THEN ELSE IF THEN ELSE IF THEN ELSE** ... but then we'd need to have a whole sequence of **ENDofIF**s (:>::>::>::>:) to finish all of them off. Using **ELSEIF** (:>#) is so much easier to get right. Be careful that you type :># and not :>:# because the latter will be understood to be **ENDofIF IF**, which will not work the same way at all!

Testing the letters

You might have been wondering whether your conditionally included or excluded sentences are going to come out right. It is all very well writing these complicated tests, but how will you be sure you've written them correctly and you haven't just demanded the wrong amounts from everyone and invited all the Juniors to the pub?

You could of course print out all the letters and check them, but that could waste a lot of time and paper. You could run your merge and from the exit menu use the `Discard result` command for letter after letter, waiting for a Junior to turn up. This saves trees, but could still take some time. The proper solution is to apply special test data to your letter to see if it runs the way you want, and the simplest way you can make this test data is to use LocoScript's **Fill** mode.

To try your letter in Fill mode you go to the Disc Manager screen, select the document containing the letter and press F (for Fill). Press `[ENTER]` to the confirmation menu which appears. LocoScript will now start processing your letter just as if it was merging it with your datafile. However, when it encounters the first item which would normally come from the datafile it will prompt you to type in what it should be:

```
┘.........1........?....▌...3.........4........└........6.....
  Dear (+Mail)NAME?(-Mail)▌-Mail) (+Mail)surname(-Mail),↵
↵
```

Type in something vaguely correct, and press `[ENTER]` (`[F10]` on a PC). You'll then get prompted for subsequent items. Check that an appropriate letter seems to be produced. If the text has scrolled up off the screen then at the end of the Fill select `Edit result` from the exit menu and cursor up to check it all. When done press `[EXIT]` (`[F10]` on a PC) to get the exit menu back again. Select `Discard result` and you will then get the following menu:

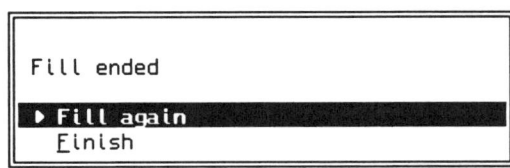

```
┌─────────────────────────┐
│ Fill ended              │
├─────────────────────────┤
│ ▶ Fill again            │
│   Finish                │
└─────────────────────────┘
```

Select `Fill again` by pressing `[ENTER]` and type in a different membership class to check that works as well. Work through all the possible combinations in turn until you are sure that your letter will work properly in all cases. When you are happy then select `Finish` (or `Abandon mailmerge`) and you will be returned to the Disc Manager.

Tips for writing master documents

Before we change topic there are a few observations to be made, the first of which is that documents such as the ones we have been dealing with in this chapter are usually called **master** documents rather than "programs". This is because you can easily think of them as a master copy of the letter which you want, which is then personalised for each individual member. Indeed, it can sometimes be easier to take an existing letter and replace the bits to be personalised with mailmerge commands, than to try and write the whole thing, text and commands, in one go.

You may have noticed that we have been writing the values we test for in a different style. In previous chapters we've made a point of having a definitions section with commands like `social="Social"` and then tests like `# class = social`. We had to do this because the **IF** commands were written inside the various `loop=" ... "` commands. If we had used " characters inside the " ... " part then LocoScript would have assumed that this was the end of the `loop=` definition and would then have got upset and told you that there were `Syntax errors` in your document. You *can* still write commands like `social="Social"` in the documents in this chapter and they will work just as well; but since the tests are not nested inside `loop=" ... "` definitions there is no need to do so, and we haven't bothered.

The third thing to notice is the way we've used carriage returns (↵) to make the tests easy to read. You need not worry that they will appear in the results document, because we have been careful to put them in a (+Mail) section. When LocoScript is processing a (–Mail) section it puts all the characters and codes (like underline or ↵) into the output document. When it reaches a (+Mail) section the characters are interpreted as commands (item names, tests and so forth) and the codes are completely ignored. So if you write ...↵(+Mail) you'll get the ↵ in the printed document, whereas if you write ...(+Mail)↵ you will not.

The final point is really just for completeness. We've been using `:<:` as **THEN**, `:><:` as **ELSE**, `:>#` as **ELSEIF** and `:>:` as **ENDofIF**. If you read the technical bits of the LocoScript manual you'll see that the colons (`:`) are not strictly always necessary. That's true for the examples in this chapter, but they are sometimes necessary in more complicated examples, and they do no harm when they aren't strictly needed. So we'd recommend that you always put them in, just as we have.

Choosing who you want to write to

If you've got any Life Members, or not all your subscriptions fall due at the same time, you've probably been worrying what sort of letter to construct for these cases, when in fact you don't want to send anything at all!

There are two ways of proceeding, which are in fact very similar techniques to those we used in chapters 8 and 9 to produce selective lists of members.

The first, and most straightforward scheme, is to start the document with a test to see if a letter is or is not required. If the letter is not required then we discard it and move on to the next record:

```
(+Mail) # class="Life" :<: * :>:↵
(-Mail)
```

IF (#) the condition (class="Life") is true, **THEN** (:<:) discard this letter (*) **ENDofIF** (:>:). Thus we avoid producing letters to Life members. Notice that * is a command, and has nothing to do with wild-card character * which we have used for some text comparisons. Also, we do not put (-Mail)*(+Mail), which would just print a * at the top of Life member letters!

TIP: Notice that we've put ↵(–Mail) at the end of the test. As we explained above, if you put (–Mail)↵ then you get an extra ↵ at the top of your letters and it may take a while before you realise where it is coming from!

Although we've said that you should start the document with the test and discard, this is not strictly necessary. The * command will work at any point. One could imagine for example changing the # town="NORWICH" :<: example we had earlier so that the **ELSE** line read:

```
:><: answer = ? ;Type (Y) to discard this letter↵
     # answer = "Y" :<: * :><:↵
              (-Mail)Mr Jones 0603-654321(+Mail)↵
        >:↵
:>:↵
```

You might type Y to avoid sending letters to people who lived abroad. But this is pretty fancy stuff, and almost every * command you ever use will be at the start of your master documents.

Writing letters to everyone

Although this test and discard scheme is straightforward it is only the best way when you are going to discard a small number of letters, for otherwise it can be awfully slow. Just as in chapter 9, we can use an index to arrange to consider only the small group of "interesting" people in the datafile.

For example:

```
_J.........1.........?.........3.........4.........5.........6.....
    (◆Mail)↵
    $="class"↵
    !mclass = ? ;Which class of membership ? ↵
    !pass = 1 : # pass = 1 :<: $$ mclass : pass = 2 :>:↵
    # class <> mclass :<: $="" : $$"9999999" : • :>:↵
    (-Mail)↵
    Dear (◆Mail) name (-Mail)  (◆Mail) surname (-Mail),↵
    ↵
```

We select membership class order (`$="class"`). We start by asking which class we are interested in (`!mclass = ?`). The `!` on this command ensures we only ask once! We then move to the first such person (`$$ mclass`), but we use the standard trick of `!pass=1 : # pass=1:<:` to ensure we only do this the first time through. (Yes, you could combine these two first pass tests if you wished, but it is much clearer set out the way in which we have done it.)

Then we test that we're still dealing with the correct class of member by the comparison `# class <> mclass`. If so then we produce a letter; if not then we discard this letter `*`, having first moved to the end of the datafile (`$="":$$="9999999"`) to ensure that we return to the Disc Manager.

In fact, everything we wrote in chapters 8 and 9 about making selections from the people in your lists applies here, so we will not repeat it. All of the various tests and tricks will work just as well on the letters we are dealing with here as on the lists which we were producing then.

As an example of a real letter, let us suppose that we want to write to everyone who should renew in September 1992. The `expiry` item in the datafile says when they are paid up until so we will have to test for 92/09. Obviously if all your members renew at the same time you need only test for the year. You should never miss out this test, in case you have some members who have already paid for the forthcoming year.

The other test which we will make is to explicitly exclude the life members, who need pay nothing. Hopefully, their `expiry` item does not contain 92/09, but we will avoid possible ill-feeling if we make *sure* we don't ask them for money!

Thus we start the letter with the tests:

```
   |.........1.........?.........3.........4.........5.........|........
(+Mail)↵
# class = "Life" :<: * :>:↵
# expiry <> "92/09" :<: * :>:↵
(-Mail)↵
```

We could combine the tests with an **OR**, but this way it is more likely to work first time!

Then for the body of the letter:

```
(+Mail)name(-Mail) (+Mail)surname(-Mail),↵
(+Mail)cr="↵
"↵
# address  <> "" :<: address  : cr :>:↵
# addr2    <> "" :<: addr2    : cr :>:↵
# addr3    <> "" :<: addr3    : cr :>:↵
# town     <> "" :<: town     : cr :>:↵
# county   <> "" :<: county   : cr :>:↵
# postcode <> "" :<: postcode : cr :>:↵
(-Mail)↵
Your subscription for 1993 is now due. (+Mail)↵
# class = "Family" :<: (-Mail)"Family" membership is £20. (+Mail):>:↵
# class = "Social" :<: (-Mail)"Social" membership is £10. (+Mail):>:↵
# class = "Junior" :<: (-Mail)"Junior" membership is £5. If you
were 16 or over on the 1st January then your dues now become
£15. (+Mail):>:↵
# class = "Full"   :<: (-Mail)"Full" membership is £15. (+Mail):>:↵
(-Mail) Please return this notice with your payment to ......↵
(+Mail)# postcode = "" :<: ↵
(-Mail)↵
PS. I don't seem to have a record of your postcode. Please
check your address is correct!↵
(+Mail):>:↵
(-Mail)
```

TIP: Notice how we've used #address<>"":<:address:cr:>: etc. to suppress the lines of the address which are blank. We could have put (-Mail)↵(+Mail) instead of setting the cr item, but it would have been rather more complicated to type in, which usually means that we will get it wrong and end up with ↵s in the wrong places!

Although we've now said all we need about writing letters automatically, that is not the end of the topic altogether. The next two chapters are also about writing letters. We have devoted the whole of chapter 16 to considering renewals properly, rather than just as an example of letter writing. We then return to general letter writing in chapter 17, where we consider other ways in which LocoScript can help with your correspondence.

16
Renewals

Although the previous chapter was apparently all about producing "renewal" letters, it was really concentrating on the techniques of automatic letter writing. In this chapter we start all over again dealing solely with renewals.

Renewals are such an important topic for the "Hon. Sec." that we've tried to some extent to make this chapter stand alone, because it may be a year since you last did any renewals and you may have forgotten the details. But if you are just starting with this book, we cannot recommend diving straight in at this chapter, however urgent your need may be. Please turn back and spend a little time on chapters 7, 8 and 9.

This chapter is not a "programming" chapter. If the simple approach we use is insufficient for your needs, you will find related material in chapters 15 and 17 to help you.

The renewal notice

Before we start on any of the programming details it is important that you know what your renewal notice is going to say. If you charge a subscription of any sort which should be renewed, it is essential that you keep the data so that you are able to identify subscribers who:

- need to renew (i.e. they are not exempt for some reason);
- are due to renew (i.e. their subscription has expired);
- and those you have asked to renew, but who have not yet done so.

It is not enough putting a note in the annual newsletter saying that renewals are due in February and then sitting back and waiting for the payments to arrive. Some people will pay but many more will mean to do it and forget.

As a minimum you should print out a piece of paper giving the name(s) of the member, their address and their membership number (if used) for reference, together with the clear message:

```
Your subscription to ...... for the period xx to xx is now
due.... £10↵
Please return this notice with your payment to...... (and give the
```
name and address of the person to whom the renewal should be sent).

These notices can be printed so that they fit in window envelopes (see chapter 12) or sent with a general mailing.

We don't think it helps much to dress up your message in flowery language or say things like "paying up time is here again". You want the person to know that:

- the subscription is due;
- how much is due;
- where the payment is to be sent.

Anything which takes attention away from these details will reduce your response rate.

To produce your renewal notices

Unless you are generating a renewal notice for absolutely everyone you will need an item in your datafile which tells you when renewals are due, which in our datafile is called `expiry`. You will need an index for this item so that you can find those members who need to renew this time. To set up this index you may need to review the section in chapter 5 about date indexes.

Create a document called `RENEWALS` and set it up to use the paper you want.

If there are a lot of notices to run off, it is worth using continuous stationery even if there is some wasted space on the sheet. If you have a sheet feeder on your printer, you can make a typical renewal notice fit onto A5 paper used sideways (landscape). If you do not own any A5 paper then you can feed in A4 sheets twice (from opposite ends) and then tear, cut or guillotine them in half.

The first thing to type into the `RENEWALS` document is a short program section to find the subscribers who need renewal notices. If you are generating renewal notices for everybody then the entire section may be omitted.

Renewals

```
_|..........1..........?..........3..........4..........5......
(+Mail)↵
!nowdue = ? ; Type in when you want renewals for ↵
$= "expiry"↵
! pass = 1 : # pass = 1 :<: $$ nowdue : pass = 2 :>:↵
# expiry <> nowdue :<: $="" : $$"9999999" : * :>:↵
(-Mail)↵
↵
```

You will see that the first command requires you to type in when you want notices for, which will be the year (1993, say) or perhaps month (92/09). Using a ? command like this means that by typing in a different year (or month or issue) you can use the same program next year and the year after etc.

The next command is a $= command which selects the expiry index, $$ moves to the first record to be processed (but only on the first pass); and the #expiry<>nowdue command deals with stopping when all the records which require renewal notices have been processed.

Follow this little program section by the beginning of your renewal notice. Start by typing in the heading – the name of your Club or Society with its address – or set up the document to run on your headed paper.

The next thing you will need to put into the notice is the name and address of your member. We can extract this from the datafile by using suitable mailmerge commands:

```
↵
(+Mail)name(-Mail) (+Mail)surname(-Mail)↵
(+Mail)cr = "
"↵
# address  <> "" :<: address  : cr :>:↵
# addr2    <> "" :<: addr2    : cr :>:↵
# addr3    <> "" :<: addr3    : cr :>:↵
# town     <> "" :<: town     : cr :>:↵
# county   <> "" :<: county   : cr :>:↵
# postcode <> "" :<: postcode : cr :>:↵
(-Mail)↵
(RAlign)          (+Mail) !? date ; Type today's date (-Mail)↵
↵
```

The **IF** (#) statements arrange that if any lines of the address are blank they are suppressed. The date is the "today's date" – the date on which the renewal notice is generated. The !? command will prompt you for the date on the first notice; and then insert it automatically on all subsequent notices. Obviously *LocoScript* Professional users can use (+DaTe) codes instead if they wish.

Follow the member's details by the text of your renewal notice. This should include the information on how much to pay, where to send the payment, and to whom cheques should be made payable.

Then put a dotted line to produce a "tear off" slip.

Below this line *repeat* the society name and where to send the payment. You want to ensure that when your member detaches the tear-off section, and then loses the main letter, the cheque will still be sent to you, rather than the previous holder of your post! You put the same information in the main letter so that it is not necessary to address the envelope before sealing the torn off slip into it!

You will need to know who has returned the slip to you, so you need to have the member's name and address on the slip as well. Once again a little program section will pull this in from the datafile:

```
(+Mail)name(-Mail) (+Mail)surname(-Mail)
(+Mail)
# address  <> ""  :<: address  : cr :>:
# addr2    <> ""  :<: addr2    : cr :>:
# addr3    <> ""  :<: addr3    : cr :>:
# town     <> ""  :<: town     : cr :>:
# county   <> ""  :<: county   : cr :>:
# postcode <> ""  :<: postcode : cr :>:
(-Mail)
```

These lines are exactly the same as the ones above (*except* that cr does not need to be defined twice), so you can copy them to a block and paste it in to save retyping them.

Now finish off the notice with the text:

```
I enclose my subscription £10
Signed....
```

Press [EXIT] ([F10] on a PC) and then Finish edit. You then merge this program with your membership datafile.

If the program fails to work first time, go back and check that you have typed it in correctly including all the colons and quotation marks, and that you put in the right names for the items on *your* datafile. If it still doesn't work, read chapter 25 on "troubleshooting".

When people have paid

How much detail you enter when the renewal is paid will depend upon how much information you want to keep in your records. If you have an item on your card for the amount paid, then if the subscription has gone up, you can change the figures from the last time it was paid. If you have decided to keep a note of when the subscription was paid, you need to move to this item and change it to the new date.

However, the important thing is that you update the item on which you run your renewal notices. If they have now paid for 1992, do not leave the entry as 1991. You are going to search on this item for people who need reminders, and eventually for those who need to be deleted from your list. Obvious perhaps, but we have seen systems where this was not done!

If payments will go to someone else, the treasurer perhaps, then you should provide them with a simple list of expected renewals for them to tick off as they are received. Use one of the simple listing programs from chapter 8 or 9 for this.

Reminders

There is no point in sending endless reminders, the postage costs soon mount up, but one reminder is worth sending as it will get results. Make a decision at the beginning as to how long you will wait before reminding those who have not yet paid. Then again print out the name and address and repeat the wording from your first notice. We do not think you should imply that your system may have faults by apologising for sending the reminder or saying "if paid within the last xx days please ignore this notice". If they have paid and you send the reminder, they will tell you soon enough!

So create a new document called REMINDER and put in the same program as you used for renewals. (Copy it from the previous time and paste it in!) This will produce the list of those who have still not renewed.

The only thing you need to change is the text, which should now be quite firm:

```
We regret that as we have not received your renewal, we are
deleting your name from our mailing list. If you wish to
continue to receive ....↵
then please send your renewal (£10) to ..... immediately.
```

You should deal with these lapsed members immediately, as we discuss below. If you delay, you run the risk of forgetting and they will remain there for another year.

If your society issues a publication, it is important to agree at the outset at what point you will stop sending issues. We would advise the earlier after the subscription lapses the better. A surprising number of people take more notice of the non-appearance of a magazine than of any number of reminder letters. It is easy enough to send back issues later, when you receive payment.

Some people will respond at one of these renewal stages, saying that they do not wish to renew – but, sadly, such considerate people are in the minority. You will, however, need to ensure that you don't send further reminders, or their politeness may wear a little thin. You should not discard their records entirely but you should keep them on file as we shall discuss in a moment.

Sending further reminders costs money but there can be times when it is worth sending one further notice. You could perhaps combine this later in the year with advance notice of a particular event or article in your publication.

It is awkward if the people who haven't paid are particular friends or relatives – but you really should harden your heart and say when you meet, "Sorry, but next week I will have to take your name off our lists." This gives them an opportunity to pay up there and then or to say that they are no longer interested.

There are also the people who pay twice! We'd recommend entering their subscriptions for an extra year and then not sending them a reminder the next time. If you know them you can always ask if this is alright – but, especially when the money is for a charity, accept it gratefully – it will be earning extra interest for the year !

Lapsed members

In almost all cases, you will want to remove inactive or lapsed members from your lists. These people are often referred to as "dead" or "dying". Of course, anyone genuinely deceased should be deleted so that you do not worry relatives by continuing to send mail to their address.

You could of course leave the lapsed records on the datafile, since unless you have a remarkably high turnover they will not occupy a great deal of room on your discs. If you do this then you will need to modify all your listing programs to add tests to exclude the lapsed members, so you don't post things to them or invite them to coffee mornings.

Renewals   *137*

Although this is not really very difficult, it is simplest to remove their records once it is clear that they will not be renewing.

But before you go mad with the delete key, there are a number of reasons why you should not just lose the lapsed subscribers from your datafiles. First, some people have the annoying habit of paying extremely late, just after you have removed them from your files. They also seem to be the people most likely to send you their cheque with a brief note saying only, "Sorry this is so late. Best wishes, Jack". You will be able to get their full name off the cheque, but you need their address and all the other details you keep about your members in order to put them back on your datafile.

Secondly, previous subscribers are one of the most profitable mailing lists you can have, other than the current members. If you mail details of meetings, publications, raffles, art shows, or special events, to previous subscribers, you should get a better response to the mailing than from any other list you beg, borrow or buy from outside. You will probably get some of them back as active members too.

As an interim measure, you can mark their renewal date in the expiry item with an x so that you do not send further reminders or put a row of xxx in their address so that you can identify labels to be removed. But the best system is to set up a separate file for all lapsed members coded by their date of expiry. We give the details of how to do this in chapter 23.

Even if you are desperate for space on your PC or PCW and don't want yet another file or another disc, *do* keep the information about your lapsed members somehow. Print it out as a report and label it with the date and what the list is. Mark it **DO NOT DESTROY** so that you don't throw it out without thought when you need to clear the spare room for a visitor. You could print the details onto labels and stick them on 5 x 3 cards and file these. If you do this, make sure that you have a date on the cards showing expiry, or you will be wasting postage on really out of date addresses. We've also found it worthwhile to keep two or three sets of these labels for use in the future – even without keeping any permanent record of them.

Although these lapsed subscribers are valuable, in many cases their useful life is about five years. It depends on the sort of membership lists you are maintaining, as some categories of people move more than others, and obviously some events will cease to interest people as they get older.

Covenants

If you are running a charity then you should be aware that there are a myriad of rules and regulations for charities. Most of them do not affect running membership lists and collecting subscriptions. However, charity subscriptions can be paid by covenant and this has distinct advantages for the charity, because the government (via the taxman) will chip in some money as well.

The subscriber pays the usual amount (or more if they wish), normally by standing order through a bank. They sign a form promising that they will pay this amount for at least four years to the charity and the form is then recorded by the charity treasurer and sent to the bank (for the standing order) and the taxman (for their records). The charity can then claim the Income Tax which the subscriber is paying on the subscription amount. Therefore the charity obtains more than the usual subscription without it costing the subscriber any more. (Obviously if the person does not pay tax, there is none to recover.)

Advice should be sought on how to word the form so that it will have the correct legal effect. Perhaps one of your members is an accountant or solicitor and can find this out for you. You should also look carefully, with a naive eye, at the accompanying material you send to your members to encourage them to use the scheme. We have seen several letters encouraging us to set up covenants that left us totally puzzled as to what we were meant to sign, what we were meant to do, and how much we would end up paying. Explain clearly and simply what to sign, where to send the form and exactly how much the member should pay. Then only the untaxed, and members who think they will not be interested in your charity for a four year period, can possibly have an excuse not to pay in this way.

TIP: You should avoid signing people up on covenants for periods longer than four years. The reason for this is purely practical – you might want to raise your subscription rates, and getting people to alter standing orders can often seem to take forever.

Although not really relevant to membership subscriptions, you should be aware that if a charity is offered a large donation (from April 1992, more than £400), it can be given by way of Gift Aid and again the Income Tax can be reclaimed on this to boost the charity's coffers.

17
Writing special letters

LocoScript is of course a word-processor and is therefore packed with features to help you write letters. Don't forget about cutting and pasting text from one document to another, or setting up permanent or temporary phrases which can be a great help with complicated terms – or even words you often mis-type.

We would strongly recommend setting up "templates" with your club name and your name, address and telephone number, all preset with margins and tabs, with suitable paper and printer selected for you. You can then Create your documents (using C) and start immediately upon your letters without having to worry about all this. A less satisfactory alternative would be to set up a phrase which is your name and address and telephone number and then paste this in at the head of each letter.

Extracting items

There will be times when you need to send pretty much the same letter to a number of people. Perhaps you send a "welcome" letter to new members, or you send reminders about meetings to committee members. You may have standing orders which have not been paid, or you may receive unsigned or wrongly dated cheques. It is foolish to recreate such letters from scratch each time. You might be able to use the techniques of chapter 15, but these are not always suitable. You should create documents for these standard letters, leaving room in each to add the recipient's name and address.

There are several ways to use these documents. You could put them into a particular group (directory on the PC) and name them TEMPLATE.STD. Any documents you Create will then automatically start with the text set up. On the PC you could use Edit to... or Select template to do the same sort of thing without having to name the document as TEMPLATE.STD. You can even copy the document within the Disc Manager and then edit the copy. However you do it, you will eventually end up in the same situation: you are editing a document into which you want to insert a name and address, and possibly some other information such as a membership number.

Fortunately this information is available to you, even while you are editing.

PCW: Press [F1] and select `Run LocoFile`. If you have used a datafile since you loaded LocoScript you'll be put back into it. If it is the wrong one press [F1] and choose `Select new file` to go into the Disc Manager. If you have not used a datafile before then you are just put straight into the Disc Manager. In the Disc Manager you move the cursor to the datafile and press [ENTER].

PC: Press [F9] and select `Open datafile`. In the Disc Manager you move the cursor to the datafile and press [ENTER]. Alternatively, if you want to use the datafile which you used last (which will usually be the case, unless you have a lot of them) then start by pressing [F9] and select `Return to datafile` - if it is not the right datafile after all then select `Open other datafile` from the datafile [F9] menu and you will be put into the Disc Manager to select the file.

Once in the right datafile use the [F5] (PC [Ctrl][F5]) `Goto` menu to move to the correct record. If necessary use the [F2] menu (or the PC `Index:` selection) to choose the right index. It will be no good looking up `Smith` if the current index is set to `town`!

You should now be looking at the correct details for your member. You could copy the information into a block (or a phrase) by hand using [COPY] ([Alt][+] on a PC) etc., but there is a special system called **extract** which will do this for you. Press [F7] which brings up the `Extract` menu, then use [+] or the space bar to put a tick against the parts of the information you want:

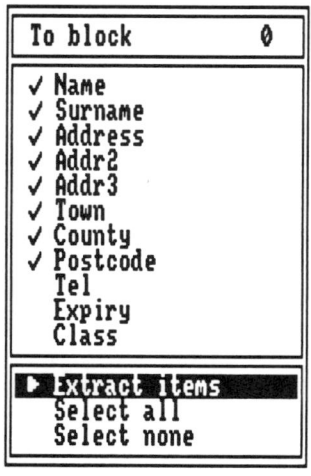 

Writing special letters 141

Once you have the right set of items press [ENTER] ([F10] on the PC) and they will all be placed into the block (usually block 0) shown at the top of the menu. You can change this to any number 0 .. 9, but remember which block is which! The block will be available when you return to editing by pressing [EXIT] ([F10] on a PC). Before returning you can, if you wish, make extracts for any further entries you want in exactly the same way, but of course you must give each a different block number.

When you go back to your letter, put the cursor where you want your name and address to start, and press [PASTE] ([Ctrl][F7] on the PC) followed by the block number. You will find that the rules which LocoScript applies when putting information into the block will cause spaces, tabs and carriage returns to be added between items in a natural sort of way. Thus an extracted name and address will usually lay itself out the way you want when you paste it in.

In the unlikely event that you get into trouble with the way that extract lays out your details then you will have to rearrange your datafile card. Go into Datafile set-up and either move the items to appropriate positions, or possibly change where their names are displayed. The full rules for how extra characters are added are set out in the manuals so we won't waste space by repeating them here.

If you find that you usually mark the same details (name, surname, address etc.) then you can get them preset for you. Go into Datafile set-up and press [F7]. You will get the same menu of items that you are used to, but this time you tick the items that you want to have ticked by default in the future.

Fill mode

There is another, much more powerful, way of basing one document upon another which is called **Fill**. We met it earlier in chapter 15 as a way of testing out a merge, but here we are going to discuss its real purpose, which is to create customised letters.

When you "Fill" a document LocoScript will move through it stopping at the mailmerge commands to allow you type in information.

To use Fill, you need to set up your standard letter, but instead of leaving a gap for information like names and addresses you mark the places it is required by ? commands:

```
(+Mail)? ; suitable prompting text(-Mail)↵
```

Your letter might start like this:

```
(+Mail)? ; Name (-Mail)↵
(+Mail)? ; Address (-Mail)↵
```

When you Fill this document LocoScript will display your prompt (the text after the semicolon) and you can type in the information. If you make a mistake then you can cursor around and use [←DEL] and [DEL→] to make corrections. When you type in the address you can just type in ↵s in the usual way, so there is no need to prompt for the individual lines of the address. When you type [ENTER] ([F10] on a PC) then LocoScript will remove the prompt, relay the text you have typed in, and move on to the next mailmerge command.

A further refinement is for repeated items like the date. You can set this on the first letter and it will be there correctly for all the following letters you create in the same Fill session. You do this by putting in:

```
(+Mail)!? date ; prompt(-Mail)↵
```

where you want the date to appear. The ! causes you to only be asked once, and date is the name of the item where your response will be stored for use in subsequent letters. Fetching the date in this way is of course just one example of the !? command; *LocoScript* Professional users would do best to put in dates using (+DaTe) codes.

When you get to the Dear ..., part of the letter you have a choice. You can just prompt again with another mailmerge ? command. However, you may well be retyping exactly what you put earlier. If so, then you can save yourself some work. Change the original prompt for name to read:

```
(+Mail)? name ; Name (-Mail)↵
```

This stores your response into the item called name. Now just put:

```
Dear (+Mail) name (-Mail),↵
```

The computer will then repeat the name, just as you typed it above. However, this will not always be suitable, because you may not wish to have Dear Joe E Bloggs, preferring Dear Mr Bloggs,.

Writing special letters

Having completed the creation of your letter with its embedded mailmerge commands you then save it to disc and return to the Disc Manager. Now press F (for Fill) and your letter will appear and LocoScript will move down through the document, stopping at the first gap which you have to fill in. In the case we are considering it will prompt you to type in the person's name.

When you have filled in the recipient's full name, press [ENTER] ([F10] on a PC) and the cursor will move down to the address, which you should also fill in. When it is complete you press [ENTER] ([F10]) again. You will next be asked to fill in the date. Before you press [ENTER] ([F10]) do check you have typed the date in correctly. The computer is stupid enough to repeat a mistake on every subsequent letter!

Once all the gaps are filled in, the text appears followed by the usual mailmerge exit menu. If you choose Edit result then you can cursor up and fix anything you mistyped, or you can make any other amendments to the letter you wish. When you are satisfied press [EXIT] ([F10] on the PC) to get back to the exit menu.

If you choose Print result, the letter will be printed but that particular letter will *not* be saved on disc. You will have no record of writing it. If this is important to you, you should Save and Print result or Save result (and print later); or you could use carbon paper for your copy if your printer is suitable; or you could request two copies be printed when you start the Fill!

Having disposed of the results of your first Fill, you will then see the menu:

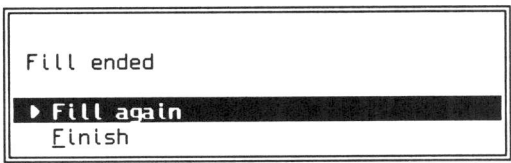

If you want to do a second letter you choose Fill again and the document reappears with the same gaps to fill (although the date will be filled in automatically for you).

TIP: If you make a complete mess of someone's name and address and fail to notice immediately then select Discard result from the exit menu and Fill again from this menu. You can then try all over again.

If your printer allows you to choose between High and Draft quality printing then you will have to take a little care when using Fill. The choice of Quality and the number of copies you want are made from the first menu you get when you press F. If the last thing you printed was in Draft then LocoScript assumes you will want Draft next time. If you want High Quality for your letter *you must change it at the start* or you will waste time and paper printing it out in Draft.

How many copies are printed is handled at the same time that the Quality is chosen. Unlike Quality the previous value is forgotten and the menu is always preset to one copy. Your only chance to change the number of copies is in the very first menu.

TIP: If you forgot to set the Quality and Copies (or if you are just unsure if you remembered) then pick `Save result` or `Save and Print result` from the exit menu so that you will have a copy of the document on disc to reprint if necessary.

You can use any and all of the features of the mailmerge language within Fill. You can use **IF THEN ENDofIF** commands to include or exclude particular paragraphs, sentences, or even individual words and letters. You can number clauses automatically or do arithmetic, calculating sub-totals, totals and VAT. But, interesting and useful though these things are, they are not really to do with processing people, and so they do not belong in this particular book.

18
Alternative item indexes I : Special interests

Up until now, whenever we have constructed indexes, each record (each person) has only appeared in the index once. This is exactly what we want for a surname index with everyone placed in alphabetical order. It is also exactly what we want for the membership class index – although there may be many members in each class (Junior/Family/Life etc.) each particular member is placed in one and only one membership class. This chapter is all about a different sort of index in which people can appear more than once. We've written it in terms of special interests that members may have, but it is equally applicable to different offers of help they may make, or special skills they can offer.

Let us suppose that your club is for nature lovers and you ask your members about their special interests. They will respond with a whole range of topics, like bird-watching, flowers, fungi, badgers and so on. You could create a new item in your datafile for these interests. Using programs like the ones earlier in the book you could produce lists of people who were interested in bird-watching, or produce a special mailshot for the mushroom specialists. But what if some people have more than one interest. How do you deal with someone who is interested in both mushrooms and bird-watching?

One approach is set up a special item for each interest. All you need to do is to enter datafile set-up mode and create the items. Then for each member you just need to mark their interests. Just typing a Y into a box is quite sufficient.

```
      Town Manchester
   County
Postcode M56 1GG        Tel 061 123 4567
   Expiry 93/05        Class Social
                       Fungi [Y..]
```

To produce a list of fungi fanatics is then straightforward:

```
(+Mail)
$= "surname"
yes = "Y+"
space = " "
tab = " → "
cr = "
"
loop = "
"
# fungi = yes :<: name : space : surname : tab : tel : cr :>:
$+
"
%loop @ surname
(-Mail)
```

Program 18A

This is pretty much the same sort of program we've written before, and the same sort of comments we've made before apply to it. In particular, if only a handful of your members are interested in fungi then this program will take a long time to run for a very small amount of output. You will recall from chapter 9 that one way of speeding this up is to use an index which puts all of the relevant people together so that you only process their records. You can do this here as well. If you were to construct a fungi index using the fungi item then your processing program would be:

```
(+Mail)
$= "fungi"
space = " "
tab = " → "
cr = "
"
loop = "
name : space : surname : tab : tel : cr
$+
"
%loop @ fungi
$= "" ; $$ "9999999"
(-Mail)
```

Program 18B

Here we list out all the names and phone numbers of the people whose records have text (anything – not necessarily Y) in the fungi item. We stop when we meet a record with a fungi item which is blank (because we've sneakily changed the %loop@ command to use fungi as the controlling item).

Alternative item indexes I : Special interests

Multiple interest items

It's all going pretty well so far – but not for much longer. The problem is that LocoScript only allows you to set up 8 indexes per datafile. You'll have several set up already (for surname, membership class and so on) so if you have more than a handful of special interests then you'll run out of indexes to use. You could set up the indexes temporarily and delete them once they were finished with – but it would probably be as quick to go back to the first program in this chapter and process all the records each time. The other problem that you might encounter is running out of items. LocoScript only allows you 50 items on the PCW (though 250 on the PC), so if your members have a diverse range of interests then you could encounter this limitation.

However, there's a much better way of setting up your datafile which avoids all these problems, and that is what this chapter is really about. Instead of creating a lot of individual items for specific interests we will create a small number of general interest items and put the particular interests into them.

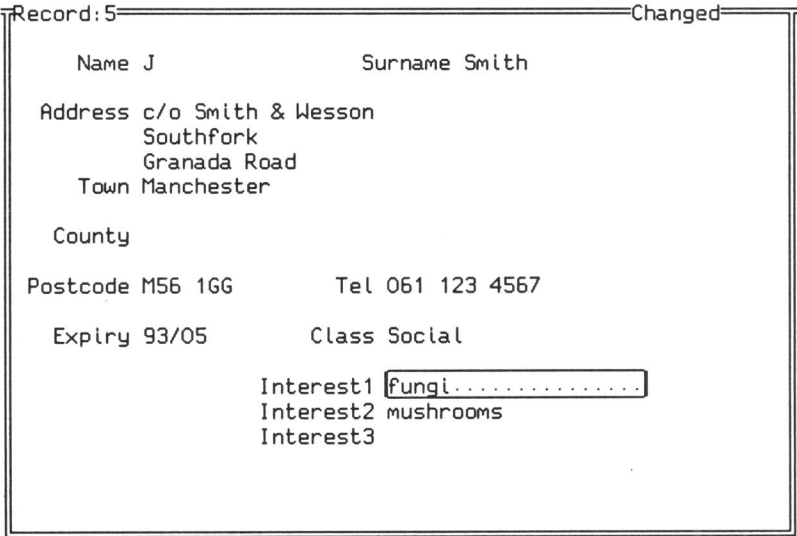

TIP: There is no need to show all the item names. Just as with the `addr2`, `addr3` ... items in chapter 3, you can hide any names you don't want to display.

How many items you set up is now dictated by the member who claims the largest number of special interests – rather than by the total range of possibilities.

To fill in the items you just type in the interests of each member into the items. There is no need to put a particular interest into a particular item, nor do you necessarily have to check that interests are on an "approved" list. If a member is interested in aardvarks then just fill this in – unlike the scheme we started out discussing there is no need to agonise over whether it is worthwhile setting up an `aardvark` item.

When you first set up the datafile you'll probably fill in the interest items in order, if for no other reason than the fact it looks neater this way. If later on a member tells you that their interests have changed, perhaps fungi lose their fascination, there is no need to "close up" the items. All the programs we give in this chapter will work just the same if there are blank items in and amongst the filled in items. Equally, there is no harm in having records with no interests filled in at all.

The programs for processing a datafile with these general interest items are just like the programs we've produced up to now, except instead of testing one item it is necessary to test several items and combine the results together using `OR`.

For example:

```
(+Mail)
$= "surname"
fungi = "fungi"
space = " "
tab = "        "
cr = "
"
loop = "
# interest1 = fungi OR interest2 = fungi OR interest3 = fungi :<:
name : space : surname : tab : tel : cr
:>:
$+
"
%loop @ surname
(-Mail)
```

Program 18C

This program assumes that you only have three interest items. If you have more then you need to extend the sequence of `OR`s accordingly. It produces the fungi fellowship and their phone numbers in just the same way as the first program in this chapter.

This program also suffers from just the same speed problems as the first program in this chapter – and you will not be surprised to learn that the solution is exactly the same; set up an index.

Alternative item indexes I : Special interests 149

Alternative item indexes

The type of index you set up is, however, a bit different. What you need is an **alternative items index**. To make this you go into Datafile set-up in the usual way and press [F2] to create a new index. Having specified the first item (interest1) and the type of sorting (alphabetic, no case is best) you will now have a menu looking like this:

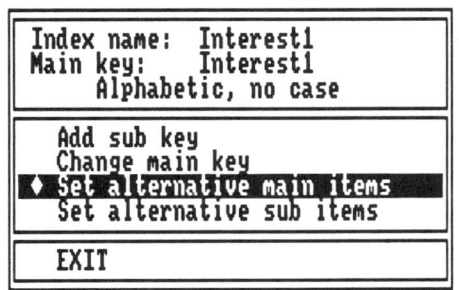
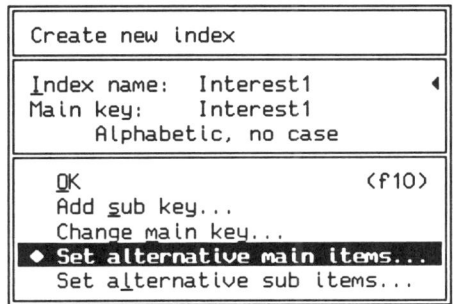

Select the command for alternative main items. You will now be presented with the item list again, with interest1 ticked. Unlike before, you will now find that you can tick more than one item at the same time. You need to tick all of the interest1, interest2, interest3 etc. items. This tells LocoScript that you want to build an index which indexes the contents of all of these items. When the ticks are correct press [EXIT] ([F10] on the PC). You will not need to alter the ordering (from alphabetic, no case) so press [ENTER] to return to the index menu which will now look like this:

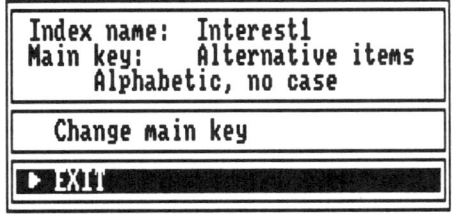
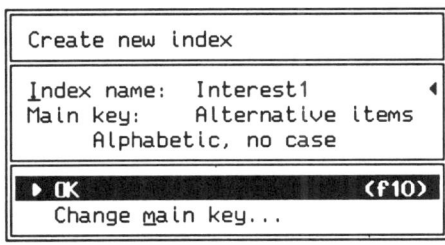

You should now cursor up to the index name line, which will have been set to the first item (interest1), and change the name to something more sensible (such as interests). Once this has been done, you can close up the menu and then leave Datafile set-up mode. LocoScript will build the new index, giving you an indication of progress on the screen.

Once your new index is set up you can use it for the fungi freaks:

```
(+Mail)
sig = "fungi"
$= "interests"
$$ sig
space = " "
tab = "→                    "
cr = ""
""
loop = ""
# interest1 = sig OR interest2 = sig OR interest3 = sig :<:
name : space : surname : tab : tel : cr
:><: stop = 0 :>:
$+
""
stop = 1
%loop @ stop
$="" : $$"99999999"
(-Mail)
```
Program 18D

This is almost exactly the same program as 9B in chapter 9. We use the $$ command to move directly to the first record with fungi in an interest item. We then generate a list of names and phone numbers, arranging to stop (with stop=0) when we encounter a person who is not interested in fungi – which we spot by seeing that no interest item contains the word fungi.

Again we've assumed just three interest items – you will need to extend the list of ORs if you have more. Just keep on typing – don't worry if you hit the right margin and some of your tests wrap to the next line.

The beauty of the alternative item index is that we can use the same index for any interest group; bird-watching, badgers, aardvarks and so on. There is no need to set up special indexes. Indeed, by changing

    sig = "fungi"

into

    sig = ? ;type the Special Interest Group

there is no need to construct different listing programs for different specialist groups.

Alternative item indexes I : Special interests

If you are using LocoScript on a PC you can use a special command `$?` to make the program a little more elegant (and a little bit quicker). This command, which is not available on the PCW, returns the name of the item which was indexed upon. This avoids the multiple test `# interest1 = subject OR interest2 = subject` etc.

Thus (for the PC only):

```
(+Mail)
sig = "fungi"
$= "interests"
$$ sig
space = " "
tab = "    "
cr = "
"
setwho = "who = "
loop = "
% setwho & $? :
# who = sig :<:
name : space : surname : tab : tel : cr
:><: stop=0 :>:
$+
"
stop = 1
%loop @ stop
$= "" : $$"9999999"
(-Mail)
```

Program 18E

This program works by executing the command `%setwho & $?` for each record. The `&` concatenates (glues together) the *value* of `setwho` (`who=`) and the *value* of `$?`, so that the actual command executed is `who=interest3` or `who=interest1` etc. depending which of the interest items contains the word which we are currently indexed upon. We can then just apply just the one test `#who=sig` to check if we are still processing `fungi` records. Making one test obviously makes it much easier if you have many `interest` items.

It is important to note that after the `$?` there are *two* command separators: a colon and a carriage return(↵). The program will not work if you leave either of them out. It doesn't actually matter whether they are colons or carriage returns – the important thing is there must be **TWO** of them – one to terminate the `%` and one to terminate the command that the `%` actually carries out (`who = interest`*n*).

Although we've used a special chapter to talk about them, alternative item indexes are pretty much the same as other indexes. You can adapt almost all of the programs which we've given in previous chapters to use an alternative item index.

So if you want to organise a fungi fair in Fakenham:

```
⌐|....↑....1.........?.........↑.........4.........?.........6.....
  (+Mail)↵
  $= "interests"↵
  sig = ? ; Which Special Interest Group do you want a listing for ↵
  $$ sig↵
  reqtown = ? ; Which town do you want↵
  comma = ","↵
  tab = "→      "↵
  cr = "
  "↵
  loop = "↵
  # sig = interest1 OR sig = interest2 OR sig = interest3 :<:↵
  →   # reqtown = town :<:↵
  →      surname : comma : name : tab : town : tab : tel : cr↵
  →   :>:↵
  :><: stop = 0 :>:↵
  $+↵
  "↵
  stop = 1↵
  %loop @ stop↵
  $= ""  : $$"9999999"↵
  (-Mail)
```

Program 18F

This program steps through the `interests` index testing each record to see if the town is the one we want. Alternatively of course, you could step through a `town` index testing if the interest is the one you want!

TIP: Set up an extra tab stop and indent the embedded **IF** (#) command as we have done. This will make it much easier to check that you have correctly matched up your **IF**s **THEN**s and **ENDofIF**s!

You might wish to speed up this program by using a `$$` command (using the main-key sub key form: `$$ interest $ town`). Unfortunately you cannot set up an index with alternative main items (such as the `interest` items) and then a sub key such as `town`. You *can* do it the other way round (main item `town` and alternative items as sub keys) and this is discussed in the next chapter.

Similarly, you'll find that your lists are always in record number order within each interest. You cannot put them into surname order because you cannot have a sub key of `surname`. If you wished, you could use the techniques of chapter 21 to extract your

Alternative item indexes I : Special interests 153

members in surname order then insert them into a new datafile. This would arrange that, until another member joined, record number order is the same as surname order.

The other tricky thing about alternative item indexes is stopping loops properly. The difficulty lies in writing **IF** (#) statements, because you do not know which item has supplied the current key. You can do it on the PC using the **$?** command we introduced earlier, but this command is not available on the PCW. Thus the program from chapter 11 which counted membership categories will not work with alternative item indexes on a PCW, but can be made to work on the PC thus:

```
⌐┘..........1..........2.........↑.........4.........5.........6.....
(+Mail)↵
$= "interests"↵
tab = "→          "↵
cr = "
"↵
current = ""↵
count = 0↵
setwho = "who = "↵
loop = "↵
% setwho & $? :↵
# who = current :<: count = [count + 1]↵
:><:↵
# count <> 0 :<: current : tab : count : cr :>:↵
current = who↵
count = 1↵
:>:↵
$+↵
"↵
%loop @ surname↵
current : tab : count : cr↵
(-Mail)
```

Program 18G

This will produce output such as:

```
⌐┘..........1..........2.........↑.........4.
            aardvarks→                  1↵
            bird watching→             21↵
            flowers→                   12↵
            fungi→                     46↵
            funji→                      1↵
            mushrooms→                 23↵
            poppies→                    1↵
            toadstools→                12↵
            →
                                        3↵
```

Obviously the `funji` is a misspelling which must be fixed. You probably also want to check that the `mushrooms` and `toadstools` people also have an entry for `fungi`.

Because of the multiple entries the total of all the interests will exceed your membership. Each record will appear at least once, and more than once if there are multiple interests. You do not, however, get hundreds of entries for unused items, only those people (three in the example) who have no interests at all are indexed at the end as "blank".

The final thing to note about alternative item indexes is that they aren't usually very suitable for producing complete lists of members, precisely because people can appear in them more than once. So if you're producing labels for a general newsletter stick to a simpler index!

Using `Find` to find things

It is not always possible to set up indexes in the way we've discussed so far in this chapter. Suppose, for example, that one of your members offered you something unusual – "I could organise a sponsored parachute drop for you if you like." At the time, you didn't think much of the idea and so you didn't set up an elaborate "Help offered" alternative items index. However, you dutifully filled in the offer in the free form `comments` item which we recommended you to create way back in chapter 3. Now the committee is keen to raise money and you vaguely recall something about the parachuting offer – unfortunately you forgot who made it. If you had an index you could `Goto` the offer, but you don't have such an index. You can't remember exactly what you typed either – so setting up a temporary index on the `comments` item will not work either.

The solution is to use the `Find` menu ([F6] on the PCW, [Ctrl][F6] on the PC). This searches through every record looking for the text you typed in, just as when you are editing a document [FIND] will search for some text in your document.

In this case you want to set the text to something like `parachut` (which will match `parachute`, `parachuting` etc.). Then select `Find first` and press [ENTER]. LocoScript will work through the records in the order of the current index (so for speed avoid using an alternative item index where records appear more than once). If the wrong `parachut` is found, just select `Find` again and this time immediately press [ENTER] to `Find next` with the same text.

TIP: `Find` is a good way of looking up people with illegible signatures who write to you with incomplete addresses (`Rose Cottage, Wednesday`) in the top right of their letters. However, it can be dreadfully slow, especially if you have forgotten to switch to a simple index!

19
Alternative item indexes II : Family memberships

This chapter, like the last one, is about alternative item indexes. In chapter 18 we used alternative main items to handle "keywords" using the example of members' interests. In this chapter we are going to be using some indexes with alternative sub key items. The example we are going to use is where several members of a family belong to our club, but instead of treating them as a group we want to deal with them as individuals who happen to live at the same address.

Obviously, we could produce multiple records for the family members. On the PCW you would have to type in every record individually (though cut and paste would speed this up a bit). On the PC there is a Create duplicate record facility which you can use to produce a new record with the same information as an old one. All you have to do then is to alter the forename, which cuts down on the typing.

There is nothing wrong with setting up your datafile with multiple records in this way. The individual family members will be handled individually by your programs, and this may be most satisfactory. The disadvantage is that although you don't *always* want to treat them as a group, you do sometimes. For instance, they will all change their address together. One payment may renew all of their subscriptions, and you may only want to send them one newsletter or one notice of forthcoming events.

The solution is put all of the members of the family onto one datafile record, but to construct an alternative item index which includes all of the members of the family.

The first thing to do is to go into Datafile set-up and construct some appropriate items to hold the names of the parents and the names of the children. You may have to use [F5] to make the card longer and move your existing items around to make room first. You can do this by using Change (Amend) item, or by pointing at each item in turn and using [ALT][SHIFT][↓] to move it interactively.

TIP: If moving items down, start with the lowest and move it down first, so that you have space to move the others into. LocoScript can get confused if you try to move one item over the top of another.

Once your card has been set up you can enter the data, giving you something like this:

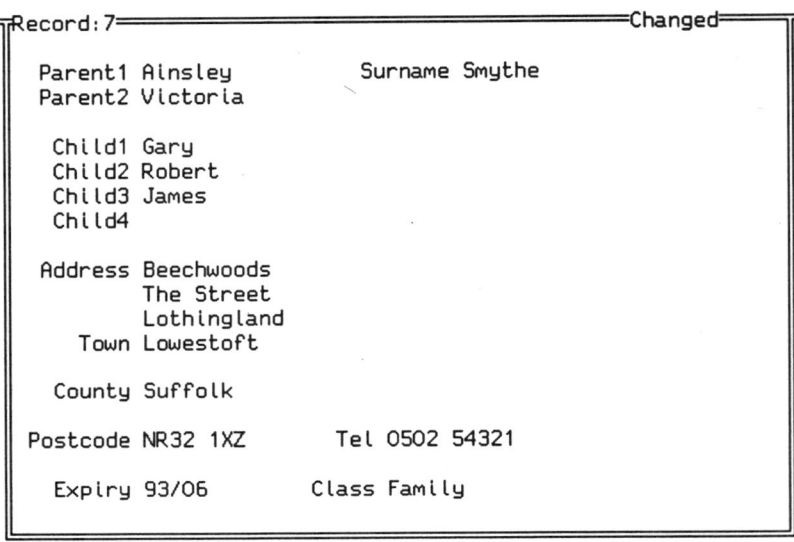

We can now build an `allperson` index which has a main key of `surname` but alternative sub key items of `parent1`, `parent2`, `child1`, `child2`, `child3` etc. To make the index, go into Datafile set-up in the usual way and press [F2] and select `Create new index`. Select `surname` as the main key and pick `Alphabetic, no case` sorting. Now pick `Set alternative sub-items` and place a tick next to all of the parent and child items. When they are all ticked press [EXIT] ([F10] on the PC), select `Alphabetic, no case` sorting again and you should get a menu like this:

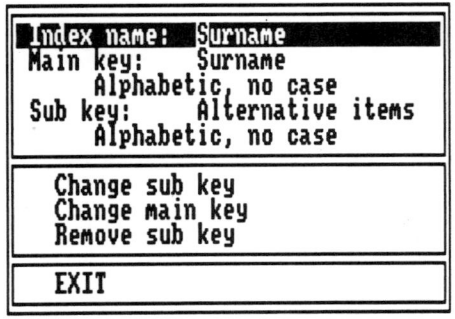
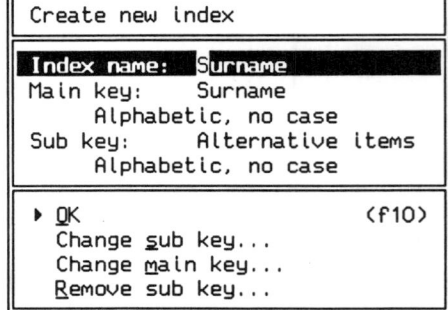

Alternative item indexes II : Family memberships

Move up to the index name line and fill in something suitable (like allperson). Apart from making the point about the nature of the index, you probably already have an index called surname! Now close up the menu and exit from Datafile set-up mode, which will cause the new index to be created.

Using alternative sub key indexes

You could now use [F2] to select this new index and step through a few records using the [PAGE] key ([PgDn] on a PC). You'll see that in general you move through in surname order, but whenever you encounter a family you stay on the same card with the highlighted "current item" hopping around from one family member to the next in alphabetical order of their first name.

If you use [F5] to Goto a record you'll be asked to fill in details like this:

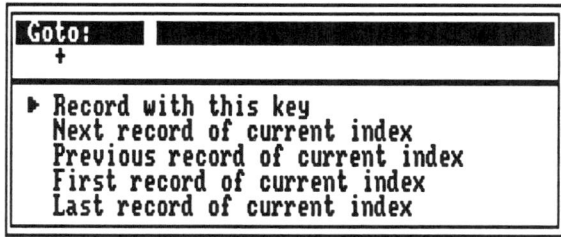

or on a PC:

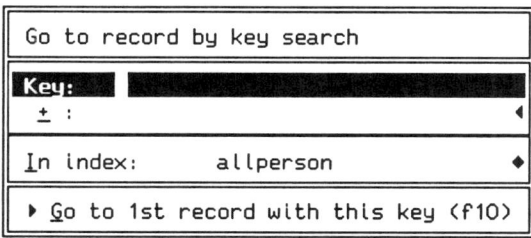

You need not fill in the second line at all – typing all (or just some) of the surname will allow you to move to a nearby record in your datafile. You can move to exactly the card you want by filling in both the surname and the forename. But remember, this index, like all indexes with sub keys, will take no notice of the sub key unless there is an exact match to the main key.

Alternative sub keys are sorted upon the text within the items, without regard as to which item is which. Therefore when looking for an individual no distinction is made between one parent, the other, or the children. For this reason alone, these are very useful indexes to set up on your datafile. Even if you never use any of the programs in this chapter you will save time in looking up `Janet Brown` if you don't have to remember that her record is indexed under her husband's name (or indeed that `John Smith` is indexed under `Mary`).

What you cannot do with alternative item indexes – and this is just a restriction which LocoScript imposes for reasons of simplicity rather than as a social judgement – is to index the same record under `George Robinson` *and* `Linda Black` where a wife has not taken her husband's name, or if the couple are just living together. You can arrange, with a little extra complexity in the listing programs, to correctly put together the right first and second names. What you cannot do is to construct indexes with anything other than two Robinsons (or alternatively two Blacks) in them.

A possible solution to this is to have two records (one for George, and one for Linda) just as if they were strangers living in different places. However, you mark one of the records so that it points at the other ("see George Robinson"), and you leave items like the address blank. This will work fine if you're looking up people "by hand". It can even be made to work in listing programs, but we won't go into the details of this because things get rather complicated rather quickly.

If you have company or society memberships then you may wish to set up an index so you can look up either the individual or the company or society name. In this case it is best to use the company/society name and the surname as alternative *main* keys.

Lists in alternative sub key order

Having made an alternative item index on family members you can use it to produce lists in much the same way as any other index, except for the same difficulties that we discussed in chapter 18. It can be rather tricky to check loop conditions and to tell which member of the family has caused you to be processing the record. For this reason listing programs using alternative item indexes are almost impossible to construct for the PCW and so the following programs are for the PC only.

However, if you are using a PCW do not let the PC orientation of the rest of the chapter give you the idea that alternative item sub-indexes are only useful for PC owners. You may not be able to use them effectively when merging to produce lists and labels – but they are very useful indeed when you are using `[F5]`=`Goto` to locate records "by hand".

Alternative item indexes II : Family memberships 159

First a complete list of members (just as in chapter 7) (PC only):

```
→|..........1..........?.........+.........4....+....5..........6..
(+Mail)↵
$= "allperson"↵
comma = ","↵
tab = "    →              "↵
cr = "↵
"↵
setwho = "who = "↵
loop = "↵
% setwho & $? :↵
surname : comma : who : tab : town : tab : tel : cr↵
$+↵
"↵
%loop @ surname↵
(-Mail)
```
Program 19A

Just as in program 18E the command `%setwho&$?` (which will only work on the PC) causes LocoScript to execute `who=child3` or `who=parent1` etc. which therefore sets the item `who` to the family member who is next in the membership list. Again, just as in 18E it is vital that there are *two* separators at the end of the command – so the colon before the carriage return cannot be omitted.

As a final example (again PC only), a list of all the children and their parent(s) names:

```
→|..........1..........+.........3.........+.........5....+....6..
(+Mail)↵
$= "allperson"↵
comma = ","↵
tab = "    →              "↵
cr = "↵
"↵
null = ""↵
child = "child*"↵
setwho = "who = "↵
loop = "↵
# $? = child :<:↵
% setwho & $? :↵
surname : comma : who : tab : parent1↵
# parent2 <> null :<: comma : parent2 :>:↵
tab : tel : cr↵
:>:↵
$+↵
"↵
%loop @ surname↵
(-Mail)
```
Program 19B

In the program we use the test `#$?=child` to compare the item *name* against `child*` which will match `child1`, `child2` etc. but not `parent1` or `parent2`. Only if we have found a child do we produce the `{{ details required }}`. For tidiness we check if there is a second parent `#parent2<>null` before generating the second name.

The program produces useful lists like this:

```
_|..........1..........?..........3..........?..........5....
    Allingham,Giles→    Mr,Mrs C E→        0603 54321⏎
    Allingham,Susan→    Mr,Mrs C E→        0603 54321⏎
    Hill,Jo→            D W→               050 88 9999⏎
    Johnson,Annette→    Mrs R→             0502 65432⏎
    Smythe,Gary→        Ainsley,Victoria→  0502 54321⏎
    Smythe,James→       Ainsley,Victoria→  0502 54321⏎
    Smythe,Robert→      Ainsley,Victoria→  0502 54321⏎
```

The alternative item indexes which we have covered in this chapter and the previous one can be rather confusing when you first meet them, but they can also be extremely useful. The main mistake made by beginners is to confuse them with sub keys (such as **main-key:** `town`, **sub key:** `surname`). The difference is that alternative item indexes allow records to appear more than once in the same index, whereas sub keys are just a way of ordering records whose main keys match.

20
How to change your mind

This chapter is about what to do when you realise that things would be so much easier "if only" different decisions had been taken when your datafile was designed or when you first entered all the details into it.

We start by discussing the simpler changes, when you want to alter the size of an item or its position on the card. We then move on to discuss adding and removing items. The next two chapters go on to deal with much more major reorganisations which involve extracting all the information from your current datafile and re-inserting it into another.

Changing size

You may want to alter the sizes of the items on your datafile card. Perhaps you are half way through entering all your member details when you suddenly discover that Major Double-Barrelled-Last-Name has too long a surname to fit into the slot designed for it, or you've forgotten about extn:2221 as a possible addition to a telephone number.

To change the size of an item you need to enter the Datafile set-up mode from the [F1] (PC [F9]) menu. Move the cursor to the item whose size you want to change and press [F3]. On the PCW select Change Item, on the PC press [Alt][F10] to select Inspect Item. The menu now displayed is very similar to the one you saw when the item was first created. You can alter the width (or possibly the height) of the item. Now press [EXIT] ([F10] on a PC) to confirm the new size. If you get a message such as:

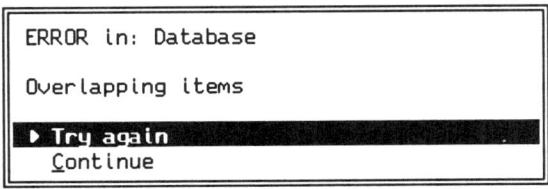

then your new size causes the item (or the item name) to overlap another item, or the edge of the card. Select Try again if you've just made a typing error and you wanted a smaller size. Select Continue if you are going to sort it out by moving another item out of the way or by making the card size bigger.

Provided you have no overlaps then you will be allowed to exit from Datafile set-up by pressing [EXIT] ([F10] on PC) and you can immediately continue using your re-sized item.

TIP: Don't get carried away making items bigger and bigger to cope with ever more outlandish names and addresses. If you make the items too big they will not fit onto labels any more. Company names are the biggest offenders – so just abbreviate them until they are a respectable size.

You can of course use the same technique to make items smaller. Don't worry that you will lose any information. If you move to a card and the information is too long to be displayed in a particular box then LocoScript will display what it can, followed by ... in the bottom right corner of the box. If the box is re-enlarged then the information will be displayed normally again. In the meantime, all the programs we've covered in previous chapters will continue to use the entire item contents – they won't take any notice of the size of the box on the card at all.

If you decide you need more room for the item boxes then you can easily alter the size of your card. Enter Datafile set-up and press [F5]. You can then change the length or the width of your card. If you do not leave room for all the items then you will be warned about overlaps, and you will have to move the items around to deal with this.

Changing the position of items

If you want to move items elsewhere on the card then this is also quite straightforward. After entering a few dozen records you might be beginning to wish you'd paid more attention when we stressed the connection between the position of items and the easy ways of typing in your members' details!

Just as we described above, you should enter Datafile set-up, move the cursor to the item and then Change (PC Inspect) the item. This time the values to be altered are those giving the item's Column position (across the card) and Row position (down the card). These are the coordinates of the top left corner.

Just as before, LocoScript will object if you make the item overlap another item or the edge of the card. Don't forget that there must also be room for the item name unless it is

How to change your mind 163

"hidden". If the name is inconveniently placed then you can alter the `Place at` value
to move it to another "o'clock" position:

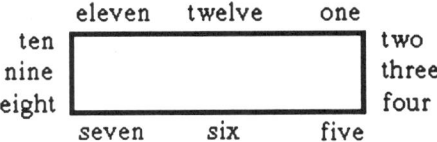

You can even change the item name, but if you did so then you would need to alter its
name wherever you've used it in any of the programs that you have developed so far.

None of these changes to size, position or even name will alter the actual information in
your datafile. However, you *must not* remove the item, because even if you create a new
item in the same place, with the same name, LocoScript still discards the old information.

Instant feedback

Before we move on, there is an alternative way of changing the size or position of items
on your card, which you may prefer. Once again you start by entering Datafile Set-up
and moving the cursor to the item you want to change. You can change the size and/or
the position of an item by pressing the cursor keys in combination with various shifts:

[ALT][→]	makes the item wider;
[ALT][←]	makes the item narrower;
[ALT][↓]	makes the item taller;
[ALT][↑]	makes the item shorter;

and [ALT][SHIFT] and the cursor keys move the item around without changing its size.

Be careful as you move the item around. If you "run into" another item LocoScript
(especially on the PCW) can get confused and you will find yourself moving the item
you collided with rather than the one you wanted. If this happens and you get two items
on top of each other then the easiest way of sorting it out is to press [F3] and use the
menus to set the position and size values explicitly.

TIP: You can't abandon changes to Datafile set-up. If you want things back where
they were you'll have to move them there yourself. In fact you won't even be
able to exit from Datafile set-up if you have overlapping items! If your
reorganisation is in the least bit ambitious you should have a recent backup to
return to in case you make things worse rather than better.

Adding new items

As your use of your datafile increases you may want some more items. Perhaps your AGM has introduced classes of membership when previously all were equal, or you need an item to hold subscription information to your new journal. Fortunately, like all the other changes in this chapter, this is particularly simple to implement.

All you do is to enter Datafile set-up, move the cursor to where you want the top left corner of the new item to be and then press [+]. Use the cursor keys to change the item size (or [ALT][SHIFT] and the cursor keys to move it around) then press [ENTER]. Type in an item name, set its o'clock position (or hide it), check the details are correct and press [EXIT]([F10]). Your new item now exists in every card – but it is always empty; you have to fill in the data yourself! Alternatively, instead of setting up the item in this interactive way you can type values into the menu in just the same way as we did in chapter 3.

Creating new items is so simple you might be wondering why we've bothered mentioning it at all. The reason is that you might have been used to other, less flexible, database systems where you have to design absolutely everything on the very first day and you cannot add new items whenever you feel like it.

Removing items

To remove an item, perhaps because you were over ambitious in your initial design, or the need to record some information has now passed, you select the item from the Datafile set-up [F3] menu. If you move the cursor to it first then it will be pre-selected for you – which will avoid accidents. Select Remove item. You will get a final chance to change your mind:

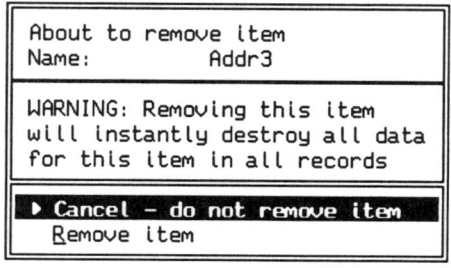

Move the cursor to Remove item and press [ENTER]. The item, and all its associated information in every record, is now gone forever.

Squashing the datafile

The way in which LocoScript achieves its remarkable flexibility in displaying datafile cards is actually achieved by holding the data and the display format completely separately in the file. Only when you move to a particular card does LocoScript decide how to put the information into the item shapes and the screen positions which you have currently chosen. If you have added new items for which there is no information then LocoScript displays an empty box. Conversely, if an item has been deleted then the information in the record is discarded and not kept.

This dynamic matching up of information and item sizes has three important consequences. First, adding lots of items to the Datafile set-up will make no difference whatsoever to the size of the datafile on disc because LocoScript does not need to use up any space to record "this item is empty" into every record. Second, it doesn't matter how big you ask for the items to be displayed, LocoScript will use the same amount of space to hold the information in each record. So don't feel that you have to stint on item sizes to keep the datafile size down. Your file will be the same size whether you have a comments item which is 3 lines by 10 or 30 lines by 65!

The third consequence of the dynamic approach is that when you remove an item the datafile does not get any smaller immediately. As you call up cards, LocoScript will remove the information from the record, so over time the file will shrink. If, however, you "Squash" the datafile then the information will immediately be removed from every record, which might be helpful if you are short of disc space.

To squash a datafile, you need to point at it with the Disc Manager cursor then select Squash datafile from the [F1] (PC [F9]) menu. You will be asked to confirm you have picked the correct file, and when you press [ENTER] the Squash will start. If there is room then a new datafile is created and the old version is left as a limbo (PC .BAK) file. If there is not room then the existing file will be Squashed "in place". It could be extremely embarrassing if a Squash "in place" failed in the middle and locked you out of your file forever. Therefore, in this case, LocoScript insists that you promise that you have a backup copy before the real work of the Squash starts. If you do not have a backup then you should make one immediately!

Once the Squash is running, various numbers will count up and down to show you how things are progressing. The PC is rather more helpful in that it counts down so you can see how long it has to go. If you change your mind about the Squash, then [STOP] (PC [Esc]) will abandon the process.

You will need some space on drive M (or the PC temporary path) to hold the intermediate information generated by the Squash. If you get a `Disc Full` in the middle of a Squash then you should read the message carefully to ensure you make room on the correct drive!

Christmas is coming!

A very common requirement with datafiles of individuals is a special mailshot. The example we will use is the sending of Christmas cards, but any unstructured list would be relevant. Suppose you decide to send Christmas cards to all the other society secretaries in your datafile, plus all the life members, plus the committee, plus several dozen others because they're really keen helpers. In principle you could write an listing program with a lot of tests (`# xxx OR yyy OR ...`) but in practice it would be much easier to go through and mark the records you want. So that's what you do!

Set yourself up a new item (see above). It need only be a little box 2 wide and 1 high. Call the item `xmas` (for example). Now go through the datafile putting an x (or some other character) into the box for every record you want to pick out.

TIP: *Do* make the box two characters wide as we suggest. When you [PAGE] (PC [PgDn]) to the next card the cursor will not move. If the box is one character wide you will need to move the cursor leftward back into the box before you can type again. If the box is two wide then you are still inside it so you can type the next x without having to move the cursor!

Now use your favourite listing or labels program, adapted with the simple test:

```
null = ""↵
# xmas <> null :<: ... {{ details required }} ... :>:↵
```

Once your labels or list is complete you can remove the special `xmas` item (unless you want to keep it for Christmas cards next year).

LocoScript will treat a new `xmas` item as holding completely different information (remember, we warned you that "erase and replace" was not the same as "move"). This means that you can remove this year's `xmas` item and immediately create a new `xmas` item in the same place on the card. All of last year's `xmas` people will be forgotten, and you will have twelve months to mark with an x all the people who deserve a Christmas card next year.

21
New data for old

The last chapter was all about how to change your mind when you wanted a new way of displaying the information in your datafile. It used LocoScript's built-in flexibility to alter the size, position or even existence of items. We stressed the way in which the information in the records was not altered, merely the way it was placed on the screen for you to look at. In this chapter we start to consider what to do when what you really want to do is to alter the information itself. We begin with some fairly simple alterations, and by the end of the next chapter build up to a rather complex example – how do you split up address items and then get the town name into the town item on your card?

For all these changes we are going to use the same basic technique:

> Step 1 is to run a special "extract" program, which is actually very similar to all the other programs we've been using since way back in chapter 7.

> Step 2 is new, and involves inserting the information we've extracted into a brand new, empty, datafile.

Let us suppose, as a first example, that you've had some delays in producing the next issue of your journal and so you want to change the expiry date of everyone's subscriptions from 92/12 to 93/03. You could of course just arrange that all of your listing programs for lists and mailshots etc. are altered to test for the old date in the datafile and generate the new date:

```
dec92="92/12"↵
mar93="93/03"↵
# expiry = dec92 :<: mar93 :><: expiry :>↵
```

This would put the expiry item into the results document unless it was 92/12 when it would be changed to 93/03. Although this would work, you'd have to change every program you own, and it is a likely recipe for total confusion. Obviously it would be better to change all the datafile cards affected. Unfortunately, you cannot do a global exchange within a datafile, but you *can* do one within a LocoScript document. So the solution is to extract the information from your datafile and save it in a document. You can then do the global exchange and insert the new version into another datafile.

The extract program is hardly different from the programs we have been using so far:

```
└┘..........1..........2..........3..........4..........5..........6..
  name ¶ surname ¶ address ¶ class ¶ expiry↲
------------------------------------------------------------
(+Mail)↲
sep = "¶"↲
ff = ""↲
------------------------------------------------------------
""↲
loop =""↲
name     : sep↲
surname  : sep↲
address  : sep↲
class    : sep↲
expiry   : ff↲
$+↲
""↲
%loop @ surname↲
(-Mail)
```

Program 21A

The first thing to notice is that the program starts with a list of items. Since these precede the (+Mail) code they will be transferred into the results document just as they are. This section is followed by the usual definitions section. The `sep` item *must* be the same character as the one used to separate the items on the first line, and *must* be a character which never occurs anywhere in your data. We've chosen ¶ because it is reasonably easy to type, but you've probably never used it before.

The next section is a standard loop. However, you will notice that it extracts *exactly* the same items as were given on the first line in *exactly* the same order. Also *every* item is followed by a `sep` item, except the last which is followed by an `ff` item.

The other vitally important thing is that you must include absolutely every item from your datafile into the two lists of item names (`name/surname/address/class...`) because if you don't extract the information then it will not be transferred into the results document, and therefore will not end up in your new datafile. In order to reduce the length of the programs in this chapter (and thereby make their function clearer) we have assumed a fairly short list of items (using `address`, rather than `address`, `addr2`, `addr3`, `town`, `county`, `postcode`); your real-life files will probably have several more items than this.

New data for old

When the program is merged with your datafile it will produce the output:

```
⌐⌐⌐⌐⌐⌐⌐⌐⌐⌐⌐⌐⌐⌐⌐⌐⌐⌐⌐⌐⌐⌐⌐⌐⌐⌐⌐⌐⌐⌐⌐⌐⌐⌐⌐⌐⌐⌐⌐⌐⌐⌐⌐⌐⌐⌐⌐⌐⌐⌐⌐⌐⌐⌐⌐⌐⌐⌐⌐⌐⌐
   name ¶ surname ¶ address ¶ class ¶ expiry▼
─────────────────────────────────────────────────────────────
   Mrs R¶Johnson¶The Old House¶Full¶93/12▼
─────────────────────────────────────────────────────────────
   Mr & Mrs¶Abson¶Pink Cottage¶Family¶93/07▼
─────────────────────────────────────────────────────────────
   E¶Anderson¶Garden Cottage¶Life¶93/05▼
─────────────────────────────────────────────────────────────
   Mr & Mrs C E¶Allingham¶Campion Meadow¶Family¶93/05▼
─────────────────────────────────────────────────────────────
   J¶Smith¶c/o Smith & Wesson¶Social¶93/05▼
─────────────────────────────────────────────────────────────
   Mr J¶Arthurson¶Belling House¶Junior¶93/01▼
─────────────────────────────────────────────────────────────
```

This will typically be even more untidy than this, but do not let that concern you. It is also unordered (actually it is in record number order); again this does not matter.

You now choose `Edit result` and perform your global exchange:

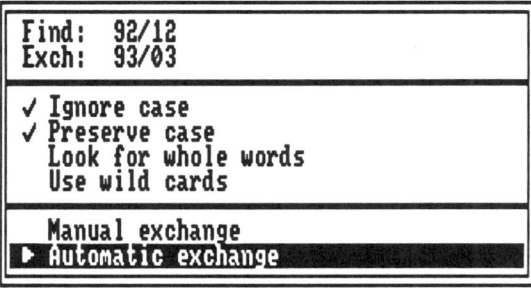

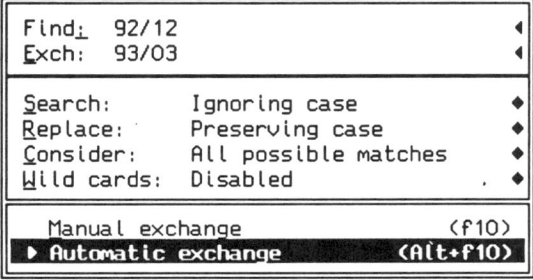

When the global exchange is complete you should then press [EXIT] ([F10] on a PC) and select the Save result option. Choose a suitable destination using the Disc Manager cursor. You will not be keeping the document for very long, so you can use the default name of DOCUMENT.nnn if you wish.

If you prefer, you could save the document first and then do the global exchange. This would be a good idea if you had a lot of editing to do which you might get wrong and so need to Abandon editing and start again.

Whilst the data is in the document it looks rather untidy. It can wrap strangely at the margins or it may contain big groups of ¶¶¶¶ characters. Do not be tempted to "tidy it up" – apart from any edits which you may be making to alter the contents of the items. If you tidy it (by adding carriage returns) then when the data is re-inserted you'll get carriage returns in inappropriate places. If you damage a sequence of ¶¶¶¶s then you'll mix up all the items! The document is laid out for LocoScript to read – not for humans!

Once your edits and global exchanges are complete the next stage is insert the document back into a datafile. In order to do this you will need an empty datafile. If you insert it back into your original datafile you will find that you get *two* records for everyone – the original, and also the inserted, global exchanged, version. This will be worse than useless.

On the PCW there is no easy way to make an empty datafile – which is why in chapter 3 we stressed that you should keep a copy of your datafile with no records inserted into it. Now is the time to find that file and take a copy of it to work with. If you didn't keep such a file then you'll need to enter Datafile set-up in your old file now and make a note of the item names and positions, and all the indexes. You can then Create new datafile from the Disc Manager screen and set up all the items and indexes afresh. This is best avoided!

On the PC there is a special option within [F9] Create datafile. If you choose the option Select template you will be allowed to pick a datafile on which your newly created datafile will be based. This lets you make a brand new datafile, with the same set-up as the original, but containing no records at all, which is exactly what you want.

Once you have your empty datafile, you should go into it, and whilst in normal mode (not Datafile set-up) press [F1] ([F9] on the PC) and select the command to Insert data. LocoScript will return to the Disc Manager to allow you to select the "data document" which is to be inserted. Point at the document with the newly edited text in it and then press [ENTER].

New data for old   *171*

The data from the document will now be inserted into your new datafile. You will see a progress menu ticking round as this happens. Once the operation has finished, the progress menu is removed and your new datafile is all ready for you to work with.

Solving problems when inserting into datafiles

In principle, nothing should go wrong with your insert. However, things can fail when you first try them. You may, for example, get a message like this:

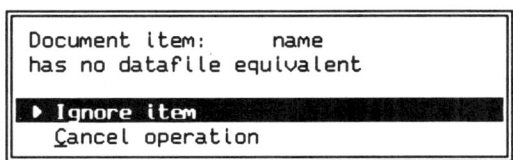

This means that the first line of your document – which was transferred unchanged from the extract program – contains item names which do not correspond to the item names in your new datafile. Of course, you will also get complaints if the second part of the extract program had incorrect item names – but these would have been complained about earlier with the usual `Name does not exist` message, which you've probably got used to by now. You should fix the item name and try again.

You may get a message like this:

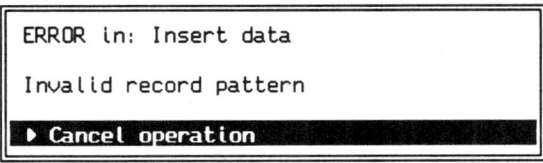

This means that the first line of the document, called the **record pattern**, is arranged incorrectly. The record pattern describes how the data in the rest of the document has been laid out. Assuming that the mistake is not obvious (e.g. a ¶ separator missing from between two items) then your item names are probably not just characters and digits, and are therefore not acceptable in a pattern. Change your datafile names into mailmerge names in the usual way (see chapter 25 for full details of this).

If your names are correct then check you don't have any extra characters in the pattern. Spaces around the ¶ characters are acceptable, but you don't need colons in this part of the document, and you cannot use carriage returns to make it look neat. If you have too many items to fit on a line then just let LocoScript wrap them onto the next line – do not force a wrap at a particular place.

You may lose items of data altogether. This is probably because you didn't extract them! Remember that you have to mention every single item twice (once on the first line, and once inside the loop). You can use the datafile [F3] menu to show you a full list of all your items, including those whose names are hidden. If a name is completely blank (not just hidden) then the item will be called @12,13unnamed or similar. To extract an item it must be given a proper non-blank name.

You may lose items of data because they have been amalgamated with another item. This will be caused by a missing sep between the items in the extraction loop.

If the items are shuffled around then you probably don't have them in the same order on the top line and within the loop. The actual order is irrelevant, just so long as you use the same order in both places.

TIP: Use the same order as the [F3] menu, so that you can check your program easily.

Another, much rarer, reason for your items being shuffled is that your data actually contains the ¶ character. The solution is to use another character for the separator. Given the huge range of LocoScript characters you should not find it difficult to choose an alternative! If you are unsure if you are using ¶ (perhaps you've inherited the datafile from someone else) then you can use Find to search for it.

If you find that every other record in your datafile is blank then you need to look at the very last item. Unlike all the other items which are followed by a ¶ (or sep) the last item is *only* followed by ↧ (or ff).

Another problem arises when you start with, say, 100 records but you now have more or less than this. This can happen if your editing removes one of the ↧ characters from the document, or inserts another. If you are concerned that you might have done this then you can check your record count by using [DOC] ([Ctrl][End] on the PC) to move to the end of the document. Your last record should be on page 101 (i.e. one more than the number of records, the extra one being the record pattern at the start).

When you extract your data and re-insert as we have just described, *this will not preserve the record numbers from the original datafile*. It was precisely because we knew we were going to show you this sort of program that we strongly advised you in chapter 2 that you should not use record numbers as membership numbers, but you should set up a special item for them!

New data for old 173

Exchanging text with mailmerge commands

Now that we've discussed a simple extract, edit and re-insert we'll consider some of the more powerful things you can do. We can, for example, avoid the global exchange part of the process by getting the extract program to do it for us. Suppose that we used to call the classes of membership by their initial letters F, J and L but now we've changed our minds and want to use Full, Junior and Life. We can do this automatically by changing the bit of the extract which reads:

```
.... : sep : class : sep : ....
```

to read:

```
.... : sep↵
# class = f :<: full↵
:># class = j :<: junior↵
:># class = l :<: life↵
:><: class :>: sep : ....
```

where we've assumed the definitions section of program has set up the old and new membership classes:

```
f    = "F"↵
j    = "J"↵
l    = "L"↵
full    = "Full"↵
junior  = "Junior"↵
life    = "Life"↵
```

Note that if the class isn't recognised we've left it alone and output it unchanged. These errors will have to be tidied up by hand.

Note also that we're allowed to use ↵s in this part of the program to make it easier to read – it was only in the pattern part at the top that they are not allowed.

This technique of altering the data as you extract it can be extended as much as you like. You can write # commands as subtle as you wish and thereby process your data into new and useful forms. However, in practice it is usually much easier to use global exchange than to get the # commands correct!

Even the example we've just discussed can be done by global exchange. You cannot of course exchange j into Junior throughout your document – because it will make rather a mess of all the other js (in Jane for example). The way round this is to exchange ¶j¶ into ¶Junior¶.

If you are worried that you may exchange some single J initials as well then you will have to be slightly more clever. There is no reason for all the separators to be the same character – it is just usually easier that way. Thus you can alter the extract program to start with:

```
.... ¶ address ¶ class § expiry ....
```

on the top line, then add the definitions:

```
sep  = "¶"↵
sep2 = "§"↵
```

and then inside the loop:

```
address : sep↵
class   : sep2↵
expiry  ....
```

Now you just need to global exchange ¶j§ into ¶Junior§.

You must make sure when altering separators in this way that you change the character in *both* the pattern *and* the loop part of the program!

Automatic processing of your data items to change their contents is not something you'll do every week, but it can be an extremely useful technique when you realise that things would be so much easier "if only".

22
New items for old

In the last chapter we showed you how you can extract all of the information from your datafile, edit it and then put it back again. In this chapter we are going to be doing much the same thing, but getting LocoScript to do the editing for us. We will show you how to combine items together, split them apart and invent new ones. The way we do this is to deliberately "get wrong" the things we warned you about in the last chapter because they might inadvertently scramble your data.

The classic example of creating new items is the task of splitting a multi-line address into individual `addr1`, `addr2` etc. items. This is essential if you want to use "n-across" labels or sheets of labels on a PCW. On any machine, if you want a town index then you again need your address split into separate items – but you also need the town in the town item! At the end of the chapter we give a program which will sort this out for you. But, before tackling that, some simpler examples are in order.

Creating extra items

In chapter 20 we discussed abolishing items and creating new ones. However, the new items we created all started off empty – and it was necessary to work through the file afterwards and fill in the details. If you want to make some extra items which are not empty then you need to use an extract program which generates extra items in the results document over and above the items from the original datafile.

Let us suppose that you have decided to publish a newsletter. Your committee in its wisdom has decreed that everyone except Juniors and Social members shall receive it, unless they write and ask to be taken off the mailing list. However, Juniors and Social member can specially ask to receive it. "Your computer can surely cope with that," they tell you firmly.

Well it surely can; all you need is a new item on every record which contains a marker for everyone who should receive the newsletter. Once you have this item then as requests to be added or removed from the mailing list arrive then you can oblige. So the only problem is to set the item up initially according to the committee's decree.

The program you will need is as follows:

```
_|..........1..........?..........?..........4..........5..........6....
   name ¶ surname ¶ address ¶ class ¶ newsletter ¶ expiry▼
─────────────────────────────────────────────────────────────────────────
(+Mail)↵
junior = "junior"↵
social = "social"↵
no     = "No"↵
yes    = "Yes"↵
sep    = "¶"↵
ff     = "▼
─────────────────────────────────────────────────────────────────────────
"↵
loop ="↵
name     : sep↵
surname  : sep↵
address  : sep↵
class    : sep↵
# class = junior OR class = social :<: no :><: yes :>: sep↵
expiry   : ff↵
$+↵
"↵
%loop @ surname↵
(-Mail)
```

Program 22A

You will see that this is just like program 21A except that the pattern on the top line contains a new item called `newsletter` and the loop contains extra instructions to generate the values automatically for this item:

`#class = junior OR class = social :<: no :><: yes :>: sep↵`

The text `No` will be generated if the member is a Junior or Social member, and the text `Yes` otherwise. Make sure that you don't forget the `sep` at the end of the line!

The first part of the procedure is just as before, you merge the program with the old datafile to produce the document with all the information in it. The second step is just the same as well; you insert the results document into an otherwise empty datafile. However, the datafile you insert into must have a new item created in it first (called `newsletter`) into which the new information can be inserted.

TIP: Create the item in your standard (empty) datafile before making a copy so that future copies will also contain the new item.

Merging items

If you want to abolish something altogether you can of course just remove the item, as we discussed in chapter 20. Sometimes, however, you want to merge items together. Suppose you originally created three separate comment items (it seemed like such a good idea at the time), but now you realise that life would be so much easier "if only" you had just one big comments item.

The program you need is:

```
....|.........1.........2.........3.........4.........5.........6....
     name ¶ surname ¶ address ¶ comments ¶ class ¶ expiry↵
─────────────────────────────────────────────────────────────────────
(+Mail)↵
sep = "¶"↵
ff = "↵
─────────────────────────────────────────────────────────────────────
"↵
loop ="↵
name       : sep↵
surname    : sep↵
address    : sep↵
comment1   : comment2 : comment3 : sep↵
class      : sep↵
expiry     : ff↵
$+↵
"↵
%loop @ surname↵
(-Mail)
```
Program 22B

We've assumed that your old comment items were called `comment1`, `comment2` and `comment3` and your new item will be called `comments`.

You can see that we have combined the items by doing what we have warned you about doing accidentally; leaving out the separator between the items! We have also put different item names in the pattern and inside the loop!

Again the procedure is to first extract all the information from the old datafile. You then need to create a new and empty datafile which has the new `comment` item defined in it. You should also remove the `comment1`, `comment2` and `comment3` definitions from this new datafile. Finally you insert the results document into the new datafile and you will have but one `comment` item in the future.

In practice, when combining items like this you will probably need to be a little bit more clever because your new comment item will look better with a ↵ between each of the old comments. However, writing:

```
comment1 : cr : comment2 : cr : comment3 : sep↵
```

will not work very well if your comments were often blank. You'll end up with a lot of new comment items with just ↵ ↵ in them. What you actually require is:

```
c = comment1↵
# c = null :<: c = comment2↵
:># comment2 <> null :<: c = c & cr & comment2↵
:>:↵
# c = null :<: c = comment3↵
:># comment3 <> null :<: c = c & cr & comment3↵
:>:↵
c: sep↵
```

which is just a series of tests to insert ↵ symbols between the comment items unless they are blank. They assume the definitions `cr="↵"` and `null=""`. The mailmerge command & concatenates (appends) things together. Do not worry if they look a little daunting at first sight; we've met all these commands before and they read moderately sensibly in "English":

c = comment1
IF c {which just holds `comment1`} **IS** blank so far
    THEN c = comment2 {easy; it may or may not be blank}
ELSE IF comment2 {which we are adding} **IS NOT** blank
    THEN c = c & cr & comment2 {the case when we need a ↵}
    {otherwise if comment2 is blank then leave c as it is}
ENDofIF
IF c {the combination of comment1 and comment2} **IS** still blank
    THEN c = comment3 {easy; it may or may not be blank}
ELSE IF comment3 {which we are adding} **IS NOT** blank
    THEN c = c & cr & comment3 {the case when we need a ↵}
    {otherwise if comment3 is blank then leave c as it is}
ENDofIF
c : sep {to insert the concatenated item and the separator}

Of course, you don't *need* to be clever like this when concatenating items, but a little extra effort will keep your datafile tidier for the future.

New items for old

Splitting up items

As we promised at the start of the chapter, we are now going to show you how to split up your monolithic, multi-line address item into separate addr1, addr2, addr3 etc. items. The new arrangement is a good idea because it lets you create town indexes, and it is essential if you wish to use "n-across" labels or sheets of labels on a PCW.

In general, LocoScript will *not* let you split up items particularly easily; if you want to separate initials from surnames you'll have to do it by hand. The special feature of addresses which enables our split program to work is that the constituent parts are separated by ↵ characters, and these can be an item separator within a pattern.

The program you need is:

```
⌐⌐....⌐....1.........2.........3.........4.........5.........6....
     name ¶ surname ¶ class ¶ expiry ¶ addr1↵
     addr2↵
     addr3↵
     town↵
     county↵
     postcode▼
------------------------------------------------------------
  (+Mail) ↵
  sep = "¶"↵
  ff  = "▼
------------------------------------------------------------
  "↵
  loop = "↵
  name     : sep↵
  surname  : sep↵
  class    : sep↵
  expiry   : sep↵
  address  : ff↵
  $+↵
  "↵
  %loop @ surname↵
  (-Mail)
```

Program 22C

The first thing to notice is that the pattern describes an address which will be made of several addr1, addr2 etc. items separated by ↵ characters. Then when you look inside the loop you can see that we generate these new items from the single address item. This mismatch between the two ways of telling LocoScript about the address is all there is to it. We *generate* the address as one item which happens to have ↵s inside it, then *describe* it using the ↵ as a separator to pick out the individual lines. All the other items use our normal ¶ separator – so it does not matter if they include ↵ characters or not.

For this technique to work the address item *must* be the very last item in the pattern. Previously it did not matter in what order the items occurred (provided that the order was the same in the pattern and in the generating loop). In this case, the order is vital because if some of your addresses are less than five lines long the terminating ↓ will cause the "missing" lines to be made blank. If you do not put the address at the end then the missing lines will be constructed from the other items and you'll end up with the membership class, expiry date and so on cluttering up the address lines!

You merge the program with the old datafile in the usual way and save the resulting document. You then take a new datafile with no records, but with the new address items set up within it. Use the Insert data command from the datafile [F1] (PC [F9]) menu and your addresses will now be split up into their individual lines.

Of course, in the program examples throughout the book we call the first address line address rather than addr1 because it looks nicer when we display cards. Feel free to alter the pattern to do this; we just wanted to make clear the distinction between the address item in the old datafile and the addr1 item in the new datafile.

How to get the town in the town item

We promised we'd show you how to get the town into the town item, and if you've just performed the address splitting procedure from program 22C this is probably one of the things which is worrying you at present.

Your problem will be that because of the splitting procedure you have addresses which look something like this:

```
address     6 Saltings Rd.
addr2       Norwich
addr3       Norfolk
town        NR80 4GG
county
postcode
```

where the town, county (if any) and postcode are on the wrong lines. You could sort out all your addresses before you ran the extract program 22C by adding extra ↵ characters to the address, but it is possible to sort it out at this stage – which will be welcome news if your problem is that you have had single line address items for some time, but have been a little slap-dash in the way you used them!

New items for old 181

You'll have a good idea by now how we propose to proceed. We're going to extract all the data into a document and then re-insert it into a new datafile. We just have to determine which item contains the town name and then rearrange the rest of the items accordingly. Unfortunately you can't write a test of the form:

```
# addr2 is a town name :<: ...
```

because there isn't any sort of general test that you can make for town names. So a human (you) is going to have to tell LocoScript which line is the town (and incidentally which line is the county and which is the postcode). The way to do this is to add some extra items to your datafile called m1, m2, m3, m4, m5 and m6:

```
┌─────────────────────────────────┐
│ Create new item                 │
├─────────────────────────────────┤
│ Name:    m1                   ◀ │
├─────────────────────────────────┤
│ Name is:    Displayed         ◆ │
│ Placed at:  3 o'clock         ◀ │
├─────────────────────────────────┤
│ Item width:              2    ◀ │
│ Item height:             1    ◀ │
├─────────────────────────────────┤
│ Column:                 49    ◀ │
│ Line:                    4    ◀ │
├─────────────────────────────────┤
│ ▶ OK                    (f10)   │
└─────────────────────────────────┘
```

These items should all be 2 wide and 1 high, and should be positioned at the ends of the various address lines in your datafile:

```
    Name ............    Surname ....................
 Address .................................... .. m1
         .................................... .. m2
         .................................... .. m3
    Town .................................... .. m4
  County .................................... .. m5
Postcode .........    Tel ................... .. m6
  Expiry ........    Class ..........
```

TIP: *Do* make the extra items two characters wide just as we have done. When you [PAGE] (PC [PgDn]) to the next card the cursor will not move. If the box is one character wide you will need to move the cursor leftward before you can type again. If the box is two wide then you will only need to cursor vertically to the item you want to type into. This will speed things up considerably.

Now work through your entire datafile. When you find records with address lines which are in the wrong items then put a T into the marker item which is on the line with the town name, put a C into the marker item which is on the same line as the county name and P into the item on the postcode line. If something is already in the correct item then you do not need to mark it (though it will do no harm if you do). If a particular address does not have a postcode, for example, then you do not put a P marker at all.

For example, the following record has three misplaced items:

```
╔Record: 1═══════════════════════════Changed═══╗
║                                               ║
║       Name Mrs R        Surname Johnson       ║
║                                               ║
║    Address The Old House                   m1 ║
║            Horning Road                    m2 ║
║            Lowestoft                  t    m3 ║
║       Town Suffolk                    c    m4 ║
║                                               ║
║     County NR32 0XX                   p    m5 ║
║                                               ║
║   Postcode              Tel                m6 ║
║                                               ║
║     Expiry 93/12        Class Full            ║
║                                               ║
╚═══════════════════════════════════════════════╝
```

It is quite possible that marking your cards in this way, then going on to extract and then re-inserting the records, will be more work than just editing a handful of offending records by hand. If so, then for goodness sake do the easier task! There's no shame in going to bed earlier.

However, to continue and do the job automatically then the program you want is on the opposite page. It is the longest program in the entire book, because the problem it solves is the most complicated one we cover.

Despite its length it just as easy to comprehend as any of the others (and just as easy to type in and use without being quite sure how it works at all).

New items for old

```
⌐|..........1..........?..........3..........4..........5..........|⌐
name ¶ surname ¶ address ¶ addr2 ¶ addr3 ¶ town ¶ county ¶
postcode ¶ class ¶ expiry▼
```

```
(+Mail)
sep = "q"
ff = "
```

```
"
null = ""
p = "P"
c = "C"
t = "T"
loop = "
a1 = address : a2 = addr2 : a3 = addr3
a4 = town : a5 = county : a6 = postcode

# m6 = t :<: t9 = a6 : a6 = null :>:
# m6 = c :<: c9 = a6 : a6 = null :>:
# m5 = t :<: t9 = a5 : a5 = null :>:
# m5 = c :<: c9 = a5 : a5 = null :>:

# m1 = p :<: a6 = a1 : a1 = null :>:
# m2 = p :<: a6 = a2 : a2 = null :>:
# m3 = p :<: a6 = a3 : a3 = null :>:
# m4 = p :<: a6 = a4 : a4 = null :>:
# m5 = p :<: a6 = a5 : a5 = null :>:

# m1 = c :<: a5 = a1 : a1 = null :>:
# m2 = c :<: a5 = a2 : a2 = null :>:
# m3 = c :<: a5 = a3 : a3 = null :>:
# m4 = c :<: a5 = a4 : a4 = null :>:
# m6 = c :<: a5 = c9 :>:

# m1 = t :<: a4 = a1 : a1 = null :>:
# m2 = t :<: a4 = a2 : a2 = null :>:
# m3 = t :<: a4 = a3 : a3 = null :>:
# m5 = t :<: a4 = t9 :>:
# m6 = t :<: a4 = t9 :>:

name    : sep
surname : sep
a1 : sep : a2 : sep : a3 : sep : a4 : sep : a5 : sep : a6 :
sep
class   : sep
expiry  : ff
$+
"
%loop @ surname
(-Mail)
```

Program 22D

After a normal sort of definitions section we start to define the loop, which starts in an unusual way. First the current contents of the six lines of address are copied into the working values a1..a6. The marker values are checked in turn for the mark P to indicate the postcode line, C the county, or T to indicate the town line. If something is found in the wrong slot then it is moved to the correct place.

The special case of finding the wrong thing in the county or postcode slots where they might be overwritten before they are moved is handled by moving them via the temporary items c9 and t9. It is just because there are so many different possible movements of the items that the program is as long as it is.

Once the items are all in the right slots the program is able to output the items in the usual way, surrounded by separators and finished by a ↲.

Having typed in the program you merge it with your marked up datafile and save the resulting document. Insert this into a new datafile (which need not have the extra little marker boxes) and the town will be in the town slot etc., ready for you to create indexes upon it!

It may look like magic, but it works! and it is not just an academic exercise; we really used it to tidy some of our datafiles.

23
Splitting up datafiles

This chapter brings together the techniques from earlier in the book for producing selective lists with the techniques for making new datafiles in the last chapter. In combination they allow you to create datafiles, rather than lists, which contain only some of your members.

In general we would not recommend splitting your datafiles this way if you can avoid it. Though it might seem attractive to keep one datafile per class of member you'll find it inconvenient to transfer the information when a Junior grows up and becomes a Full member, or if a Full member moves away and downgrades to become a Social member. It might also seem attractive to split your datafile into A..M and N..Z, but when Miss Brown marries and decides to take the name of Mrs Smith you'll have to move her record from one file to the other. It will be much more convenient to keep all your members together.

If your membership file grows too large you will have to decide whether to split it or upgrade your machine. On a PC you are only likely to run out of room on floppy discs. The only practical option is to purchase a hard disc. It is difficult to find a hard disc smaller than 40MB (40,000,000 characters!) these days, so you'll not run out of space again until you have a membership equivalent to a medium size town.

On a PCW, 3 inch floppy discs are 180K double sided (the top drive on an 8256 or 8512) or 720K (all other models). 180K should allow for about 400 members and 720K over 1600. If your datafile becomes too big on an 8256 then you should consider purchasing a second drive. At present the only readily available second drives are of the 3½ inch type : which means the discs are different (a minus) but cheaper (a plus). The other relevant restriction on PCWs is that it is often preferable to work with the datafile on drive M. You can expand drive M by plug-on packs up to 2MB. The other possible expansion for a PCW is to add a hard disc. The economics of doing this are rather dubious; you might well find that you can get a cheap PC for only a few pounds more, and you will get a much better deal from a price/performance point of view.

Having said firmly that splitting datafiles is not to be generally recommended, there is one reason for splitting files which *is* a good idea. In chapter 16 we discussed lapsed members and indicated that although they could be left in your main file, it would be better to extract them all from time to time and save their details elsewhere.

The program to do this is like those in the last chapter, but with an **IF** command in the loop to decide which records to extract, just like the **IF**s in the loop in chapter 8 et seq.

```
_|..........1..........?..........3..........+..........5..........6....
 name ¶ surname ¶ address ¶ expiry ¶ transfer▼
.........................................................................
(+Mail)↵
today = ? ;Date of transfer (fill in today's date)↵
xfer  = ? ;Records to be transferred : e.g. 93/02↵
sep = "q"↵
ff = "▼
.........................................................................
"↵
loop ="↵
# expiry = xfer  :<:↵
name     : sep↵
surname  : sep↵
address  : sep↵
expiry   : sep↵
today    : ff↵
:>:↵
$+↵
"↵
%loop @ surname↵
(-Mail)
```

Program 23A

As you can see, we have assumed that you are extracting records with a particular expiry date. You could equally well rewrite the **IF** command to extract those members whose membership class you have changed to lapsed.

When a record matches the expiry date then the relevant details for the ex-member are generated in the results document. It may not be worthwhile generating every item – the important thing is that this information must match up with the pattern on the first line. We would recommend generating the whole address, so you probably need the addr2, addr3, town, county and postcode items as well, if you have them.

You will note that you have to type in the date that the transfer is made, and that this is placed into the output document along with the other details of each ex-member. The reason for this is that instead of inserting the document into a new datafile you are going to insert it into the "lapsed members datafile". In adding these ex-members to the others

Splitting up datafiles

already in the file you may create a duplicate record, because, for example, Mr. Smith joined and left, rejoined and has now left again. (He may not actually be leaving and rejoining, he might just be seriously incompetent about paying his dues promptly.) Anyway, these duplicate records won't worry you because untidiness in the lapsed members datafile is of little importance. However, when Mr. Smith rejoins *again* and you find two records for him with different addresses then it could be useful to know which is the older. Similarly, if you want to use the lapsed members datafile for a special mailshot then you might well wish to distinguish between people who left just a year ago and those who haven't belonged for most of the decade.

TIP: Even though you don't mind duplicate records in your lapsed members datafile you don't want it messed up. So always insert your new data into a *copy* of the actual datafile, so you can retry with a fresh copy if anything untoward happens.

Although you have now extracted the ex-member details from the current datafile and saved them away, they are of course still cluttering up the original datafile. You can now clear them out. If there are only a few people involved, you can work through and delete the records "by hand". Alternatively, you can do a further extraction (of everyone else) and insert the result into a new datafile. This will definitely be quicker if you suffer from mass resignations! The program you would need is:

```
⌐⌐.........1.........?.........3.........◆.........5.........6....
    name ¶ surname ¶ address ¶ class ¶ expiry▼
─────────────────────────────────────────────────────────────
(◆Mail)⏎
xfer' = ? ;Records not to be kept : e.g. 93/03⏎
sep = "¶"⏎
ff = ""▼
─────────────────────────────────────────────────────────────
"⏎
loop ="⏎
# expiry <> xfer :<:⏎
name    : sep⏎
surname : sep⏎
address : sep⏎
class   : sep⏎
expiry  : ff⏎
:>:⏎
$+⏎
"⏎
%loop @ surname⏎
(-Mail)
```

Program 23B

Note that this time it is important to keep *all* of your existing information (so you must extend the pattern part of the program and the generated details accordingly).

Resurrecting lapsed members

As a final word on the subject we'll briefly consider how to resurrect your lapsed members. The simplest scheme is probably to forget about their presence in the lapsed file and just create a new record for them and fill in the details! Alternatively, look them up in the lapsed file and note their details. While you are in the file you might as well delete their record since they no longer belong there. Now enter your current datafile, create a new record and type in the details.

You could in principle use the [F7]-Extract menu to pick out the information from the lapsed record and [PASTE] ([Alt][Ins] on the PC) to put it into the new record. However, this will only work if you are prepared to extract each item into a separate block. Although extract can append several items together into one block, paste will not split them up again. It can be useful, though, for comment items or complicated numbers or references which you may mis-type.

If you have a mass return (undoing the mass resignation) then you can do an extract on the lapsed file and an insertion into (a copy of!) the current file. You should use much the same program as you used to transfer the details to the lapsed file in the first place.

Assuming not everyone has come back, you will need to mark the returnees. The simplest scheme is to create a special temporary return item in Datafile set-up, as we did for Christmas cards in chapter 20, and then alter the program to something like:

```
loop = "↵
        # return = yes :<: ....
```

rather than the # class = lapsed test that we had before.

It won't matter to LocoScript if the details that you insert back into the current datafile have fewer items than the rest of the records because it will just make the missing items blank. It might matter to you though, so you'll need to work through and check them all.

TIP: The inserted records will have the highest record numbers in your datafile, so select the record number index in order to work through them as a group.

Of course, if you knew the mass return was on the cards you'd have transferred absolutely every item to the lapsed datafile, but then if you'd expected the mass return you'd have saved a copy of your datafile before you split it up!

In any case, you'll deserve your vote of thanks at the AGM!

24
Taking over an existing list

This chapter is all about what to do with an existing list of people. If your society has been running for some time it must already have some sort of membership list. What state it is in can vary enormously.

If you are lucky, the lists have been kept on a computer. This chapter explains how you can transfer these lists to your computer and use our LocoScript programs. Perhaps they have even been kept on a LocoScript system and you wish to amend it. In this latter case you should have another look at chapters 20 and 21.

The major advantage of taking over a computerised list is that, although it is not always straightforward, you can almost always avoid retyping the list from scratch. This helps in two ways. First you avoid spending the typing time, and second you will not introduce errors into the data which will have to be checked and corrected.

Taking over a manual list

It is rather more likely that you will take over lists that have been kept manually, and perhaps have not really been kept at all! The responsibility for manual lists is often spread between several people, so you may find it hard to determine which of several lists is current, or you may find inconsistencies between the details held by the membership secretary and the treasurer.

The first thing to do is to pick the list you have most faith in and put these names and addresses onto the computer along with any other details that are recorded. Now use the programs we gave earlier in the book to produce a report of all your "members". Annotate this report by cross-referencing it with any other lists you may have and then update the records on your datafile.

Once this process is complete you will be able to produce a list of people who are apparently members but, for example, do not seem to have paid for at least a year. Check that they do not pay by standing order, because this often results in their payment being a secret between themselves and the treasurer!

When you are satisfied they are in default send them a polite reminder letter asking for payment. Such a letter will have two benefits – those with guilty consciences will pay up quickly, and those who do not pay even now can have their names removed, which will cut the mailing costs!

An unexpected advantage of putting the list on the computer in this way, is that people are more likely to complain about errors in their names or addresses when they return a slip which has their name already on it.

Putting a manual list on to the computer involves a fair amount of typing. If you are a two finger typist this may appear a daunting task – but it will improve your keyboard skills no end! However, if it really seems too much, perhaps you can persuade someone with typing skills to do some, if not all, of the typing for you.

If your helper is a trained copy typist then they might prefer to type into a LocoScript document rather than directly into a datafile. This is acceptable. The rest of the chapter is about transferring lists from one computer system to another. The last step of that process is to insert a document into a datafile, just as we have been doing in chapters 21, 22 and 23. There is no reason why this document should not be generated by a human, providing they are consistent in the way in which they put in carriage returns and form feeds to separate the names and addresses.

If you are changing over from a manual to a computer system then there are some legal implications. You may need to inform your membership that their records are now held on a computer. See chapter 26 for a discussion of this.

Taking over a computer list

There are three distinct parts to the problem of transferring a list from one computer to another. You have to generate a complete list of all the data on the old system. You have to get the old list onto your machine (a "physical transfer") and you have to insert the list into a LocoScript datafile (a "logical transfer").

In order to know what is needed in the earlier stages we will start by considering the end of the process. Ideally what we would like is a file in the sort of format which we were

Taking over an existing list 191

using in chapters 20 and 21 to insert records into a datafile. At the time we rather glossed over the exact form of the file, but it was in fact of the form:

```
pattern details
end of record
member 1 details
end of record
member 2 details
end of record
etc.
```

Previously, these files were always LocoScript documents which we generated ourselves in order to rearrange our own data. It is not in fact necessary for these files to be LocoScript documents, with codes and formatting information of all kinds. It is equally acceptable to use **ASCII files** which just contain characters (a..z, 0..9 and so on), along with just spaces, tabs and carriage returns. ASCII means that the encoding used for the characters (a = 97, b = 98 etc.) conforms to an industry standard. The advantage of using ASCII files is that it is much more likely that you can get data in this form than as a LocoScript document.

In order to make things a little simpler we will use a feature of LocoScript which allows us to keep the record pattern separate from the data itself. We will type it into a LocoScript document and not attempt to transfer it with the data from the old system. The ASCII file will just contain:

```
member 1 details
end of record
member 2 details
end of record
etc.
```

So, the very last stage of our transfer will be to insert an ASCII file into a LocoScript datafile using a LocoScript document as a pattern. This sounds impressive, but is in fact rather easy. All you do is to press [F1] ([F9] on the PC) whilst in the datafile. Select Insert data and press [ENTER]. The Disc Manager screen will appear. *Select the pattern document* and press [ENTER]. LocoScript will read the pattern and then almost immediately prompt for the real data (on the PC you get a friendly intermediate message telling you the pattern has been read successfully). Move the Disc Manager cursor to the ASCII file and press [ENTER]. The data from the ASCII file will now be inserted into your datafile.

Now we know the end of the story we can consider the previous stage. Exactly what does the datafile we insert into look like? This is easy – it looks just like the sort of datafiles we've been using throughout the book. Chapter 3 explains how to set one up. You'll need an item for every piece of information coming from the ASCII file. Because you haven't necessarily seen the data yet you may not know exactly how big to make some of the items. This is not a problem because as we discussed in chapter 20 you can easily adjust the item sizes later. If you forget an item then when you start inserting the data you will see a message like this:

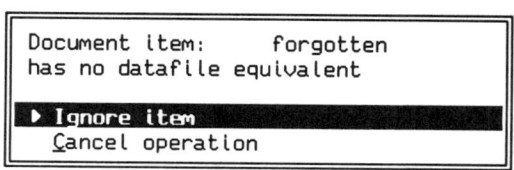

and you can cancel the insert, fix the datafile set-up and then try again. However, and this is very important for PCW users. You must always insert the data into a *copy* of your datafile. The reason is that if you have to try again you will need another clean, empty, datafile – otherwise you'll just get all your members in the datafile twice and this havoc will take some considerable time to sort out! Using a copy is less important for PC users who can create a new datafile using an existing datafile as a template.

Moving further back in the story, the next thing to consider is what the record pattern must look like. In principle this too is easy. The record pattern looks like the data, but in a stylised form. Instead of actual names, surnames and addresses the record pattern contains the item names for these pieces of data. An example will make this clearer. Suppose your ASCII file was of the form:

```
Brown, Arthur, 32 The Road, NORWICH, Norfolk↵
Smith, Mary, 27 The Lane, LOWESTOFT, Suffolk↵
etc.
```

and these details are to be placed into the datafile items: `surname, name, address`. Then the pattern record would be:

```
surname,name,address↵
```

You should type just this one line into a document and save it on disc:

Taking over an existing list

What the record pattern actually tells LocoScript is that the data starts with the item surname. LocoScript is further told that the end of the surname is marked by a comma. This comma will not be part of the surname when it is stored in the datafile. The next piece of data is name, and again the end of it will be signalled by a comma. The last item is the address which ends with a carriage return (↵). Since that is the end of the record pattern that completes the details for that member. LocoScript then restarts the record pattern at the beginning as it starts fetching the details for the next member.

The key point is that it is the record pattern which is in control of the process. Suppose you unwisely used the pattern:

    surname,name,address,

Everything would proceed as before, except that the address item for Arthur Brown would be just 32 The Road and the comma after this would terminate the first record. LocoScript would then decide that NORWICH was the next surname, Norfolk↵Smith the next name, Mary the next address and so on. When this sort of thing happens to you, then the first thing you will need to check is that record pattern is correct!

If the first few people are inserted correctly but everything goes wrong thereafter then you will need to look at the datafile. Maybe it is not as regularly laid out as you thought. Perhaps organisations have a different layout than individuals.

    The RSPB,,Sandy,Bedfordshire↵

is OK – the two commas mean that the name item is blank.

    The RSPB,Sandy,Bedfordshire↵

is not OK – Sandy will be treated as the name and not as part of the address.

You will have to decide for yourself how to sort this out – you may be able to regenerate the file, or perhaps you need only edit a handful of offending records. If you choose the latter course then on the PCW you need to Create a new document and use the [F1] Insert Text option to insert the ASCII file into LocoScript (on the PC you can edit the ASCII file directly).

Once you have fixed the problems there is no need to convert the file back to ASCII again – you can insert it just as well in its new form as a LocoScript document, and you can continue to use the separate record pattern document.

CSV format

A common format for ASCII files which many other programs can generate is called **CSV** (which stands for comma separated values). All this means is that each piece of data is followed by a comma. Text items are surrounded by double quote marks ("), and within these quote marks a comma is just a character like any other.

The same data as before in CSV form might be:

    "Brown","Arthur","32 The Street, NORWICH, Norfolk"↵
    "Smith","Mary","27 The Avenue, LOWESTOFT, Suffolk"↵
    etc.

If you are using a PC then this is no problem because CSV data is catered for. You simply use the pattern:

    "surname","name","address"↵

and all will work as before. The PCW cannot handle CSV directly and so it will reject this pattern with an `Invalid record pattern` complaint. On the PCW you must use a pattern like this:

    dummy1"surname"dummy2"name"dummy3"address"dummy4↵

What this does is to treat all the data up to the first double quote as the item `dummy1`. Since there is nothing before the double quote this just makes a blank item. All the data up to the next double quote is put into the `surname` item. This is just what we want. The data up to the next double quote is put into the item `dummy2`. Since this is just the comma which we didn't want anyway there is no problem. Similarly the address data is put into the `address` item and `dummy4` is blank. Thus we have got all the real data into our real items and all the spurious commas have ended up in the dummy items.

When you use this record pattern LocoScript will complain about the dummy items:

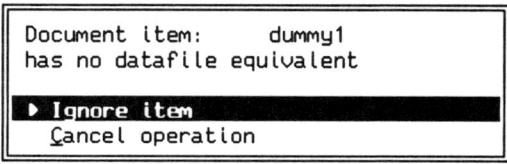

Select `Ignore item` and the commas will be discarded for you.

Taking over an existing list 195

Unfortunately, CSV files are not always as simple as this. Sometimes the program that makes them is "clever" and only puts the quote marks around text if it contains a comma. Thus you get:

    Brown, Arthur, "32 The Road, NORWICH, Norfolk"↵
    Smith, Mary, "27 The Lane, LOWESTOFT, Suffolk"↵
    etc.

You might try using the record pattern:

    PC: surname,name,"address"↵
    PCW: surname,name,dummy1"address"dummy2↵

However, the "clever" program can also make records like this:

    The Mayor,,NORWICH↵
    Robinson,"Mr, Mrs & Family","14 The Close, CAMBRIDGE"↵

This is not a problem to the PC because it knows that the double quotes are optional in CSV and so the original pattern "surname","name","address"↵ will still work. However, there is no way of specifying optional dummy items to a PCW. You will have to either persuade the original program to be less clever, or you will have to edit the exceptions by hand to make the data into a standardised form.

Optional items

There is one last problem concerning patterns, which is how to deal with optional data items. We've been stressing that all the data in every record must be the same, but what if it is not. Do you need to edit the data by hand to make it regular? The answer is no, LocoScript can be made to cope, *provided that the optional data is at the end of the record.*

Consider the same sort of data as before, but with some extra information added:

    Brown, Arthur, "32 The Road, NORWICH, Norfolk", Fungi↵
    Smith, Mary, "27 The Lane, LOWESTOFT, Suffolk", Flowers↵
    Davis, Angela, "10 The Parade, IPSWICH", Fungi, Mushrooms↵
    etc.

You must be able to tell where the address ends and the interests start – either the address has to be a fixed number of lines, or there must be some sort of unique ending to it. In practice you will find that this works out and you can construct a suitable pattern. On a PC this would be:

    surname,name,"address",interest1,interest2

and on a PCW:

    surname,name,dummy1"address"dummy2,interest1,interest2

where in each case you need as many interest*n* items as in the longest list.

But, you will object, this won't work! And indeed it will not as it stands. Since Arthur Brown only has one interest Mary Smith will become interest2 and interest3. This is prevented by marking the end of each record with a form feed (↓) character. The form feed acts as an unconditional end of record forcing all the items still remaining in the pattern to be made blank. You can either arrange for the form feed to be present in the ASCII file (as ASCII value 12) or you can convert the data into a LocoScript document and use global exchange to swap ↵ into ↓. Type [RETURN] ([SHIFT][↵] on a PC) to get a ↵ into the exchange menu, and [ALT][RETURN] ([Ctrl][SHIFT][↵] on a PC) to get a ↓.

If you are using form feeds as unconditional record terminators then there is a small trap you can fall into. If your data look like this:

    Brown, Arthur, 32 The Road, NORWICH, Norfolk↵
    ↓
    Smith, Mary, 27 The Lane, LOWESTOFT, Suffolk↵
    ↓
    etc.

Then using the pattern surname, name, address↵ will generate all the correct member details in your datafile *plus* an equal number of totally blank records! This is because the pattern finishes with the ↵. Therefore the first record ends with the ↵ at the end of the first data line. The next member record is started, but the ↓ immediately makes all the items of the second record blank. One solution is use the pattern:

    surname, name, address

i.e. without the final ↵. This will incorporate the ↵ into the address item. If you wish to discard it then use the pattern:

    surname, name, address↵
    dummy

Making the ASCII file

Having now considered the end result of our transfer (which is to insert data into a LocoScript datafile) we can now see what the first step must be. We have to generate the data using the original software on the old system. We are afraid we can't help you much with this: you need to consult an expert – such as the previous Hon. Sec whose data you are taking over. Of course, they'll grumble (after all they thought their job was over) and they'll also try to persuade you to use the same system they did (they might have a point here – but do they own a book as useful as this one?).

It is quite possible they've never had to generate an ASCII file before – so get them to dig out their manual. Look up ASCII, Text-file, CSV, Export and things like that in the index. If their system is too primitive to generate files it will surely print the data. Can you print to a file rather than to a printer? Have they got a utility of some kind which will intercept printer data and save it on disc? Can you send the printer output to a serial port and connect that serial port to your computer? There will be a way of getting the data out somehow; you just have to find it.

Physical transfers

So finally we get to the tricky bit, the physical transfer. You have exactly the data you want on one sort of computer disc and now you want it on a LocoScript disc – either a PCW 3 or 3½ inch disc or a PC disc of an appropriate size for your machine. Perhaps you are both using the same type of machine and can read each other's discs, but you will probably find that they are of different sizes or different formats.

There are four different ways of doing the transfer:

1. Send it to a specialist. A number of companies offer data transfer services. Charges vary as do the formats they support. If you are convinced that you only need one transfer (and you won't have to reformat the data and try again) this could well be the best solution. Chapter 27 gives some further details.

2. Read the data off disc. If you both use the same size of disc then you will find that programs exist to read and write data to different filing system formats. These programs may be system software (a Macintosh, for example, can handle MSDOS discs using Apple File Exchange), they may be utilities which were shipped with the drive (as with 3½ inch drives for the PCW) or they may be extra programs you can obtain. Many such programs are "Public Domain" or

"Shareware", obtainable from shareware libraries or user groups. Everyone will know about MSDOS format discs. PCW discs are more unusual. If you're asked then explain that they are:

180K discs: CP/M format. 9 sectors of 512 bytes per track. 40 tracks per side. 1 reserved track. 64 directory entries. 1K block size.

720K discs: CP/M format. 9 sectors of 512 bytes per track. 160 tracks as 2 sides * 80 tracks, in the order (track 0, head 0), (track 0, head 1), (track 1, head 0), (track 1, head 1) etc. 1 reserved track. 256 directory entries. 2K block size.

All 3½ inch PCW discs are the 720K format, but 3 inch discs are 720K format if for drive B, 180K format if drive A.

3. Transfer the data by serial cable. If both machines have serial ports then you can connect them by a wire and transfer the data. You will need a suitable program at each end to send and receive the data. At a pinch, on a PCW you can just about get away with using the CP/M program PIP to read the data (load CP/M and use the command PIP A:FILENAME=AUX:) but in order to avoid data loss you may need to use a very slow baud rate and you should use SETSIO to turn on interrupts.

If the preceding paragraph was full of jargon you did not understand then this method is not for you without the help of an expert. Most "comms" programs are far harder to use than they should be, and even with the right test equipment it can take ages to wire a serial link correctly. Go back and reassess the attractions of scheme 1 above!

4. Transfer the data by a customised link of some kind. There are a number of products for linking specific machines together. LocoLink will link a PCW and a PC, and there are programs and cables for linking different models of PCW. Unlike the previous method, these programs are designed for use by non-experts and therefore there is much more likelihood of success.

TIP: However you transfer the data, we have one last piece of advice. Ask that the previous datafiles and programs are preserved for a little while until you're up and running – preferably until a complete year has gone by. If you forget to transfer the list of life members across it might be some time before you realise!

25
Troubleshooting

> **How I hate this damn machine,**
> **I wish that they would sell it.**
> **It never does quite what I want,**
> **But only what I tell it.**
>
> **Anon**

This chapter is all about what to do when things start going wrong. You may be reading it in sequence, immediately after chapter 24, but it's more likely you've turned here because you've got a real live problem in front of you. Unfortunately, we're not there to look over your shoulder and advise, but in this chapter we've set down as much as we can about how we'd look at your problem and how we'd set about solving it.

The first thing to decide is what your problem is! Is nothing happening at all? Are you getting messages on the screen which you don't understand? Or is that LocoScript is apparently working properly, but you just aren't getting the results you want?

Nothing (much) is happening at all

If your problems relate to loading LocoScript, editing documents, or accessing your datafiles then our advice is for you to do a little homework first, and then come back to this book. In writing this book we've had to assume a basic level of knowledge, because otherwise it would be twice the size. All the LocoScript products come with manuals, one part of which (in some cases almost all of which) are tutorials, which have been specially written to show you how the product works, and to take you through the fundamentals.

If you've typed in one of the programs from this book and merged it with your datafile and nothing much has happened then what has gone wrong? Check you typed it in correctly. Did you type (+Mail) and (−Mail) codes using the [+] and [−] keys? Typing these as text will not work!

Is the program being "swallowed up" in the usual way when you start the merge, but you are getting no results, but just the "exit" menu? If so then what may have happened is that you've got one of your definition commands wrong. Definitions need to be of the form: value = " text ". If you leave off the trailing double quote then LocoScript could "eat" the rest of the document while vainly looking for it.

Alternatively, the double quote may be present, but you've got some mismatched (+Mail) or (–Mail) codes. When looking for the closing double quote LocoScript counts +1 for every (+Mail) code it passes and –1 for every (–Mail) it passes. It will only accept a double quote at level zero as the end of the definition. The way we have written the programs in this book mean that we hardly ever use (+Mail) and (–Mail) codes so the main thing to check is that the double quotes match up.

You may get nothing at all if you fail to balance your **IF THEN ENDofIF** commands. If these are wrong, especially inside loops, then you often find that the program is "eaten" in the usual way. Then nothing happens, or you may get just one line of output. You may not even get an "exit" menu until you press [STOP][STOP] ([Esc][Esc] on a PC).

Check carefully to ensure every **THEN** :<: is balanced by its own **ENDofIF** :>:. The **ELSE** :><: and **ELSEIF** :># are neutral, because they both finish a **THEN** section, but they immediately start the next section which must, eventually, be terminated by an **ENDofIF**. Check that all these characters occur in a (+Mail) part of the document. Make sure that if they occur inside a loop then *all* of the command is within the loop! The error might be that you've written loop="IF .. THEN ...":ENDofIF, so both the quotes and the **IF** are balanced, but when the loop is performed the **ENDofIF** is somewhere else entirely! If you've "nested" your **IF** commands one inside another then check that you have indeed put the whole of the inner one inside one part of the outer.

You will also get nothing if you make the %loop@ command the very last thing in your document. For the programs in this book to work it must be followed by at least a ↵.

One of the commonest ways to get nothing at all is for this to be the right result! You may not actually have any Red-haired Life members living in Norwich! On the other hand, you may have stopped looking too soon. In many of the programs we've performed loops using the command %loop@surname. What this does is to perform the commands within the loop until the surname item is blank or zero, or until the end of the datafile where all items are made blank. If you are using our programs on your own datafile make sure that you have altered this loop control variable to something which can never be blank or zero. If you're using a PC then we'd strongly recommend writing %loop @ $#, using the record number ($#) for loop control because this can never be blank or zero on a real record. Unfortunately $# is not available on a PCW.

A general error message has appeared

If you get an error message then the first thing to do is to read what it says. Sounds simple, but not everyone manages it successfully!

LocoScript error messages come in two parts. The first line tells you where the error occurred: Error with file: SETTINGS.RSC, Error in database: etc. The second line tells you what the error is: Disc full, Disc is write-protected, Command syntax error and so on. Finally there will be one or more commands giving you various options: Cancel, Retry and perhaps some further possibilities, depending upon the sort of error you've got.

We deal with specific mailmerge errors later, but you can get all sorts of other errors reported whilst using running the programs from this book. The following messages usually indicate that your problem lies with your discs:

```
Bad call format
Bad command
Bad unit
Data error (CRC)
Disc address mark missing
Disc data error
Disc format cannot be handled
Disc format not recognized
Disc is unsuitable for drive
Disc is write-protected
Disc media error
Disc sector not found
Disc seek failed
Drive is not ready
Drive does not exist
General failure
Invalid function code
Non-DOS disc
Read comparison error
Read fault
Seek error
Unexpected end of file
Unknown disc error
Write fault
Wrong disc type
```

These messages describe the various different ways in which LocoScript is unable to read or write documents and data. The first line of the message will tell you which file or drive is involved. Read this! or you'll worry about the wrong drive or file. You should also read chapter 6 about backups (regretting as you do so that you never bothered before!)

Apart from the fact that they've happened whilst you were running a program, these messages are nothing really to do with this book, because they're just telling you that your discs or drives aren't fully functioning.

Our general advice is that if you get these errors from just one floppy disc then you should copy any useful files off it, then reformat the disc. If reformatting fails then discard the disc because it is probably physically damaged. If reformatting succeeds then the disc had merely acquired the wrong electrical pattern for some unknown reason, and it is now working. If you get these errors from many discs all at once then the chances are that you've got a problem with your machine. You should consult an expert, your dealer or a third party maintenance company for advice.

The same principles apply if errors are reported on your hard disc. If only one or two files are involved there is some sort of flaw, temporary or permanent, on that part of the disc. If everything throws up errors then your problems may lie elsewhere. However, since taking off all the valid data and reformatting are both more time consuming and more complicated than with floppies you should in all cases obtain some expert advice before proceeding.

The messages:

```
File checksum error
Not a LocoScript document
Page too big
```

mean that LocoScript does not recognise your documents.

Perhaps when a disc error occurred in the past you typed Ignore? When you Ignore a disc error you are telling LocoScript not to bother retrying, but to struggle on using whatever it managed to read last, however incomplete. This can be a sensible thing to try with your own documents, where you can retype any damaged sections. It is not sensible with LocoScript's system files!

If you feel that the messages are unreasonable then perhaps you have some sort of RAM fault (so that your machine's memory cannot remember things properly). Perhaps you have damaged the file in some way by trying to alter it with another program?

The message:

    Invalid datafile

means that although LocoScript has recognised your datafile there is something wrong with it internally. This is not good news, and you should start considering why you never read chapter 6 about backups! The reason for the internal damage could be ignoring disc errors or RAM faults, as we have just been discussing. The other, and more likely, reason is that you have turned off your computer whilst the datafile was still open. In order to work as fast as possible LocoScript does not always write all of the changes to a datafile immediately. If you fail to return to the Disc Manager screen before you switch off you can sometimes leave the datafile in a state where some changes have been made, but others have not. If LocoScript detects this inconsistency then it will reject the datafile.

If you have an up-to-date backup then you should use this. Otherwise you should try the Squash command in the Disc Manager [F1] (PC [F9]) menu. One of the things that Squash does is to completely recreate the index information in the datafile. If the internal damage was caused by switching off the computer then Squash will usually fix it up for you. If the damage is more severe then Squash may only be able to recover some of your records. It will warn you about this, and you will have to make up your own mind, when you see how many records remain, as to whether you will be better off restarting from your backup copy or the squashed version.

TIP: Do not squash your only copy of the datafile! If you end up sending the datafile to someone like David Smith (the PCW "Disc Doctor") then the original datafile will be required, not the squashed version.

The messages:

    Disc is full
    Directory is full

mean exactly what they say! Check the first line to see which disc or drive is involved. If your problem is Disc full then it may be because you're generating too much data at once. We usually give an alternative version of the program which doesn't generate all of its data all at once, so it will not need so much disc space.

If you get Directory full then this means that you've used up all the "slots" for filenames on the disc. On a PCW, 180K (drive A) disc there is a limit of 64 filenames, whereas 720K (drive B) discs are limited to 256 filenames. Slots are also used by group names, and files bigger than 16K can take more than one slot.

On a PC there is also a limit to the number of files which can be stored in the "root" of a disc. Sub-directories can be as big as you like, but the topmost level has a fixed size which varies depending on the version of DOS and the type of media, but can often be only 100 or so files, even on a 300MB hard disc! Most people don't encounter the limit because they sub-divide their files into sub-directories to make them easier to handle.

If either of the following two messages appear when you start a merge or a fill, then LocoMail is not available on your PCW:

```
LocoMail is not available
Incompatible version
```

The first means you haven't added LocoMail to your start-of-day disc. The second means that you added it incorrectly. Purchase the product if necessary, and make sure that you follow the "Upgrade" instructions which come with it!

The message:

```
Editor data buffer full
```

means that your mailmerge program is too complicated, or it is trying to store too much data into items. None of the programs in this book will get anywhere near generating this message; the data buffer mentioned is very large. The only likely modification which might pose difficulties would be if you set incredibly wide margins and lots of tabs to extract your data. Even then, you'd be pretty unlucky to encounter this message.

Mailmerge error messages

Having described the rather exotic messages which you may never see, we now get to the everyday messages which users of the LocoScript mailmerge facilities become all too familiar with.

```
Name does not exist
Duplicate name definition
LocoMail command syntax error
Mail merge command syntax error
LocoMail command type mismatch
Mail merge command type mismatch
Invalid record pattern
```

Troubleshooting

You can probably get rid of these messages, without ever knowing what they mean, by correcting the typing mistakes in your program!

If you've copied a program from this book you can be certain that it should work! One of the last things we did when we were writing it, was to try every single example to ensure that it didn't go wrong. We then made an electronic "screen dump" of the program, precisely as it appeared on our machine. When we typeset the book on our computer we then "pasted in" these screen dumps so that the illustrations show you exactly what we had in our programs.

So if you think you've copied a program exactly then look again! Have you missed out a character? Do you have colons where we have colons? Did you type a semicolon rather than a colon? Do you have carriage returns where we do? Have you typed S+ rather than $+? Have you spelled all of the names absolutely correctly? Have you used a (bracket when we put a < character?

To find what is causing an error message, you need to understand a little bit more about how the mailmerge handles a program. What it does is to work through your document character by character, line by line. It starts in a "switched off" state, but turns itself on when it sees a (+Mail) code and turns itself off when it sees a (–Mail). While it is "switched on" it is obeying the contents of the document as commands, and then discarding them – hence the way it which it appears to "eat" the document.

If an error occurs, mailmerge stops immediately and shows you an error message. The error has occurred immediately before the current position, in the bit which has just been "eaten". If you are unsure where the current position is then take the menu option to Edit document. This will take down the error message and show you the current position as a flashing cursor. You can then abandon using the Exit menu and edit the program document to look at, and fix, the previous command. Of course the actual error may have occurred several lines earlier – but it cannot have occurred any further down the document than the stopping point.

In practice, you'll find that most of your problems occur in the command %loop @ ... i.e. when the mailmerge repeatedly executes the commands which have been stored in loop. Unfortunately, you can't tell where inside loop the problem occurs. There are some techniques to help you here, which we discuss later in the chapter in the **Looking for errors** section; but the first thing to do is to understand the error message, then if you examine your program you can usually see what the cause is.

Name does not exist

The `Name does not exist` error is generated when you use an item name and mailmerge does not recognise it. The item should either be defined by the program in a command like `tab="→"` or it can be one of the items in your datafile.

You'll get this message if the items in your datafile do not have the same names as ours, and you fail to change the programs to compensate.

You'll get this message when you've decided to adapt a program and you've added some more formatting ("let's put a comma between these items"), but you've forgotten to set up the `comma` item in the definitions section.

Perhaps you are trying to use a datafile item and you've spelled its name wrong (was it `telephone` or `phone` or `tel`?). You should be particularly careful if you did not follow our recommendation and your datafile item names are not solely made of letters and digits. We discuss this specially in **Converting datafile names**, later in the chapter.

Trying to use a non-existent index in a `$=` command will also generate a `Name does not exist` error. This is usually easy to spot because this command is seldom inside a loop. You will also get this error if you write `$=town` when you meant `$="town"`.

You will also get a `Name does not exist` error if the loop control variable has not been defined when the `@` part of a `%` command is executed. Beware of **IF THEN ENDofIF**s which set the loop control variable, but leave it undefined when the **IF** condition is not satisfied. Our programs avoid this by, for example, always presetting `stop=1` just before the `%loop@stop` command.

Duplicate name definition

A `Duplicate name definition` error is just the opposite of the previous error! You have tried to define an item for the second time, or you are trying to give one of your program items the same name as something in your datafile, or indeed you are trying to assign a new value to a datafile item.

If this message occurs before the merge even starts then you have two items in your datafile with identical names as far as mailmerge is concerned. See the later section on **Converting datafile names** for more about this.

LocoMail command type mismatch
Mail merge command type mismatch

These two messages (the second is the PC form) usually mean that you're trying to do some sort of comparison and the items involved are not suitable.

Remember you can only compare text for equality or inequality. You cannot write:

    # surname > "BZZZZZZ" :<: ...

and you cannot compare dates such as 93/12 for "greater" or "less".

On the PCW you can get a command type mismatch error if you do arithmetic with a blank item because blank items are treated as being text not numbers. On the PC this is not a problem because a blank item is treated as zero in a sum. We haven't really discussed processing numbers with arithmetic commands, but you may branch out on your own. If so then PCW programs will have to treat blank items specially.

However, you have to be careful how you handle the blank items. If, for example, you wanted to do a sum on the item tithe you might try to write:

    # tithe = "" :<: tithe = 0 :>:↵

Unfortunately, if this item comes from the datafile, this command will be rejected with a Duplicate name definition error! The solution is to use a temporary variable which can be set to zero:

    # tithe = "" :<: temporary = 0 :><: temporary = tithe :>:↵

and then do all further sums on the variable temporary.

LocoMail command syntax error
Mail merge command syntax error

These two messages (the second is the PC form) are general purpose messages to the effect that you've got the format (the "syntax") of your mailmerge commands wrong.

Apart from typing incorrect characters, which you will just have to look for, there are two slightly more subtle ways of getting a syntax error. The first way is to use a datafile item name which contains characters other than letters and digits. How to alter these names is covered later in the **Converting datafile names** section. The second way to get syntax errors is to fail to follow a command by either a colon, a carriage return (↵) or a (–Mail) code. This often happens when you decide to "tidy up" a program and remove all the excess carriage returns. If you do remove a ↵ then you must replace it by a colon to separate the commands.

In particular, it is essential to have a command separator at the end of a loop. The effect of a %loop @ control command is to start taking commands from loop rather than from the next line of the document. When LocoScript fetches the last character from loop it checks the control item. If this is not blank or zero then it immediately moves to the first character of loop again. This means that there has to be a separator between the last command of loop and the first.

In this book we've always been most careful to build loops of the form:

```
loop = "↵
...
$+↵
"
```

so that we have a suitable separation between the commands. Actually there are two separators (the two ↵ characters)! The last one is the vital one, but we added the first one because it does no harm, and it made all the programs look neater.

Invalid record pattern

This message occurs when you are inserting data into a datafile, and means that the first record which describes the format of the data records has not been constructed correctly. You will find a lot more about this in chapters 21–24.

Looking for errors

You can almost invariably find errors just by looking, but it is obviously much quicker if you know where to look. As we discussed earlier, the error has always occurred just before the current cursor position in the document. However, in practice problems always seem to occur inside loops where they are harder to pin down.

Things are not as bad as they might seem, because there is usually some clue to guide you. Look at the output which was produced. This tells you how far the program got before failing. For example, if you can see a name, then a surname, then a Name does

Troubleshooting

not exist error, then the mistake has to be after the output of the surname and before the output of the next item.

If you are still stuck, perhaps because there are several suspect commands, then the solution may be to add some extra output to help you.

Alter your program to add:

    h=999:h:cr:

between two of these commands. If the program gets this far then you'll get 999↵ shown on the screen. Add a few more such commands (with different numbers to avoid confusion) and you'll pretty soon pin down where the problem must be.

If you are still absolutely stuck then you could try expanding the loop. Since the effect of %loop@control is to execute loop many times, you could replace this command by many copies of the contents of the loop item.

Make a copy of the program and edit the duplicate. Use LocoScript's "cut and paste" facilities to copy the loop definition into a block. Copy from just after the opening double quote to just before the closing double quote. Now paste this in a couple of times just before the % command. You can now try this alternative program, and your error will no longer occur inside a % command, where its exact location can only be guessed at. Instead you can see exactly where things go wrong, and you can then fix it.

When you get the wrong results

When you run your program and you do not get the output that you expected, the reason is invariably that you asked LocoScript to do something other than what you had in mind. We can't really help you much with this, apart from giving a general principle and then suggesting few classic mistakes to check for.

The general principle is to look at the output. Think about how this differs from what you wanted. Look at the way the program made this decision, and examine some records which were (or were not) included to try and see why.

Maybe the problem is that too many people are included on the list or too few. If so then look at the **IF** commands and the condition you were testing for. You should also be looking for some common factor amongst the people who are missing. Maybe you are testing for Mar 92 whereas some data items contain March 92.

If people are missing altogether then maybe your loop is being stopped incorrectly, because the loop control variable becomes blank before the end of file. You will probably remember that we keep on stressing that if you write `%loop@surname` then it is vital that no-one has a blank `surname` item.

If the first person of each group is missing then something is wrong with your handling of `$+`. Maybe you have forgotten the `$-` to disable the automatic move to the next record which occurs when your merge takes more than one pass?

If you are getting the wrong people on the list then look hard at the conditions. Have you written `town="NORWICH" OR class="JUNIOR"` when what you really meant was `town="NORWICH" AND class="JUNIOR"`?

Is the order of your output incorrect? If so, then look at the out-of-order records. Is that a zero or a capital O? Have you, on the PCW especially, got leading or trailing spaces on your items. Did you sometimes type `92` and sometimes `1992`. Did you sometimes add a full stop after the town name? Have you got invalid dates like `31/2/93`? Invalid dates are all sorted together at the end of the month or year.

If your output is laid out incorrectly then check if you put ↵ at the end of items instead of pressing [ENTER] (or [TAB]) to move to the next item. If your tabs go to the wrong place then check that you've set up the tab positions you want in the layout.

Is there no apparent connection between the missing people? If so then look for an unnecessary `$+` which is skipping every other record.

If alphabetical order is OK for a while, but then goes random it is likely that you've forgotten to select an index using `$=`, or chosen an index which does not have `surname` as a sub key. If you've just created your datafile then the original list was probably in alphabetical order. Thus, surname order will be the same as record number order until you start getting new members!

Are you getting some people in the list more than once? This is often useful (see chapter 18), but if you did not intend it, then you should *not* choose an index with alternative items for your `$=` command.

If, after staring at the list for some time, you are still puzzled, then the best way to proceed is to alter your program. Add some extra commands to output some more information, or some `h="999":h:cr:` markers to show what the result of an **IF** command was. Eventually the penny will drop.

Converting datafile names

You may recall that in chapter 3 we advised you to avoid spaces, colons and other punctuation in datafile item names. You may have gone ahead anyway because you thought it made your cards look nicer. Fair enough, but you will have to use slightly different names in your mailmerge programs.

To convert a datafile name to a mailmerge name:

- Change spaces into underlines. Thus `first name` becomes `first_name`.

- Discard any characters which are not digits or alphabetic. (On a PCW this means discard Greek and Cyrillic – a PC is more tolerant: see the PC Reference manual Appendix II for the full story). In particular you must discard any colons, apostrophes, hyphens, dots, commas and pound signs. Therefore `tel:` becomes `tel` and `Amount£` becomes `Amount`.

- Discard any leading digits (i.e. any at the front). Thus `1address` becomes `address`, whereas `address1` stays as `address1`.

If two or more items end up with the same mailmerge name (as would happen if you named some items `1address`, `2address` etc.) then you will not be able to merge with this datafile because you will get the error message:

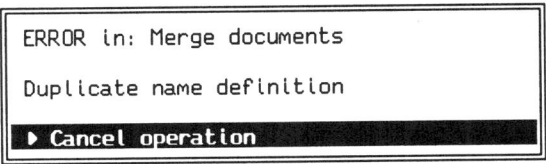

In such a case you will need to change the item names in the datafile. Just go into datafile set-up and from [F3] Change (Amend) the item. You can now alter the item name. *Do not* remove the item and recreate it with the new name because this will also remove the item's data from your records.

Note that in order to be able to refer to items from within a mailmerge program they will have to have names. If the name is left blank then the datafile menus will refer to the item by its coordinates, for example, `@12,15 unnamed`. If you have items like this you will have to Change (Amend) them to have non-blank names (possibly hidden) before they can be used in lists etc.

If you are still stuck ...

If, after trying everything in this chapter, you are still stuck then you will need to consult an expert. There is always the possibility that you are using an out of date version of the program or even that you've encountered a previously unknown problem in LocoScript.

In the absence of any other expertise, you can write to:

Customer Support, Locomotive Software Ltd., DORKING, Surrey. RH4 1YL.

You *must* enclose a disc containing your datafile and the program which is not working. They will not be able to work out what is wrong from just printouts or a fax message. If you use a PCW you should also send a copy of your start-of-day disc. If you use a PC you should also send copies of the files:

```
AUTOEXEC.BAT     in the root of your boot floppy/hard disc
CONFIG.SYS       ditto
SETTINGS.RSC     in LSPRO.PC\LSPRO.ETC
```
all the files in your printer directory.

In a covering letter you must explain the problem, how to demonstrate it, and (given that LocoScript almost invariably does what you tell it!) why it seems to you that this is in fact wrong.

If there are a lot of programs on the disc then *do say which one fails*! If you need to type particular responses to get a failure then do say what these are.

You also must give details of the machine you are using, and you **MUST** give the full version number of the LocoScript you are using. On the PCW you also need to give the version numbers of LocoMail and LocoFile. All the version numbers are on the title screen as you start the program.

If you don't include all this information, then it makes it far less likely that Locomotive can help you. Remember also that Customer Support exists to support the LocoScript program, not to provide a consultancy service, so *do not expect to get your programs written for you*.

If what you need is in fact a consultant, or indeed just some training, then Locomotive keep extensive lists of people who offer such services, usually for a quite reasonable fee. Alternatively, you may find there are evening classes in your area which cover LocoScript, especially on the PCW.

26
Legal implications

When you keep your records manually using books or record cards, there are no restrictions on how or what records you keep. However, when you keep your records on any sort of computer, you should be aware of the conditions of the **Data Protection Act 1984**. You will need to register your use of computerised records unless you qualify under one of the various exemptions.

This Act was set up to protect the public against hidden and unfair information about them being held on computers. The Act places obligations on those who record and use personal data. They must be open about that use and follow sound and proper practices. The Act allowed the United Kingdom to ratify the Council of Europe Convention on Data Protection so that data can flow freely between the United Kingdom and other European countries which have similar laws. Cynics might say that this ratification was the sole purpose of the Act, but it is, nevertheless, the law of the land.

The Act gives legal rights to individuals concerning the personal data held about them. An individual is entitled to be supplied with a copy of any personal data held about them, although the data user may charge a fee of up to £10 for supplying the entry. The "data subject" may complain to the Registrar or apply to the Courts for correction or deletion of data, and may seek compensation through the Courts for damage caused by inaccurate data.

You are storing "personal data" even if you are just recording names and addresses! **There is no exemption on size**, but nevertheless we believe that most small clubs and societies can avoid registering. We give below a summary of the information put out by the Registrar's Office, but what it amounts to is that you are unlikely to need to register if:

       you are keeping the personal data on file for the purposes of informing your members of activities and sending renewal notices;
&   you have told the membership that the records are now held on computer;
&   you do not wish to sell your mailing lists to outside interests.

If you wish to sell your mailing list for advertising purposes, then you *will* need to register. You should also note that if you are not registered then any member who objects to their records being held on the computer will have to be processed manually.

If you read the list of exemptions and you find that your club or society does not qualify, then you have no option but to register. The current cost (1992) is £75 for three years.

The descriptions of the exemptions and requirements are taken from the series of eight Guidelines published by the Data Protection Registrar:

    Guideline 1. Introduction to the Act
    Guideline 2. The Definitions
    Guideline 3. The Register and Registration
    Guideline 4. The Data Protection Principles
    Guideline 5. Individuals' Rights
    Guideline 6. The Exemptions
    Guideline 7. Enforcement and Appeals
    Guideline 8. Summary for Computer Bureaux

These publications, which set out the Registrar's view of the law, are available free of charge. The Registrar also publishes a Guidance Note Series. These are shorter than the Guidelines and deal with specific issues in more detail. A list of the current Guidance Notes is available from the Registrar's Office:

    Office of the Data Protection Registrar
    Springfield House
    Water Lane
    WILMSLOW
    Cheshire
    SK9 5AX

Further information is available from the Registrar's Enquiry Service on Wilmslow (0625) 535777, who will also try to answer specific questions.

TIP: The Enquiry Service is extremely helpful. There is no need to write to them; you can just ring them up to get your questions answered.

Legal implications 215

Summary of the Data Protection Registrar's Guidelines

Registered data users must comply with the Data Protection Principles in relation to the data they hold.

1. It must be obtained and processed fairly and lawfully;
2. It must be held only for the lawful purposes described in the register entry;
3. It must be used only for these purposes and only be disclosed to those people described on the register entry;
4. It must be adequate, relevant and not excessive in relation to the purpose for which it is held;
5. It must be accurate and, where necessary, kept up to date;
6. It must be held no longer than is necessary for the registered purpose;
7. An individual shall be entitled to access any data of which they are the subject and where appropriate have such data corrected or erased;
8. It must be surrounded by proper security.

There are a number of exemptions from the need to register.

1. Personal data held by an individual for personal, family or household affairs, or held for recreational purposes.

    This exemption does not apply to an individual who keeps records on behalf of a club, church or voluntary organisation. Then the organisation rather than the individual will be the data user.

2. Information that the law requires to be made public.

    For example the Companies Act 1985 requires every registered company to make its register of members available for public inspection.

    The electoral registration officer may be exempt in respect of those parts of the electoral register he is required to publish. However, other data users who hold copies of the electoral register cannot rely on this exemption.

3. Payroll, pensions and accounts are exempt as long as they are held by a data user only for payroll and accounts purposes. Any small business seeking exemption should read Guideline 6 where more detail is given.

4. Unincorporated members' clubs are exempt as long as two conditions are observed.

    a) All members of the club must be asked whether they object to the personal data relating to them being held by the club.

    If any member objects then either:

> > the personal data relating to that member should be taken off the computer. The information can be held and processed manually.
>
> or the club should register in respect of the personal data. Having registered, it may continue to hold the personal data whether or not members object.
>
> b) The second condition is that the personal data about members may only be disclosed in very limited circumstances. These are:
>
> > when the member has requested or consented to the disclosure. This consent may be given either generally or in the circumstances in which the disclosure in question is made.
> >
> > when the disclosure falls within one of the non-disclosure exemptions set out in Guideline 6.
>
> To comply with the second condition it would be sensible for the club to identify the circumstances in which it may wish to make disclosures and to obtain the consent of the members. Such occasions might include:
>
> > the publication of a list of members;
> >
> > disclosures to affiliated clubs and societies;
> >
> > disclosures due to computer maintenance or software changes.
>
> This exemption does not apply:
>
> > to personal data held about individuals who are not members of the club;
> >
> > if the club is a registered company;
> >
> > to a club not owned by its members.

5. Mailing lists are exempt if the personal data is held only for the purpose of distributing (or recording the distribution of) articles or information to individuals. There are four conditions which must be met:

   1. The personal data must consist only of the names and addresses of the individuals or of other details needed for making the distribution. These might include, for example, telephone numbers but if more information is held – such as occupation, status, interest or preferences – this exemption does not apply.

   2. The personal data must only be used for the purpose as defined above. If used for any other purpose, the exemption is lost.

   3. All individuals must be asked whether they object to the personal data being held on computer. If they object they must be taken off the computer records or the data user should register.

   4. The fourth condition is that personal data may only be disclosed in very limited circumstances. Full details are set out in Guideline 6.

If the above exemptions do not apply to you, then you need to register.

27
Supplies and suppliers

This chapter contains the details of various suppliers and services which we have mentioned throughout the book. You will also need some "office supplies" in order to communicate with your members. Describing what you will need is a bit like defining how long is a piece of string, but everyone will need paper, labels and envelopes. We don't give many prices because these go out of date quite rapidly – in the computer world things get cheaper as often as not!

Continuous paper

Continuous paper comes in a range of different weights and sizes. You almost certainly need plain white continuous paper rather than lined "computer paper". Boxes of continuous paper contain either 1000 or 2000 sheets. When comparing prices always remember to ask how many sheets in a box!

The paper you should use is "fan-folded" with tear-off sprocket holes at the side. Even if you are just sending a standard renewal reminder letter, people are flattered by the individual attention they appear to be getting. Once the sprocket holes are removed, most of the people you write to will not realise that the paper was ever anything but a single sheet.

You can have continuous paper printed with your society heading – but most printers will produce wider or taller characters, perhaps in several pitches, with which you can construct a suitable heading on the top of every document you produce. Even the 9512 daisywheel can be asked to underline or print in bold to give some distinction to your society name and address. If the "official" heading matters, you will do best by feeding in headed notepaper in single sheets.

You will probably want "single part" paper. You can also get multi-part carbonless paper which, provided your printer is suitable (inkjets do not make much of an impact!), will give you two copies at the same time. However, if you need a second copy, it is simple enough to repeat the printout, perhaps in Draft Quality the second time.

The usual sizes for continuous paper are:

>11 x 9½ inches (279 x 241 mm) with a weight of 60 gsm.
>>This is the typical weight of paper for photocopiers.
>
>11⅔ x 9¼ (295 x 235 mm) which is A4 paper size.
>>This is readily obtainable in 70 gsm to 90 gsm weights. Some paper companies also make this size in 100 gsm but it costs more and usually has to be ordered specially.

The weight of paper you use depends on what sort of document you are producing. Reports and ephemeral items are quite satisfactory on the lighter papers, but if your document is to be photocopied for publication in large numbers, heavier paper gives a much sharper image whatever sort of printer you are using. This is particularly true of the PCW matrix printer. Really "good" papers do not photocopy well and do not give an even print.

The size of paper you use also depends upon the final use made of your documents. If you use a smaller size of paper and then photocopy onto A4 then you are wasting space that you could have filled.

Labels

Peel off labels can be bought either in sheet form or as continuous stationery. Which you choose will depend on the type of printer you have and the number of labels you need to print at any one time.

Laser printers, DeskJets and printers like the Canon BJ-10e (which comes with the 9512+) cannot use continuous paper. For these printers you will *have* to buy sheets of labels. For any other printer we recommend you stick to continuous labels, one wide. Everything else makes things more complicated, though of course we have given you the programs you need in chapters 13 and 14.

Make sure that any continuous labels you buy have sprocket holes down the sides, and that the sprockets on your printer can be set near enough together for the paper width. Readjusting the position of labels every dozen or so is not an experience you will ever wish to repeat!

Supplies and suppliers 219

If you are buying sheets of labels then of course the size of each label determines how many there are on a sheet. For names and addresses you really need labels which are 3½ or 4 inches wide x 1½ inches high (90/102 x 38 mm). This will provide 30 or 36 characters across by 7 lines down. At this size you get 14 labels on each A4 sheet.

If you purchase sheets of labels, you can also use them in a photocopier, but this gains you little. Your records are always being updated, the label program and the report programs are repeatable as often as you need them, so why bother? If you are considering using the labels in a photocopier or laser printer then do make sure that they are guaranteed to be suitable for this purpose.

Continuous fan-folded labels come in the same sizes but you have a choice of one wide, two wide, three wide or four wide. One wide labels are the simplest to use, especially if you have a PCW. Details are given in chapters 13 and 14 for all possible variations.

Envelopes

Brown envelopes tend to be associated with bills, so some businesses think that expensive, top quality, white envelopes are good for their image. If you are running a society we think your members will be more impressed with your ability to keep down expenditure! Unfortunately, envelopes made from recycled paper are often more expensive than the others, but of course money may not be the only criterion that you use to judge cost.

Envelopes are described with the flap edge as the second measurement. There are two basic sizes of "long brown envelopes":

>9 x 4 = 229 x 102 mm (i.e. flap on the short end);

>4¼ x 8⅝ = 108 x 219 mm (i.e. flap on long edge).

The "long flap" or DL envelopes usually cost a little more, but they will justify the additional expense because they are so much easier to fill when you have more than one sheet of paper to insert. They also take an A4 sheet folded into three, whereas you have to fold in half and fold again to fit in a 9 x 4 envelope easily.

Larger sizes of envelope are most easily described in relation to paper sizes:

>C5 envelopes take A5 sheets flat or A4 sheets folded in half;

>C4 envelopes take A4 sheets flat.

Both C5 and C4 envelopes usually have their flaps at the short end.

Depending on the number of members, you should try to buy in bulk. The smaller size envelopes usually come in boxes of 1000 and the larger ones in boxes of 250 or 500. Usually the most expensive way to buy is in packets from a stationers or W H Smith's. Office suppliers will charge less per envelope, but you will need to buy more at a time. Always ask if there are discounts for larger quantities, but do bear in mind that you may have to store the unused boxes for some time – where will you put them?

Press Seal or Self Seal envelopes are easy and quick to use, *but* if you wish to make economies by buying larger quantities, they do not keep. The stickiness deteriorates quite quickly and you should reckon to be able to use what you buy within six months.

Using window envelopes is a great saving – you don't need labels and you know that the right letter has gone in the right envelope. It may mean taking a little more care in positioning the address on the letter and in folding the paper, but once you have got this right you save a lot of time. See chapter 12 for more on this.

Envelopes come in different "weights" – i.e. quality of paper. If you are sending a single sheet newsletter or a renewal notice you do not need strong envelopes. However, if you have a publication, you will want it to travel safely through the post, and you may need tougher envelopes.

Our advice would be to visit your office stationer taking a copy of your publication (or a mock-up if you have not yet produced it). Choose a size of envelope into which it fits, but not one which is so tight that you will have difficulty inserting the issue, nor so loose that it will slide around. Ask for samples of everything they have in that size which is a reasonable price. Take them back home – or to a committee meeting – and then, having put the issue in and sealed it, throw them around to see how long they will survive!

The other thing you should do is to weigh the issue and the envelope to see if using one envelope rather than another will make a difference in postage costs. The weight bands for postage in the UK are:

> 60g, 100g, 150g, 200g;
>
> then by 50g to 500g;
>
> then by 100g to 750g; which is the limit for second class postage.

The biggest jump in cost is from 60g to 100g and this is where the choice of an envelope can make the most difference. If you cannot weigh accurately enough at home, take the envelopes and the issue to a Post Office and ask them to weigh them for you.

Padded envelopes will cost more, but if what you mail is valuable, then the costs will be worth it. Again phone around for costs and also phone the manufacturers. They will supply you, but check what their minimum order is and consider storage carefully. Padded envelopes are very bulky.

If you are mailing a publication which is being professionally printed, it is worth asking the printer the charge for dispatching as well, using labels provided by you. The printer may well have the equipment necessary for using clear plastic envelopes. These must have areas of white or grey which can be written on if necessary and which take the postmark. You can also buy them to fill yourself but they can be fiddly. They can also be as expensive as cheap brown envelopes, although their light weight may mean a saving on postage.

Prices

Look up the Office Stationers in your Yellow Pages and telephone round to find the best prices. Ask for prices per box, how many in the box, and how many boxes before you get a discount. Quantity and price are strongly connected in this world. Do check if they are quoting the price including or excluding VAT!

You could also try the computer stationery suppliers who advertise in the computer magazines. You can get some very good bargains from them, but remember to ask what they charge for carriage. Perhaps understandably, if they are really cheap they may have ceased trading when you next need supplies.

Data recovery

If you corrupt data on a PCW disc (any data, not just LocoScript documents and datafiles) then **Dave's Disk Doctor Service Ltd** will get it back for you if it is possible. Dave Smith has been salvaging data since 1987. 100% of the profits go to charity, at first just the cancer charity BACUP, but now many other patient support charities as well. They work "no-fix no-fee" and "return of post" whenever possible. You should ring first to discuss your problem and get a quotation: **0892 835974**.

BACUP now market a backup program (called BACKUP) for the PCW. Because it only copies altered files it is usually much faster than the standard disc copying facilities provided with the PCW. Again, all profits go to charity.

If you lose data from a PC floppy or hard disc then the experts are Dr. Alan Solomon's company – **S & S International** a commercial organisation. Their Data Recovery Service (again "no-fix no-fee") can retrieve corrupted and reformatted discs. They can even get "dead" hard discs spinning again to recover the data! They claim a 95% success rate and provide a fast and totally confidential service. Ring for a quotation on **0442 877877**.

If you erase a file or directory on a PC there are a number of "disc editor" products which will recover lost or deleted files for you. MSDOS version 5 even includes its own UNDELETE command. These can work very well; but Dr. Solomon is particularly eloquent on the subject of easy-to-solve problems which turn up at his company as major corruptions because an unskilled user of a disc editor has made matters a hundred times worse. If you use such a product, then a few minutes reading the manual will be time well spent!

Transferring data

If you need software to read/write PCW 3½ inch discs on a PC then contact:

> **Timatic Systems Ltd**, 7 Palmerston Business Park, Newgate Lane, FAREHAM, Hants. PO16 0LB. **0329 236727**

or: **Moonstone Computing**, Fleming House, Renfrew Street, GLASGOW, G3 6ST. **041 353 2223**

To transfer data between 3 inch PCWs and a PC then LocoLink is a connecting wire plus suitable software. It works within LocoScript PC or $^{Loco}Script$ Professional, so you have to own one of these as well. Contact:

> **Locomotive Software**, DORKING, Surrey, RH4 1YL. **0306 740606**

To transfer data between a 3 inch PCW and a 3½ inch PCW then you can use a LocoLink style cable and special software called PCW Linkit from:

> **Wellington Business Services**, 129 High St., HENLEY-IN-ARDEN, B95 5AU. **0564 795025**

At greater expense, but more convenience for general use, a number of companies sell extra drives. Look at the advertisements in a PCW magazine such as **PCW Plus** or **PCW User**.

In particular, for drives (and also for a range of PCW memory upgrades):

Silicon City, Postal Buildings, Ash Street, WINDERMERE, Cumbria, LA23 3EB. **05394 88707**.

More generally, to transfer practically any size or format of disc or magnetic tape (PC, Macintosh, Amiga, etc. etc.) to any other:

A.L. Downloading Services, Voysey House, Barley Mow Passage, LONDON W4 4PT. **081 994 5471**.

Software

If you own a PCW, then to run the programs in this book you need LocoScript 2, LocoMail and LocoFile. You may have the first two "bundled" with your machine. These are all available from any good computer dealer or:

Locomotive Software, DORKING, Surrey, RH4 1YL. **0306 740606**

If you own a PC then you need LocoScript PC or *LocoScript* Professional, available from your dealer or Locomotive as before. Both these programs have the mailmerge and database facilities built-in, so no extras are required. This book assumes that you are using *LocoScript* Professional. A quick glance at the chapters on labels ought to convince you why this is!

If you already own LocoScript PC, the older version of the program, then you do not need to buy *LocoScript* Professional "from scratch" you can upgrade your existing program to the new version for (1992) £29.95+VAT, provided you are a registered user. If you are not registered then ring Locomotive to sort this out.

If you are upgrading from a PCW to a PC then you should purchase *LocoScript* Professional for the new machine. You can transfer your programs and datafiles via LocoLink. LocoScript will automatically convert your documents and programs. A quick Squash will convert your datafiles, and you will be up and running.

You will have to adjust to a PC keyboard which does not have the special purpose "word processing" keys of a PCW. Apart from that, everything you are used to on a PCW will require no relearning on the PC; and of course you get a wide range of powerful new facilities. All your programs will work unaltered, and so your new machine will be *LocoScripting People* just as before, but of course a great deal faster!

Glossary

ASCII	Loose term for files which contain characters but limited formatting information. People often assume their "ASCII" files use the values from the American standard they are named after.
backup	Duplicated data kept for safety purposes.
concatenate	To combine two text strings together (using the mailmerge & command).
cr	Conventional name for an item containing a carriage return (↵).
datafile	Computer file which contains information. A collection of records.
ff	Conventional name for an item containing a form feed (↓).
field	Term generally used by computer people for what LocoScript (and hence this book) calls an item.
fill	Mailmerge facility. A merge operation which does not use a datafile, but fetches all information required from the keyboard.
form feed	Character ↓ which moves to the next page; called End of page in LocoScript menus.
global exchange	Exchanging text through whole document.
index	A method of grouping information in order.
item	A datafile "box" which contains data. Usually known to computer people as a field. A collection of characters.
key	The item you are seeking within an index.

merge	Mailmerge facility to combine a document and a datafile to produce a result document.
null	Conventional name for an item with nothing in it at all.
pass	One run of a program. When the program is complete LocoScript will do another pass if there are more records to be merged (or in Fill if the user selects Fill Again).
pattern	Description of arrangement of items and records in data which is being inserted from a LocoScript document or ASCII file.
record	A collection of pieces of information about one person. A collection of items.
result document	The document produced by a merge or fill operation.
screen dump	Illustration of the contents of a screen.
space	Conventional name for an item containing a space.
squash	To remove "empty" space from a datafile.
string	A sequence of characters.
tab	Conventional name for an item containing a tab.
tab stop	The destination of a tab, as set in a LocoScript layout.
template	A pattern used to set up information the same each time.
$$	Mailmerge command used to define starting point in index.
$=	Mailmerge command used to define which index to be used to order a list.
&	Mailmerge concatenate command.

List of programs

Page Program Description

Page	Program	Description
37	7A	list: all members by surname
44	7B	list: all members by town
45	7C	list: all phone numbers by surname
46	7D	list: all members by surname; surname underlined
46	7E	list: all data on file
50	8A	list: only life members
51	8B	list: phone numbers of social members
54	8C	list: coffee morning; fixed details
55	8D	list: coffee morning; with optional details
58	8E	list: all members except life members
59	9A	list: all members by surname from C onwards
60	9B	list: all members with C surnames
61	9C	list: coffee morning; fast version
65	9D	list: all members by surname for a range of letters
66	9E	list: all members due for renewal
67	10A	list: all members by surname splitting into batches
69	10B	list: splitting into classes
72	10C	list: splitting by date
73	10D	list: splitting by date for a range of dates
74	10E	list: splitting by first letter of surname
77	11A	count: counting by membership class
85	13A	labels: PCW not recommended
92	13B	labels: PCW 1-across continuous
93	13C	labels: PCW 1-across continuous without blank lines
94	13D	labels: PCW 1-across single sheets
96	13E	labels: PCW n-across continuous
99	13F	labels: PCW n-across single sheets

Page	Program	Description
101	13G	labels: PCW 1-across single sheets in batches
103	13H	labels: PCW 1-across continuous; life members only
104	13I	labels: PCW n-across continuous; life members only
106	13J	labels: PCW 1-across continuous; range of dates
107	14A	labels: PC not recommended
114	14B	labels: PC
116	14	labels: PC adaptation for batches
118	14C	labels: PC life members only
118	14D	labels: PC for a range of dates
120	14E	labels: PC without blank lines
122	15	letter: using datafile items
123	15	letter: typing from the keyboard
124	15	letter: optional sections
129	15	letter: using an index for speed
130	15	letter: renewal notice
133	16	letter: renewal notice
134	18A	list: interest in fungi
134	18B	list: interest in fungi using index for speed
135	18C	list: interest in fungi using multiple items
136	18D	list: interest in fungi using alternative items
151	18E	list: interest in fungi using $?
152	18F	list: interest in fungi for given town
153	18G	count: interests
159	19A	list: members including family members
159	19B	list: children and their parents
168	21A	extract: all data
176	22A	extract: all data and add new item
177	22B	extract: all data and merge items
179	22C	extract: splitting addresses into separate lines
183	22D	extract: putting the town in the 'town item'
186	23A	extract: lapsed subscribers
187	23B	extract: current subscribers

Index

A

Abandon LocoMail   40
Abandon Mailmerge   40
addr2 item   15
addr3 item   16
Address
  how to enter   21
  how to make items   15
address item   15
Alternative
  main keys   149
  sub keys   156
AND command   56
Apple File Exchange   197
ASCII file   191, 197, 225
Automatic merge   68, 102, 117, 122

B

Backup
  definition   31, 225
  use of   35
Batches   67
  of labels   100, 116
BJ-10e   88
Blank lines   93, 119
Bubblejet. *See* BJ-10e

C

Card
  changing size   12, 162
  designing   12
  displaying items   165
  recording layout   18
Christmas cards   166

Columns   113
Comma separated values. *See* CSV
Comparisons   56
Concatenate   75, 225
Continuous paper   217
Copying
  discs   33
  files   34
Corporate members   8
Counting
  alternatives   153
  records   77
county item   16
Covenants   138
cr item   225
Create duplicate record   20, 155
CSV datafile   194
Customer Support   212

D

Data   11
Data Protection Act   213
Data recovery   35, 203, 221
Database   11
Datafile   11
  creating new   12
  definition   225
  names   13, 211
  standard layout   18
Date
  comparisons   66
  entering   8
  index   28
Definitions section   42
'Directory is full'   203

Disappeared records 30
Disappearing people 22
Disc
   editor 222
   sizes 185, 198
'Disc Doctor' 35, 203, 221
'Disc is full' 203
Discard result 40
'Duplicate name
   definition' 204, 206, 211

E

Edit result 40
'Editor data buffer full' 204
ELSE command 61
ELSEIF command 125
Empty datafile 18, 170
EndCol code 115
ENDofIF command 50
Envelopes 219
Error messages 201
Existing lists 9, 189
Extract
   items 140
   program 167

F

ff item 225
Field 11, 225
File 11
'File checksum error' 202
Fill mode 126, 141, 225
Find 30, 154, 172
Form feed 225

G

Gift aid 138
Global exchange 168, 225
Grandfather, father, son backup 32

H

Hard disc 185
Hardware 2
Header/footer text 90, 112
Height code 114

I

Ignore disc error 202
'Incompatible version' 204
Indenting 63, 152
Index 25, 225
   creating 25
'Index name is not unique' 28
Initials item 14
Inkjet. *See* BJ-10e
Insert data 170, 191
'Invalid datafile' 203
'Invalid record pattern' 171, 204
Item
   additional 164
   amending contents 21
   change (amend) 161
   create new data 175
   definition 225
   how to enter 16
   instant feedback 163
   merging data 177
   moving 162
   names 14
      mailmerge conversion 211
      positioning 13
   splitting data 179
   unnamed 172

K

Key 27, 225
   main 26
   sub key 26
'Key item has been changed' 78

L

Labels 82
   1-across continuous 92
   1-across sheets 94
   fan-fold 88, 110
   n-across continuous 95
   n-across sheets 98
   purchasing 218
   roll 87, 109
   selection 103, 117
   sheets 88, 111
   use for lapsed members 137
Lapsed members 136, 188
Left offset 88, 90, 110, 112
Letters 121, 139
Limbo record 22
LocoFile 2, 223
LocoLink 198, 223
LocoMail 2, 204, 223
'LocoMail command syntax error' 204, 207
'LocoMail command type mismatch' 204, 207
'LocoMail is not available' 204
Locomotive Software 212, 223
LocoScript 1 3
LocoScript 2 2, 223
LocoScript PC 3, 223
LocoScript Professional 3, 223

M

'Mail merge command syntax error' 204, 207
'Mail merge command type mismatch' 204, 207
Mailing list 137, 214
Master document 127
Membership classes 8
Membership numbers 7
Merge 38, 226
   halting 38, 76

N

'Name does not exist' 39, 42, 204, 206
Names and addresses 5
New paper type 87, 89, 109, 111
'Not a LocoScript document' 202
NOT command 57
null item 226

O

Off-site backup 32
Optional items 195
OR command 56
Overlapping items 161

P

'Page too big' 202
Paper type 41, 86, 90, 108
Pass 68, 226
Pattern 192, 226
Physical transfer 197
Post Office 83
postcode item 16
Print result 40
Prompting 52, 53, 72

R

Record 11, 226
Record number index 25
Record pattern. *See* Pattern
Reminders 135
Remove
   index 80
   item 164
Renewals 131
Result document 226

S

Save and Print result 40
Save result 40

Screen dump   205, 226
Separator   168
Serial transfer   198
Software   2
space item   226
Squash   165, 203, 226
Stamps   83
Start-of-day disc   87
Stopping a merge   38, 76
String   226
Subscription numbers   7
Surname
   non-empty   19
surname item   14
Syntax error   39, 204, 207

T

tab item   226
Tab stop   226
tel item   16
Telephone number indexes   28
Template   139, 226
Temporary path   116
Tests. *See* Comparisons
THEN command   50
title item   14
town item   16, 180
Transferring data   222
Troubleshooting   199

U

Undo alterations   22
Unique   30
Unnamed item   211

W

Wildcard   55, 61
Window envelopes   81, 220

Symbols

!? command   123, 142
#. *See* IF
$– command   71
$$ command   59, 152, 226
$$"9999999" command   62
$= command   41, 226
$? command   151, 153
%loop@surname   43
& command   226
* command   128
? command   123, 142
? item command   142